IMPLOSION AT LOS ALAMOS:

HOW CRIME, CORRUPTION AND COVER-UPS JEOPARDIZE AMERICA'S NUCLEAR WEAPONS SECRETS

Geri & Bill —
Best Wishes
& Bless —
God Bless —

Glen

IMPLOSION AT LOS ALAMOS:

HOW CRIME, CORRUPTION AND COVER-UPS JEOPARDIZE AMERICA'S NUCLEAR WEAPONS SECRETS

GLENN A. WALP, Ph.D.

JUSTICE PUBLISHING, LLC | AZ 85118

This book is dedicated to the Glory of God,
in whom all things are possible,
and to all Americans who expect
federal contractors to be wise stewards
of their tax dollars and whom they trust to ensure
their country's top security facilities and
secrets are well guarded and safe.

"To those who cling to power through corruption
and deceit and the silencing of dissent,
know that you are on the wrong side of history..."

President Barack Obama,
Inauguration Speech, January 20, 2009

TABLE OF CONTENTS

AUTHOR'S NOTE xiii

PROLOGUE xv

CHAPTER I:

Security and Safeguards Los Alamos Style 2002 1

CHAPTER II:

New Horizons 7

CHAPTER III:

Close Perils 13

CHAPTER IV:

The Winds of Change 17

CHAPTER V:

Let the Changes Begin 25

CHAPTER VI:

Cracks in the Ethical Wall 31

CHAPTER VII:

 Theft at Los Alamos 37

CHAPTER VIII:

Doran Comes on Board 49

CHAPTER IX:

Inklings of a Cover-Up 55

CHAPTER X:
The Hawk Has Landed 67

CHAPTER XI:
The Wind Picks Up 75

CHAPTER XII:
Interference Begins 85

CHAPTER XIII:
The Evidence 95

CHAPTER XIV:
The Sleeping Dog Awakens 103

CHAPTER XV:
Fall Guys 107

CHAPTER XVI:
Forgery Too 115

CHAPTER XVII:
Appendix O 129

CHAPTER XVIII:
Ostracized 133

CHAPTER XIX:
Halloween Assault 139

CHAPTER XX:
Deep Cover Informant 147

CHAPTER XXI:
Bull's Eye: Los Alamos 157

CHAPTER XXII:
Going Down Slow 187

CHAPTER XXIII:
'Not Suitably Fit' 195

CHAPTER XXIV:
Media Exoneration 203

CHAPTER XXV:
Beheading the Organization 215

CHAPTER XXVI:
Doran and Walp Speak, Congress Listens 225

CHAPTER XXVII:
Media Blasts 237

CHAPTER XXVIII:
On the Eve of the Hearings 243

CHAPTER XXIX:
Turbulent Congressional Hearings Begin 249

CHAPTER XXX:
The Hearing Heats Up 261

CHAPTER XXXI:
Red Flags of Cover-Up 269

CHAPTER XXXII:
No Gain? Not Exactly 275

CHAPTER XXXIII:
Fallout, Aftermath 281

CHAPTER XXXIV:
Missing Plutonium – Missing Keys – Missing Security 293

CHAPTER XXXV:
Our Settlements 297

CHAPTER XXXVI:
Past Failures 305

CHAPTER XXXVII:
Will LANL Ever Be Secure and Safe? 317

CHAPTER XXXVIII:
Meth Lab Connection 325

CHAPTER XXXIX:
Clear and Present Dangers 2009 329

CHAPTER XL:
A Nation at Risk 335

ACRONYMS 341
ABOUT THE AUTHOR 345
ACKNOWLEDGEMENTS 349
ASSOCIATED FEDERAL AND STATE LAWS 353
INDEX 359

AUTHOR'S NOTE

This book is based on the recollected experiences of Glenn A. Walp and reflects his perception of his life and work at the Los Alamos National Laboratory, in Los Alamos, New Mexico. The personalities, events, actions, and conversations portrayed within the story have been taken from his memories, and some conversations/dialogues have been reconstructed for clarity and grammatical consistency using extensive interviews, taped notes, research, court documents, letters, personal papers, congressional testimony, press accounts, and the memories of participants.

In an effort to safeguard the privacy of certain people, some individuals' names and identifying characteristics may have been altered. Supplanted names and characteristics are fictitious. Thus, any similarities to actual persons, living or dead, are purely coincidental. Events involving the characters happened as described. Only minor details may have been changed.

This book was written, authored, produced, published, distributed, and marketed under the authority, responsibilities, rights, indemnities, and protections of Justice Publishing, LLC, State of Nevada, Glenn A. Walp as Operating Manager/Managing Member and Secretary.

All nuclear weapons research data and associated security information contained within this writing are in the public domain.

PROLOGUE

At the dawn of the twentieth century, humankind was in the throes of a scientific revolution. Whereas the Renaissance advanced scientific thinking, science now stepped beyond the box into a new world of discovery that included the splitting of the atom. Lise Meitner and Otto Frisch called that process fission. Within a few months of their discovery, physicist Enrico Fermi theorized that a pound of fissionable isotope uranium would unleash the power of 15,000 tons of exploding TNT.

At roughly the same time Meitner and Frisch had unwittingly opened the door to the possibility of an unprecedented weapon of mass destruction, fascism walked through it in the form of Adolf Hitler and Benito Mussolini — dictators who had fixed their sights on ruling the world with brutality and genocide. With the threat of a Second World War looming — along with the persecution of his fellow Jews — Albert Einstein wrote to United States President Brianlin D. Roosevelt, hinting that it would be in the United States' best interest to develop a nuclear, chain-reaction bomb before Germany did. Initially alarmed by Einstein's admonishments, with the Japanese attack on Pearl Harbor, Roosevelt began to realize that the United States had better begin to harness a power that heretofore had belonged only to God. Roosevelt subsequently mandated the development of a nuclear-weapons program, which would be code-named the Manhattan Project, after the Manhattan District of the Army Corps of Engineers. Leadership duties in fulfilling the task of developing a nuclear weapons laboratory fell to United States Army General Leslie R. Groves.

I was just a few months old when Groves, U.S. Army Major

John Dudley, Edwin McMillan, and J. Robert Oppenheimer debated over where the new laboratory would be located. The selection of Site Y on the isolated Pajarito (*"Little Bird"*) Plateau in Los Alamos (*"The Poplars"*), New Mexico was mainly chosen because of its inaccessibility. Groves knew he was dealing with a committed radical enemy and believed that if Adolph Hitler got the slightest inkling of what was happening on the plateau, he would send spies into the land. As a result, Groves established controlled access roads, guard posts, fences, and armed personnel. He also ordered departmentalization of research functions; each scientist would have access only to information relevant to their specific work. Many of the scientists were angered at Groves' dictate, demanding academic freedom so they could share their knowledge. Nevertheless, Groves' hard-core military security perspective prevailed.

As Oppenheimer, the first lab director, and General Groves wrangled over the organizational structure of the operation, they decided to select an outside contractor that could handle the lab's procurement and administrative tasks. Oppenheimer would be responsible for the science, and Groves the security. The University of California, Oppenheimer's employer, was chosen as the contractor, signing a contract with the federal government in April 1943.

Twenty-seven months after the first scientists arrived at the Los Alamos National Laboratory, the world's first atomic bomb was developed.

On July 16, 1945, at 5:29:45 a.m., Mountain Time, in a place named Trinity in central New Mexico, the scientists finally and fully tested their theory on splitting atoms as the force of 21,000 tons of TNT exploded, evaporating the tower on which the device stood.

Scientists and military personnel watched this world-changing event. Scientists such as Fermi described, with elation, the technical aspects of the explosion. U.S. Army General Thomas F. Farrell noted that seconds after the explosion there was an air blast, immediately followed by a strong, sustained awesome roar, "...which warned of doomsday and made us feel we puny things were blasphemous to dare tamper with the forces heretofore reserved for the Almighty."

Oppenheimer quoted from the Bhagavad-Gita, "I am become Death, the Destroyer of Worlds."

The United States had attained its goal of beating Germany to the atomic punch.

Although the Manhattan Project mission had been accomplished, that was not the end of the Los Alamos National Laboratory. The University of California contract had a proviso that allowed the federal government to extend the contract for the duration of the war, plus six months.

Those "plus six months" evolved into 61 years without competition.

Consequently, from July 17, 1945, research into maintaining and enhancing the United States' nuclear-weapons arsenal has become a perpetual task, with the University of California at the helm. The basic concept has always been that, by staying at least one step ahead of the enemy and by keeping our national secrets out of their grip, threats against America's security will decrease and, hopefully, disappear.

But from the very beginning of these covert operations, security of Los Alamos' secrets has met with significant failures. These failures included a Los Alamos scientist selling nuclear secrets to an arch enemy of the United States; another Los Alamos scientist illegally downloading classified weapons information; an unknown lab employee losing hard drives that contained the world's most classified nuclear weapons secrets; and a laboratory contract employee walking out of the lab's front gate with classified nuclear weapon data secreted upon her person.

The University of California and the Los Alamos National Laboratory had survived the scientist's confession that he was a spy and withstood a raging 2000 Cerro Grande forest fire that destroyed or damaged lab buildings. But gross theft, corruption, mismanagement, and cover-up that began to unravel at the Los Alamos National Laboratory in 2002 was too egregious to surmount. It would prove fatal to the University of California's exclusive grip on nuclear-weapons research.

I was the Office Leader of the Los Alamos National Laboratory's Office of Security Inquiries, and Steven (Steve) Doran and James (Jim) Mullins were my top two Security Specialists-III. Steve, Jim, and I quickly learned that certain Los Alamos lab leaders wanted the laboratory run like a college campus, allowing employees and visitors to experience a campus environment, not a military installation. This approach was a quantum leap from the security and safeguard perspective mandated by General Groves.

Like Groves, Steve, Jim, and I were acutely aware that as members of the lab's Security and Safeguards Division the essence of our responsibilities was to help to protect the secrets of our nation. We were dedicated to helping preserve the United States' nuclear-weapons stockpile, a stash vital to the protection of all Americans, especially in these times of rogue nations and fanatical terrorists.

But what had begun in the mid-1940s as an operation committed to security and safeguards had degenerated, Steve, Jim, and I opine, into lackadaisical, cavalier nonchalance.

Within a few months of arriving at the Los Alamos National Laboratory, I uncovered major in-house thefts amounting to millions of taxpayer dollars, the loss of millions of dollars in federal property, waste, fraud, abuse, and ultimately, by some laboratory leaders, corruption and attempted cover-up. The more Steve, Jim, and I attempted to correct the wrong, which we fervently believed threatened America's security and put the lab's top secrets at risk, the more some of our bosses resented us. Some interfered with our investigations and those of the FBI; some attempted to intimidate us; some eventually proposed that unless we obeyed the laboratory's corporate philosophy of looking out for the lab, its image, and its contract with the Department of Energy, we could be leveled or fired – as Steve and I eventually were.

In writing this book, I have multiple aspirations. These include that the new leaders and management of the Los Alamos National Laboratory become wise stewards of America's secrets, that they will be standard-bearers for honesty based on principles of managerial ethics, and that they make their main concern *iron-clad protection* of our national secrets.

With a new course of direction, perhaps the managers of all other American national laboratories will adopt a new, more focused mission to protect national security and our top secrets.

I hope that this ensures the protection and permanence of these United States, a great land that God has blessed, and for which hundreds of thousands of Americans continue to be so willing to sacrifice their lives.

GLENN A. WALP, Ph.D.

I

Security and Safeguards Los Alamos Style 2002

"Steve Doran, OSI, may I help you?" Doran said, as he picked up the clamoring telephone at the Office of Security Inquiries (OSI) at the Los Alamos National Laboratory (LANL) in Los Alamos, New Mexico.

On the other end of the line was an excited lab employee. Some guy just came out of X-Division, took a roll of white papers from beneath his jacket and hid them in the back seat of his car, and removing anything from this division is strictly forbidden because X-Division deals with secret nuclear weapons plans, said the now frantic employee.

Steve snatched the keys to a company vehicle and headed for the door. Marty Farley, a fellow security inquirer also assigned to the Office of Security Inquiries, stopped Steve and asked where he was going in such a hurry. Steve explained and was informed by Farley that a lab attorney had told him that there was nothing to be done in such cases, but that he would go with Steve anyhow.

The two found the empty car in the X-Division parking lot and saw the rolled-up documents on the back seat floor area. Farley repeated his position, indicating that the lab attorney told him that OSI had no authority to take action in these types of circumstances, so if the guy came out and drove off, there was nothing he or Steve could do.

"Marty, we have a witness who is telling us about possible espionage that could affect the security of America, maybe the world," Doran argued. "We found the car, we can see the papers, and you say we can't do anything?"

Farley replied that he was following the attorney's direction, and was not going to get sued or fired.

Doran retorted, "I can tell you this, Marty. That car is not leaving until I find out what those documents are." Marty retreated to the company vehicle while Doran stood watch over the suspect vehicle.

Soon a male approached the vehicle in question and Steve swooped in. "What's the roll of paper on the back seat floor of your car, sir?" Doran asked.

The man was visibly frightened. They're just blueprints of my house, he said, stammering. I copied them on a lab Xerox machine and I didn't want anyone to know because I could get in trouble, the employee continued.

Doran inspected the vehicle thoroughly, and confiscated the documents, which were in fact blueprints of the employee's house.

Doran contacted me later stating, "Glenn, if this is the way OSI has been operating, then God only knows what secrets have disappeared off this hill."

Alarming and incomprehensible to Steve and me, yes, but nothing we hadn't dealt with before in our few months of employment with the Los Alamos National Laboratory.

A few weeks before this incident I was in my office when I received a similar excited call from Rich Gitto, a leader within the lab's Business Operations Division. Rich told me to contact Jason

Matthews in the ESA (Engineering Sciences and Application) Division because Jason told him he thinks he has a major theft, but he wasn't going to contact me because he wanted to handle it himself. Gitto continued, that he told Jason to call me, because since I took over OSI things have changed and were not like they used to be.

Within seconds of Gitto's call, Doran received a call from Matthews who told Doran about the alleged theft.

Steve and I parleyed, and I immediately arranged a meeting between Matthews, Doran, and me. Matthews grudgingly explained the details of the possible theft, and after much prodding, also admitted that he believed he might have another theft case. Matthews acknowledged he did not intend to tell me about the possible thefts, but Gitto scared him into calling me.

I asked Matthews why he would not call me about these incidents since lab policy mandates that he must do so. Matthews' response, "We haven't reported any similar type incidents to OSI in the last three years, so this time it wasn't any different."

"Are you saying you had multiple similar type issues in the past three years, Jason, and you never told anyone, and you handled them yourself?" I said strongly.

"That's right," Matthews responded.

"But why Jason", I asked. "Why would you not call us?" Besides violating lab policy and perhaps federal law, I continued, do you see how important it is to report this information to OSI immediately? We need to be involved from the very moment you have knowledge of a problem, because by now evidence could have been destroyed, suspects warned, and alibis established, I stated.

I understand, Matthews said, and I agree things have been flung too far to the right and there is too much freedom; it's too loose around here. There are not enough checks, balances, and controls, continued Matthews, and according to my bosses, the customer is always right, and they consider the employee the customer; so they tell me to let them alone, and I do.

Gitto was in full panic mode when he called me a few days

later to check up on what was happening with Matthews and ESA. "UC (University of California) could lose the DOE (Department of Energy) contract if this information is exposed", Gitto said. My boss is scared about losing his job because of the property control problems that you are uncovering, continued Gitto, and I warned him before, that in normal business operations there is a contract administrator and then another person for oversight of the contracts, but here at LANL the contract administrator and the oversight person are the same person. That setup is prone to create circumstances in which crime can occur, and that's what is happening at the lab, concluded Gitto.

From another security perspective, Steve and I had befriended multiple lab security guards who expressed their personal displeasure with the way security was being handled at the lab. They alleged that at some posts they didn't carry guns; at times, they walked around with empty holsters; and on occasion, they had to respond to potential violent issues without a weapon. They also alleged that their supervisors told them that although they didn't have guns at some posts, people would think they had them because they wore uniforms. Another guard stated that in his opinion, he worked under a security concept of no guns and no bullets.

When Steve, Jim, and I independently accepted offers of employment at the Los Alamos laboratory, we expected to join forces with an organization united to ensure ironclad security and safeguarding of America's nuclear secrets. To our startling surprise, what we found instead was, in our opinion, an organization that reeked with arrogance, mismanagement, incompetence, corruption, and failed security. Although the vast majority of the lab's nearly 14,000 employees and contractors were honest, dedicated, hard-working individuals, corrupt and enervated attributes permeated a significant number of lab administrators, directors, managers, supervisors, and rank-and-file personnel; all of which placed America's nuclear weapons secrets at great risk.

The springboard that propelled the uncovering of the illegal

4

and corrupt events at the Los Alamos National Laboratory in 2002 and beyond had its launching a few months before, December 2001 to be exact, while I was employed by the State of Arizona.

II

New Horizons

Three months after the calamitous tragedy of September 11, 2001, I was offered and accepted the position as Office Leader of the Office of Security Inquiries at the Los Alamos National Laboratory.

At the time of the offer, I was employed as Chief of the Arizona Capitol Police. After some quick domestic deliberations, my wife Mary and I set our sights on a new horizon — veiled as it was — and were deep into relocating our lives 523 miles from Scottsdale, Arizona to Santa Fe, New Mexico.

As I drove our family car into the *City Different*, Mary turned to me half smiling, half frowning, as we encountered heavy snow falling on Santa Fe's Cerillos Road, stating, "Bathing suits yesterday; snow boots today; you didn't tell me we were moving to Alaska, Colonel Walp."

My new job was to help protect national security interests while assisting in the safeguarding of all Americans. The position description included conducting investigations into theft, harassing/threatening letters and telephone calls, vandalism/unauthorized tampering, illegal/controlled substance, property protection, strategies and tactical planning for office activities, coordinating the drug detection/deterrence program, and supervising, directing, and conducting inquiries into national security matters. My area of responsibility encompassed forty-three square miles of property with more than one hundred different security areas, approximately 2000 classified computers, and seven million classified documents. It was for me a momentous, but easy, decision. The Los Alamos National Laboratory housed our nation's top secrets, and I wanted to serve my country, which was in the midst of one of its greatest challenges, by helping to protect those secrets.

What type of person, I *now* ask myself, would be willing to risk a six-figure job, a career, and a work reputation for the sake of ideals like truth, justice, and righteousness? Who would be inclined — perhaps foolish enough — to take on solving what was rumored to be the heavy problems and tainted atmosphere of a facility grown into a corporate giant and perhaps an even larger beast, which was supposed to be dedicated to protecting America's security by keeping its top secret defense safe, but, had major flaws, which put those secrets at risk.

For better or worse, on that frigid, January moving day, it was I, Glenn Arlen Walp.

Mary and I quickly settled into our new Santa Fe surroundings. I was now ready to begin my new adventure at the world's most famous nuclear research lab.

Driving to my first day on the job, I proceeded north on U.S. Highway 84/285 through the magnificent splendor of the Tesuque and Pojoaque valleys; I turned the truck west on New Mexico State Highway 502. There I crossed the Rio Grande, advancing upward into the formidable Jemez Mountains. My 4-cylinder, 4x4 dark blue Toyota pickup truck grumbled as it eked up the incline that led to the top of a plateau where the birthplace of the Manhattan Project lay. At that moment, I was gripped by a sensation from my West Hazleton, Pennsylvania high school football days, the gut-wrenching anticipation between kickoff and the first crack of my stalking shoulder pads against the juking thigh pads of my opponent.

My ponderings were suddenly interrupted. All around me were inspiring sights of God's magnificent grandeur: high desert plants encased in earthen hues of pale coral, muted red, green, and calming shades of tan. Mountain peaks glistened while the sun's rays ricocheted off sheets of new snow. Above was the frame of a crystal blue heaven. I drank in the beauty gratefully.

Within that awe-inspiring moment, my thoughts traveled back to Pennsylvania, my beloved family, and my wonderful upbringing.

My parents, Josephine J. (Horn) and Silas E. Walp, raised their brood — William, Rollin, Allen, Richard, Nancy, Eileen and Glenn — on a small farm in Drums, a quaint, secluded agriculture region in northeastern Pennsylvania. Ours was a typical American rural upbringing; my parents worked hard on our 22-acre truck farm raising cattle, chickens, swine, turkeys, and ducks while at the same time instilling in us the virtues of truth and honesty regardless of cost as well as a deep love for and obedience to God. In addition to my dad's working the farm, he also worked fulltime in the anthracite strip mines located near Hazleton, Pennsylvania. Inspiring stories of my great-uncle George Wagner, a member of the first Pennsylvania State Police class, added greatly to my value system; so early on I decided I wanted to grow up to become a Pennsylvania State Trooper.

In addition to my house and farm chores, I held a series of jobs as I grew up: farmhand at Hilliard's Dairy Farm in Sugarloaf, Pennsylvania; delivery boy for Risenweaver's Country Store in Drums and for Henry's Cleaners in Hazleton, Pennsylvania; and a member of a surveying team for Gannet and Fleming in Harrisburg, Pennsylvania. I also worked in multiple positions for the drug company Merck, Sharp and Dhome in West Point, Pennsylvania, and, in a portent of things to come, as a security guard for Miley's Detective Agency, also in West Point. During the restless late 1950s and early 1960s, I wrote and sang rock-n-roll in a few bands, and even cut a record in the mecca of rock-n-roll, Philadelphia, Pennsylvania. These diverse, adventurous roads had brought me to my childhood goal: the Pennsylvania State Police, where I served for nearly three decades.

In 1996, I refocused my career from the Pennsylvania State Police and accepted a position as Chief of Police in Bullhead City, Arizona. After five years in Bullhead City, I again decided to refocus. This time I left active duty to concentrate on completing my Ph.D. course work. After achieving that educational milestone, I embarked on another job-hunt.

The job I most aspired to was a nationally publicized position as Office Leader of the Los Alamos National Laboratory Office of Security Inquiries. I applied but didn't hear back from the lab, so I accepted an offer to become chief of the Arizona Capitol Police in October 2001. Then after just a few weeks on that job, the call I had been hoping for came, and I was asked to interview for the Los Alamos position. I was happy where I was, but here was the opportunity I had been searching for to make a real difference, while serving the citizens of the country I loved. On November 19, I traveled to Los Alamos for an interview. Among the nearly dozen people with whom I spoke that day was the Security and Safeguards Division Leader Douglas (Doug) Madison, who told me he would make the decision on the hire in mid-December.

Having studied the available information on the facility, I told Madison that I felt the Office of Security Inquiries was inadequately staffed. Madison agreed. He told me that if I were hired, they would provide me with all the staff and resources I needed to perform the tasks described in the job description. He felt the Office of Security Inquiries was in disarray, that multiple OSI personnel were not performing their jobs adequately, and they desperately lacked professional leadership and investigative expertise. Madison told me that drastic changes needed to be made, and that's why they had launched a nationwide search for a professional criminal justice leader. A few weeks later, I was told the position was mine if I wanted it. I did.

About a month before I moved to Santa Fe, Michael Wismer called me at my Arizona home and introduced himself as the new Deputy Office Leader of the Office of Security Inquiries. Wismer said he was calling to let me know who he was, and to ask if there was anything he could do to help me in my move.

Mike came across as an intelligent, congenial, sincere individual who was glad to be part of the new management at the Office of Security Inquiries. He explained that he had already identified many things that needed to be changed in OSI, but would wait until I arrived to ensure that I agreed with him. "I can't wait until you get here," said Wismer. "There's so much that needs to be done."

With twenty-one years of United States Air Force service and two master's degrees, Wismer was well qualified. He had served as an aerospace control and warning systems operator, security police officer, law enforcement program manager, and commander-in-charge of the Air Force unit responsible for security of 200 intercontinental ballistic missile sites strategically located in United States. I realized I would be extremely fortunate to have him as my second-in-command. Nevertheless, I was already getting an uneasy feeling about the possible pitfalls and trials of the job that I had agreed to undertake. I was unaware these feelings would grow with each passing day.

III

Close Perils

All new employees of the Los Alamos National Laboratory receive an obligatory historical overview of the laboratory at the Bradbury Science Museum in downtown Los Alamos. The museum is rich with photographs of atomic explosions, vitas of the lab's founding fathers, along with plaques that explain the tedious research that went into developing the first atomic bomb. With muted emotion, I touched the replicas of "Fat Man" and "Little Boy." I became entranced with the idea of playing a part — how significant unknown — in this theater of weighty world history. I didn't know what new steps I would need to learn in this fresh dance, but I was determined to adjust to the new beat.

After two days of introductory training, I reported to the Security and Safeguards Division (S-Division) Headquarters. Not being Department of Energy Q-cleared (Department of Energy background clearance that allows unescorted access to certain classified areas and/or classified information), I was quarantined to a 12 x 12 room within the Office of Security Inquiries double-wide office trailer adjacent to S-Division Headquarters. Beyond the perimeters of my office, I had to be escorted by a Q-cleared person, even to the restroom. Although the escort did not enter the portals of privacy, he, and sometimes she, waited outside the door. Thus, my baptism into a world of secrecy and intrigue began.

My first morning at my new job, Ken Schiffer, the leader of the laboratory's Office of Internal Security, visited me in my office. Ken was a retired FBI agent and accomplished rodeo rider who favored cowboy duds over dark suits. He and I had several mutual FBI acquaintances in the eastern United States. Smiling as he offered his enthusiastic vice grip handshake, Ken told me how glad he was I had taken on this assignment. Then his face turned sober as he transitioned to the real purpose of his visit.

He told me that he had limited knowledge, but he strongly believed there was significant theft occurring at the Los Alamos laboratory. Ken proposed that the lab never had an OSI Office Leader with my background, training, and expertise to do the professional policing job that needed to be done to address this theft. The current OSI inquirers are nice people, continued Ken, but most of them don't have the know-how, drive, or desire to investigate the flagrant crime I feel is occurring within the lab.

Schiffer next said that he'd immediately arrange a meeting with S-Division's Deputy Division Leader, Matt (Mack) Falcon, my immediate supervisor, during which the three of us would discuss the lab's theft issues. He quickly kept his word, arranging the meeting for the next day.

Walking into Falcon's office, I observed a neatly kept space filled with memorabilia of his career as an officer in the United States Air Force. Falcon's office was located in a doublewide trailer that served as S-Division's Headquarters. The walls were packed with pictures of atom bomb explosions, an appropriate representation of what the Los Alamos National Laboratory was all about. Schiffer, Falcon, and I sat down around Falcon's small metal gray conference table and spoke for nearly two hours. During this conversation, Schiffer expressed concern that a large number of thefts had been occurring at the lab for many years. No one in the past has done anything about it, said Schiffer, shaking his head and grimacing, and I think it is time the lab makes a serious effort in attempting to address these major thefts.

He paused, and added, "It is possible the thefts are connected to the drug trade in the north part of the state."

Illegal drug use and trafficking were rife in northern New Mexico. Schiffer postulated that lab employees might be stealing government property to either buy or trade for drugs or for more infamous reasons. Either way, said Schiffer, these threats could severely undermine the lab's overall security, to include "the protection of our nuclear secrets." One theft, of which he was aware, was the documented stealing of truckloads of government lumber. Just the few thefts he knew about could be hundreds of thousands of dollars.

Schiffer shifted his eyes directly toward Falcon and proposed that something needed to be done about the thefts, and thus far, the laboratory has not done enough to deal with these and other major crime and security issues.

Schiffer recommended taking a task force approach that he said could include the New Mexico State Police, the FBI, the Drug Enforcement Administration (DEA), the Los Alamos County Police Department (LAPD), and perhaps someone from the Office of Security Inquiries.

I watched closely as Falcon remained largely mute during Schiffer's presentation, occasionally nodding his head in agreement. I had been trained to be aware of my gut reactions when first meeting others, and, at that moment, I made a mental note for future reference. Ken then asked Falcon if I could begin the project by conducting an analysis of the theft problems and profiling the criminal acts at the lab, similar to the FBI's Uniform Crime Reporting (UCR) system. This would entail detailing the types of crimes as well as the time of day and day of the week they're most likely to be committed in order to help obtain a lucid profile of the criminal activity.

I took a deep breath, let it out slowly and then opened, "Before digging into the thefts and other criminal issues, I need some time to get settled in my office and learn about OSI operations." Falcon agreed, directing me to evaluate, at my convenience, the laboratory's theft problems, then report back to Schiffer and him on my findings.

Falcon then moved to close the meeting. Theft is so bad at the lab that "it has been making the valley green for years," he said frowning. Falcon was referring to the Española/Pojoague Valley, an area near Los Alamos, where many lab employees resided. "For all the Leathermans (a pocket multi-tool, costing approximately $70.00)", Falcon said giving an example "we have purchased in S-Division alone, every member should have at least three." Falcon concluded his thought, indicating that S-Division personnel keep ordering Leathermans, and I needed to find out what was going on.

Returning to my office, I began making notes. Thirty-five years in law enforcement had seared into my mind the importance of keeping a comprehensive journal. I began, simply enough, "If thefts are so bad and have been occurring for such a long time, why hasn't someone done something about it?" Suddenly to my mind sprang the question, "And what else lies beneath the surface here?" It was, I was soon to learn, a fateful question.

At that point, I didn't realize that the massive buried problems at Los Alamos had resulted in mounds of corruption, criminality, treachery, and mismanagement; or, that Steve Doran, James Mullins, and I would meet with furious opposition and interference as we sought to uncover the infamy and stealth present at the United States' pre-eminent laboratory of nuclear-weapons research. But I had just had my first awakening to the fact that what lay in wait could put America's top secrets at risk.

I leaned back into my chair reflecting on what else was occurring here, going over in my mind the lab's history, my own history, and my preparation to meet what I had begun to find out was going to be the greatest challenge of my life.

IV

The Winds of Change

The day after meeting with Falcon and Schiffer, I had my first staff meeting with Madison and Falcon at S-Division Headquarters. This meeting proved to be a fascinating and thought provoking occasion. Madison's office was the largest in the building. Like Falcon's, Madison's workplace exuded a sterile military feel, dotted with photographs of atomic bomb explosions and filled with manuals, bound reports, charts, and diagrams. At Security and Safeguards Division meetings there was never a doubt who was in charge; it was always Madison, the retired Air Force Colonel and now division leader responsible for administering all security and safeguards at the Los Alamos National Laboratory.

Madison had authored a scathing October 2000 report titled "S-Division Re-engineering" in which he identified problems within the Special Projects Office, which would soon be renamed as the Office of Security Inquiries. The Special Projects Office, he wrote, reluctantly, if it ever, cooperated with local law enforcement; did not conduct property protection incident investigations in a thorough or timely manner; completed inadequate investigations and inquiries; was wedded to ineffective past policies and procedures; needed a new infusion of personnel; and needed a new Office Leader to organize investigations and inquiries.

Welcoming me to the lab, Madison took quite a bit of time detailing why I was hired.

Madison postulated that for quite some time OSI has been in dire need of a professional criminal justice person with an extensive background in policing leadership and criminal investigations to lead the office, and that was the reason they hired me. Madison continued, that I was a lot smarter than Matt and he as it pertained to police-type activity. "We believe we have chosen the right person to do the job," said Madison.

Madison repeated what some others were asserting about the past inadequacies of the Office of Security Inquiries. He explained that the office's inquiry staff consisted of nice people and good outstanding individuals, but some lacked the drive, ability, or wherewithal to accomplish the daunting tasks now facing the laboratory.

Madison not only again promised to hire more qualified people to help me in my new job, but he told me I'd be able to make my own hires with the assistance of Victoria Snelling, S-Division's Human Resources Director, and Carol Estes, S-Division's Chief of Staff. He told me the winds of change were needed and went on to say, "You will play a major part in that change."

Because Office of Security Inquiries current work ethics and productivity seemed to him severely deficient, Madison said my first task was to professionalize all OSI operations as quickly as possible. I would learn a few weeks later that the reason they wanted fast action — what was behind the impetus for my hiring and my $10,000 bonus for an early start — was the result of something called the Appendix O mandate concerning OSI's professionalism. S-Division was preparing for an upcoming Department of Energy (DOE) audit and the Security and Safeguards Division needed to show that they could meet these Appendix O standards. Madison declared that the University of California's ability not only to gain extra funding, but perhaps to maintain its decades-old contract may depend on the success of the audit. As a first course of action, I was directed to meet and establish working relations with the Los Alamos County Police Department chief, local FBI office leaders, a liaison with the DEA, Immigration and Naturalization Service personnel, Indian Affairs officials, and assorted other criminal justice agencies.

And then, I heard a warning, which brought an icy chill to the room. There are three inquirers in OSI who applied for your job, but never got an interview, Madison said. According to Madison, they didn't get an interview because they were unqualified, and they were really pissed because I got the job, and especially because I was coming in from the outside. So, continued Madison, you will need to be on your toes when dealing with them. I suspect these three will not be helpful in assisting you getting organized and understanding the issues and problems in OSI, while some, Madison warned, as he looked right into my eyes, may even willfully misguide you if they have the opportunity, so be careful.

As the rundown from Madison and Falcon continued, I began to think that the actions I would need to take would be complex and arduous. However, Madison did say that there were other security specialists who could be counted on to provide valuable assistance, and the office administrator had been in that position for some time and would be one of my greatest assets. Madison also said that a part-time college student would be helpful, and in addition, a well-credentialed, solid individual, Mike Wismer, who had been hired specifically to assist me, was busting at the seams to do the job, and would work very hard for me.

Finally, Madison told me that I had free reign to do as I deemed necessary to professionalize and bring expertise to the Office of Security Inquiries.

And so, four days into the job, I already had two major tasks to complete: (1) to critically analyze the lab's theft problems, and (2) to professionalize all Office of Security Inquiries operations. I didn't have a specific timetable, but I knew the tasks I was being asked to pursue were top priorities to Madison, Falcon, and Schiffer.

As I reviewed my early impressions of Madison and Falcon, I had positive feelings. There seemed to be a good fit with my own characteristics in terms of personalities and methodologies; they were retired military personnel, and I had spent most of my career in a quasi-military environment.

Madison, a tall, impressive commander-type, with a strong bear-like physique, was clearly an intelligent warrior and capable leader who was not afraid to take charge. I later learned that Madison associated closely with the military and war as a guiding life metaphor. Madison had casually mentioned that he loved the taste of battle, and because of that, some may call him crazy, but he loved it notwithstanding.

Using the Robert Duvall line from *Apocalypse Now*, I replied, "You must be one of those individuals who love the smell of napalm in the morning."

"You bet," he countered.

Falcon, a man of average stature exuded a crisp military look with a clean-cut bearing. My first impression was that he was a precise decision-maker not afraid to command even if the decisions were not popular with the rank-and-file. Falcon obviously loved his job and was dedicated to his command.

It was clear to me that Ken Schiffer was a dyed-in-the-wool cop, who exemplified unwavering dedication and integrity, with a rock-solid commitment to serve — a person I immediately felt comfortable with; a person I could trust.

The way I work is to tackle new assignments head-on. Under normal circumstances, I would have been in my office all weekend arranging drawers, files, and bookcases, while consuming manuals and regulations so I could best understand the lab's operations. But Madison told me that since I was not yet Q-cleared, I was not allowed access to my office on weekends – and I could only be in the facility between 6 a.m. and 6 p.m. every weekday.

When Madison saw my visible disappointment, he chuckled and told me to take advantage of my lack of clearance, because the day would come when I would spend so much time there I would wish I was uncleared.

And so, I mentally absorbed my new assignments, taking them home to mull over that first weekend. All Saturday and Sunday, I anxiously anticipated what I would do when I returned to work on Monday morning. I was intrigued with my tasks and pleased that Madison and Falcon offered me their complete confidence and full support. I knew I would need that, along with full authority, to execute the tasks they not only wanted me to complete, but also *demanded* that I complete. I couldn't wait to get back to work.

Early on Monday morning, I began to dig in to the task of organizing my office, learning the basics of Office of Security Inquiries operations and the fault lines associated with those functions. Though an analysis of the lab's theft problem was of major importance to Falcon and Schiffer, there were other more pressing concerns to which I would direct my attention.

I wanted to meet individually with all Office of Security Inquiries employees and get to know their backgrounds, tasks, assignments, and aspirations. That's what I did whenever I took over a new command, and that's what I would do here. During these personal meetings, two factors became clear. Some OSI employees were not happy with my presence. Others agreed with Madison and Falcon's assessment that it was time for change. I recognized it would take significant effort to get some Office of Security Inquiries employees to accept change, and at the same time, I understood, as Madison and Falcon had earlier implied, that I would have to rely upon my instincts if I were to survive and do what needed to be done.

After concluding my first meetings with all Office of Security Inquiries personnel, I met with Mike Wismer, with whom I had briefly spoken prior to starting my new job, to discuss our mutual ideas of professionalizing the Office of Security Inquiries. Wismer told me he felt the first order of business was to evaluate OSI inquiry reports. According to Wismer, some OSI personnel had a reputation for being incompetent inquirers. I have a feeling some OSI inquiries are totally insufficient, said Wismer. Continuing, Wismer stated that as a starting point, he would like to analyze all OSI criminal inquiry reports for the last three years and then advise me of his findings.

Wismer then made reference to some inquirers who had a reputation for "bungling" criminal inquiries. I told Wismer to let me know his determinations as soon as possible. Two days later, he returned.

"Glenn," said Wismer, "you aren't going to believe this, but you can't even classify these reports as inquiries." Wismer proposed that major thefts have one or two small paragraphs addressing the total inquiry, and in most cases, the inquiries are closed out on the first contact without follow-up. Not only that, Wismer continued, most of the work is being done by OSI office staff, not inquirers, and it looks like some inquirers don't even go to the scene of the crime; they just have the office staff telephone the complainant or victim and get whatever information they can, and that's it. Most of these inquiries are a disgrace, alleged Wismer, because they are incomplete and unprofessional, and I recommend this is the first thing we address. It's embarrassing to think this is the type of work OSI does, concluded Wismer.

Regretfully, I concurred with Wismer's conclusions after reviewing the reports, and soon approached two office staff members to ask if it were true that they prepared most OSI criminal inquiries— meaning they called the complainant/victim, typed the report, and then had the inquirer just sign the report. Both told me that was true, further informing me that they were ordered to do it that way.

Now I was sure Wismer had been right in his earlier observations. I decided the first area of change that needed to be made was to conduct professional inquiries and prepare professional inquiry reports.

Shortly thereafter, Schiffer arranged a meeting among the two of us and Senior Agent Mike Lowe of the FBI Regional Office in Santa Fe to discuss OSI inquiries. Lowe wasted no time in expressing his thoughts. OSI criminal inquiry reports are so poor that a member of my support staff was going to go to the media about it, Lowe said.

The person wanted to express her perspective from the view of a United States citizen who was disgusted with what she was reading, explained Lowe, but I talked the person out of it, for now, but I agree with her. Glenn, OSI inquiry reports are just terrible, concluded Lowe.

Lowe supported Schiffer's opinion that theft of major proportions had been occurring at the lab for quite a while. Lowe said he didn't know if anyone else at the lab cared besides Schiffer, because every time his agents attempted to work with lab personnel, they were stonewalled. My agents are completely frustrated with the lab's sidestepping, continued Lowe, and it appears some laboratory personnel don't like the FBI at the laboratory, perhaps not wanting the FBI to know what is going on, or maybe to keep negative information from going public.

Lowe closed the meeting with a prophetic statement, which brought an ominous mood to the room. "Glenn," said Lowe, "I only hope they let you do the job that you were hired to do, and needs to be done."

V

Let the Changes Begin

Digging into my work, I asked Falcon how many criminal suspects S-Division personnel had identified in the last decade that ended up in prosecution and punishment. His answer shocked me.

"None."

It was difficult to comprehend that of the hundreds, perhaps thousands of thefts and other crimes that had apparently plagued the lab in the last ten years, not one suspect was ever identified by an S-Division member that ended up in prosecution and punishment.

"None?" I repeated shaking my head in disbelief.

With a sense of urgency, I began making changes. Making changes and taking charge was not new to me. In my tenure with the Pennsylvania State Police, I spearheaded the department's national accreditation program, resulting in the force becoming the largest accredited police agency in the United States in July 1993. I implemented a minority recruitment drive that resulted in a 42-percent increase in minority recruitment, and created the first-ever

Heritage Affairs Officer position and Civil Tension Task Forces that were highly successful in defusing potential violent social issues throughout the state. In addition, I initiated a statewide criminal psychological profiling program that interfaced with the Federal Bureau of Investigation's Violent Criminal Apprehension Program, instituted the first-ever State Police community policing programs consisting of town hall meetings and trooper robots, while directing the department's first-ever Strategic Planning program. I was also the Assistant Task Force Commander of the 1977 Johnstown Flood, and the Task Force Commander of the 1989 Camp Hill Prison Riot.

After leaving the Pennsylvania State Police, I took the position as Chief of Police in Bullhead City, Arizona, where I launched a variety of first-ever criminal justice programs in the city. These included a Colorado River Safety Task Force, a gang intervention program, nationally recognized traffic safety programs that concentrated on speeding and drunk driving, multiple community policing programs that emphasized establishing positive relationships with a quickly increasing Hispanic community, initiating preliminary efforts towards national accreditation, and creating programs to address critical criminal problems regarding aggressive begging, shoplifting, prostitution and illegal drug use. As with many issues on my agenda, a significant group of people stood impenetrable as roadblocks, saying such programs could never be initiated. Yet within a few months, I had created multiple proactive programs that were catalysts in helping clean the city from these vexations. Now I thought back on these accomplishments to give myself reassurance in spite of what I knew could be outspoken controversy and criticism.

I began making my initial changes. I created a new reporting system to replace what had substituted for one in the past. Leaning upon my law enforcement experience, I looked to the police reporting system used by the Pennsylvania State Police. The Office of Security Inquiries was responsible for two major types of inquiry efforts: crime-type incidents and security incidents. Criminal incidents involved such matters as theft, workplace violence, trespassing, and illegal drug use. For the most part, security incidents involved classified information. Violations included the generation of classified information on unclassified computers, sending classified information through the normal lab mail distribution system, and leaving a safe containing classified information open and unattended. Approximately fifty circumstances involving classified information could be considered violations, ranked 1-4 according to what was known as the Impact Measurement Indexes with IMI 1 being the worst violation. All violations required an OSI inquiry to determine the facts of the incident, if an employee had committed an infraction, and, whether that employee should be sanctioned for that violation.

Within a month of starting at the lab, I issued my first OSI Special Order: 02-01, titled "Inquiry Policy," meant to address the most annoying habit of the past. Special Order 02-01 emphasized complete, thorough, and concise reporting. No inquiry stone was to be left unturned. No longer would inquirers be allowed to base their inquiry conclusions solely on telephone interviews. Now, they would have to go to where the incident occurred so they could do what investigators are supposed to do: analyze the scene, take photographs, conduct interviews, etc.

The new reporting system required all off-site thefts to be fully investigated in conjunction with the applicable local police department, with a copy of the police department's report placed in an Office of Security Inquiries file. Before I was hired, for example, if a lab computer was stolen in Albuquerque, the lab inquirer was not mandated to follow up with the local police. Indeed, in the vast majority of the cases Wismer and I reviewed, no inquirer contacted the local police department to determine if the theft was ever reported or investigated by the local police department. Inquirers, in many cases, simply took the word of the lab employees that the item had been stolen and that they had reported the crime to the relevant police department. The inquiry consisted of a cursory lab theft report, based on the employee's statement alone, with the inquirer immediately closing out the case. Imagine how easy it might have been to steal anything, with this type of system in place.

I followed Special Order 02-01 with several others in an effort to enhance Office of Security Inquiries investigations and reporting processes. All were made with the following goals in mind: to determine if a criminal activity occurred, to develop a list of suspects if a crime did occur, to pass this information to a relevant law enforcement agency for follow-up investigation, and to assist the criminal justice agency, if relevant.

So, for the first time in the Los Alamos National Laboratory OSI history, inquirers were responsible for conducting professional inquiries and preparing professional inquiry reports in *all* incidents, with the specific intent of identifying criminal suspects for referral to an appropriate law enforcement agency, hopefully resulting in prosecution.

As I had anticipated, Special Order 02-01 was not met with pleasure by some Office of Security Inquiries members even though I wanted to make the reporting system as user-friendly and efficient as possible. I sent several inquirers to professional training classes in various locations throughout United States where they were to learn contemporary strategies in criminal inquiries, with an emphasis on reporting and interviewing techniques. Some of my staff helped me create a computerized reporting process to coincide with the new reporting system. This worked pretty well—about three days—before a multitude of problems arose. At times, the program could not be opened, formats would change, blocks would disappear and a plethora of other problems emerged. The system continued to deteriorate. We brought in an S-Division computer programmer to troubleshoot the system.

I can't fix the system easily because someone tinkered with it, the programmer told me. That someone, the programmer continued, was very knowledgeable on how to disrupt the system, because they created blocks attempting to prevent a programmer from getting in and fixing it. The programmer showed me how the person skillfully placed blocks so it would not be easy for anyone, regardless of abilities, to quickly fix the system.

Finally, we were able to institute some necessary counter blocks to prevent further alterations to the system, thanks to special efforts by several S-Division computer experts.

Who was the miscreant who apparently sabotaged the program?

A few weeks after I had taken over lab operations, I walked in on a conversation between a few Office of Security Inquiries staffers who were discussing how important it was for the University of California to maintain the Department of Energy contract. In a nonchalant, inquisitive manner, I asked, "What does it matter who has the contract?"

One of the staffers responded that it could affect their salaries, retirements, and benefits; a response that was a little too sharp for my tastes or expectations. "I'm nearing retirement and need the income", he said.

It was then suggested by another staffer that it was important for OSI inquiry reports to *reflect positively on the lab* so they wouldn't negatively affect the upcoming contract.

I could understand that employees would be concerned about salaries and benefits; but proposing that reports should be manipulated was so unconscionable that, in my naïveté, I truly believed these employees were toying with me; the new kid on the block.

I wouldn't be so naïve much longer.

VI

Cracks in the Ethical Wall

Homeland Security Director Tom Ridge was scheduled to visit the Los Alamos National Laboratory on February 21. Falcon had been directing VIP visit operations for years and took advantage of Ridge's coming visit to train me to assume those duties. Wismer, whose ability I already respected, was also helping Falcon. During the planning stages, Wismer told me Falcon was going to activate emergency lights on the Office of Security Inquiries vehicles transporting Ridge from the Los Alamos Airport to the lab. Aware that most state laws normally have tight restrictions on the use of emergency lights, I asked Wismer if it was legal for Office of Security Inquiries vehicles to "run code" off Department of Energy property for this type of operation.

I don't know, but that's what Falcon is directing, responded Wismer.

Reviewing New Mexico's traffic laws, I determined it was illegal for Office of Security Inquiries vehicles to run code off Department of Energy property for this type of function, unless of course there was an actual emergency, which this was not. I told Falcon, "Not only would it be illegal for OSI vehicles to run code, but it opens up the lab to civil liability if an accident occurs." After some wrangling, Falcon acceded to my position, saying that not only would OSI vehicles be directed not to run code during the Ridge visit, but that they'd also be disallowed for any future similar operation.

A few days later, Wismer told me that Falcon had advised him that he'd run code whenever he wanted to, regardless of the law or my stance on the matter. Falcon, Wismer added, had originally gone along with my determination only to appease me. As it turned out, Falcon didn't order a code run during Ridge's visit, but the situation continued to concern me.

Later, Wismer reported to me that Falcon commonly directed Office of Security Inquiries personnel to *fix* parking tickets issued by the lab's security force, Protective Technology Force of Los Alamos (PTLA), and that PTLA was keeping a running record on those cases. If true, it would be in violation of Laboratory General Administration Policy AM-617, Parking, dated December 31, 1999, to be exact. The policy clearly defined the method of resolving a parking violation notice: either by paying a fine up to twenty dollars, or by scheduling a hearing before the Laboratory Parking Enforcement Hearing Officer, who could dismiss the cite if he wanted to. The policy also stated that a person with repeated parking violations, serious parking violations, or who had failed to pay the fine could receive disciplinary action. In the most severe cases, this could actually result in termination of employment. Nowhere in the policy did it state that a parking violation could be voided by anyone other than the hearing officer.

In order to handle this problem, I authored and issued OSI Special Order 02-16. The order clarified that except for the Parking Enforcement Hearing Officer, no OSI member, or any other lab employee, had the authority to resolve parking violation notices. The order mandated in part that, if a person felt a notice was unwarranted and approached an Office of Security Inquiries staffer, that individual was to be told that he had the option of just paying the fine or requesting a hearing before the Parking Enforcement Hearing Officer. I also told Falcon about my position on voiding notices and provided him with a copy of Special Order 02-16.

Exactly one week later, a lab exec called me to request that I discharge a parking violation notice issued to one of his employees. I explained to him that OSI did not discharge parking violation notices, and that lab policy would be followed. I advised him that the individual who received the notice should request a hearing before the hearing officer.

His curt response was, not I, or anyone else in my staff, will attend any hearing. I will contact Matt Falcon, and Falcon will take care of it.

I then received a copy of a parking violation notice from Falcon, which Falcon directed me to cancel. The notice included a notation from the exec who called me, asking Falcon to *take care* of the violation.

This necessitated another meeting with Falcon. I told him, as I had previously, that canceling a parking notice violates lab policy. I also said, not mincing words, that I did not condone this activity, and that I wouldn't allow any OSI employee to be involved in such an unethical, discriminatory and, perhaps, illegal practice. In most environments fixing a parking ticket is a significant crime, I said, and reiterated a tale about arresting a judge for attempting to fix a State Police speeding ticket when I was a member of the Pennsylvania State Police. "I will not change my position on this crucial issue of work ethics," I said my voice hardening.

Falcon responded that this is the way he had always done it, so what do you recommend I do?

There's only one way to do it I believed; "Matt, follow the lab policy."

After some discussion, Falcon appeared to agree with me, and then directed me to create a document that could be forwarded to lab employees who were requesting cancellation of a parking notice.

I proceeded to write the order (OSI Special Order 02-19), clarifying the mandates of Policy AM-617. Giving Falcon a copy of the order, I attached a note explaining that this order could be forwarded by Falcon to those requesting a cancellation of their traffic cite. This, I felt, should make it to clear to Falcon, all lab employees, and with specificity, all Office of Security Inquiries personnel, that OSI employees could not resolve a parking violation notice, but rather, that the lab's General Administration Policy AM-617 would be strictly followed.

A few days later, I received another parking violation notice from Falcon, who again asked me to void it.

Perplexed, I called in Wismer to discuss the issue. Wismer alleged that Falcon has been voiding parking notices for years, and the people responsible for the program in PTLA always felt it was improper, perhaps illegal, and they've been keeping computerized records of all the notices Falcon voided. According to Wismer, the PTLA personnel have always believed that someday this matter would come up, and they wanted to ensure they had the evidence to show that it was Falcon's decision, not theirs.

Wismer also mentioned that voiding the notices might be a federal issue because all monies received from lab parking violations are designated for return to the federal government (taxpayers) and not back to the lab.

Unfortunately, Mike Wismer's stay in the Office of Security Inquiries was short-lived. Wismer told me that when he accepted the position Falcon told him he would be the deputy officer leader, second-in-command. However, continued Wismer, when he noticed that his first few paychecks did not correspond with the salary associated with that position, he approached Falcon who told him he had made a mistake, that he thought the position was for deputy, but Madison told him maybe someday, but not now.

Wismer was highly upset, telling me he felt he was duped

34

into taking the position. One of the major reasons I took this job, Wisner said, was because of the position level. I felt Falcon was very clear what the position was and what my salary would be, continued Wismer, but now he is reneging and says he can't do anything about it.

At the same time this happened, the chief of staff position within the Protective Technology Force of Los Alamos opened up. Wismer applied for the job, and in short order Wismer left the Office of Security Inquiries. His departure didn't make my work any easier.

Meanwhile, I continued to receive a slew of petitions from lab personnel requesting that I void parking violation notices. Four of them came from S-Division personnel. I promptly rejected all requests. I was quickly becoming unpopular — or at least an annoyance — to some laboratory employees.

In response, Falcon asked me to come to his office to discuss some personal matters. His tone was conciliatory. Falcon told me he was happy I had taken such a strong stance on the emergency light and parking notice issues, and that I had established a new reporting system that requires OSI personnel to perform their functions with professionalism and expertise.

Falcon went on to praise me, saying he should have been upholding lab policy regarding parking violations for a long time. I just never stood up for what was right to do in this matter, said Falcon. But I do respect you Glenn for your strong stance, and ask that you continue to do what you are doing, concluded Falcon.

That little talk gave me the impression that these breaches of ethics, minor as they were, could and would be repaired. I also felt that anyone, and certainly Falcon, should be allowed the courtesy to correct areas where old customs prevailed and which I now correctly called into question.

However, these ominously *venial* ethical cracks, manifesting themselves to me at first as requests to Office of Security Inquiries personnel to improperly void parking violations and overlook minor traffic laws, would prove to be harbingers of major ruptures to the lab's ethical infrastructure. As investigative interference and cover-ups emerged over the coming months, I knew how this polluted philosophy took root, continued to grow, and then flourish, spreading across much of the Los Alamos National Laboratory environment.

VII

Theft at Los Alamos

When I entered the Pennsylvania State Police Academy in Hershey, Pennsylvania, and graduated as a trooper four months later at the age of 24, I ranked No. 2 in the class – three-tenths of a point away from No. 1. I also served as class speaker, and on graduation day, I spoke of my lofty goals to make my state and its people safer and to diminish crime by keeping lawbreakers off the street. In addition, I confided my eventual aim to become Commissioner of the Pennsylvania State Police.

Beginning as a patrol officer with the force, I was naturally aggressive and liked to dig into things, so I was drawn to criminal investigations. Within three years, I became a criminal investigator pursuing cases of homicides, armed robberies, rapes, burglaries, and the like. In fact, my professional persona seemed instantly sealed on my very first day on the job as a criminal investigator when I arrested twelve suspected felons all of whom were eventually convicted. Upon returning to police headquarters at the end of my shift, criminal investigation corporal John Redigan dubbed me "The Hawk."

Within five years, I was promoted to corporal and to sergeant within six - an unprecedented accomplishment at that time. I made lieutenant in ten years; captain in seventeen years; and major two years after that. By 1987 I was promoted by the Governor of the Commonwealth of Pennsylvania, Robert P. Casey, to Lieutenant Colonel; the Deputy Commissioner of all state police operations. In 1991, Governor Casey made my graduation day wish a reality by appointing me as Commissioner of the Pennsylvania State Police, which was unanimously confirmed by the Pennsylvania Senate. With that title, I became only the second commissioner in State Police history to have held every rank in the department. I had, by the grace of God, reached my goal.

In the spring of 1993, Pennsylvania State Representative Peter J. Daley II of Donora, Pennsylvania, asked if I'd be interested in running for governor of the Commonwealth of Pennsylvania on the Democratic ticket. Daley, on behalf of a group of Democrats from western Pennsylvania, told me he thought I had what it took to make a successful run. Ultimately I respectfully declined, telling Daley, that I preferred to stay within the arena of criminal justice. The eventual party nominee would be Lieutenant Governor Mark Singel.

The Republican Party front-runner was the state's attorney-general, Ernest Preate, Jr. Preate looked to be a shoo-in to win in the primary election, even though the Pennsylvania Crime Commission and the Pennsylvania State Police had begun investigating him on corruption allegations. I was chairman of the commission at the time, had completed the commission's report on Preate in April 1994 and was preparing to make my presentation before the Pennsylvania Senate soon after. However, one week before that presentation, I received a call from a politico, asking me if I would hold off releasing the report until after the May primary election. The reasoning for the delay was that if the report were released during the general election runoff against the Democratic candidate Singel, Preate wouldn't have a chance to win. And — oh, by the way — if I did hold off on releasing the report, there might be the possibility that I'd continue as the state's police commissioner for another eight years.

I adamantly refused, bringing the report before the senate in late April 1994. In short order, Preate's political dreams crumbled and United States Congressman Tom Ridge filled the Republican void as candidate for governor. Ridge went on to defeat Singel and eight years later, in the turbulent wake of the Sept. 11, 2001 terrorist attacks on the United States, Ridge became the country's first Homeland Security director. The first time I saw Ridge, up close and personal, was when he visited the Los Alamos National Laboratory in February. I pondered the man as I performed my security functions for his visit.

I've always been a no-nonsense administrator and I've always believed in sticking to department rules. In an April 13, 1994 editorial about the ongoing Preate investigation, the *Philadelphia Inquirer* newspaper referred to me as "the ramrod-straight figure of Colonel Glenn A. Walp." As a result, I've been the frequent recipient of plenty of cold shoulders and outright ostracism from those beholden to the law-enforcement culture that often places peer pressure above all requirements, and from unprincipled politicians. Nevertheless, if my job is to follow the rules, then I will do my job.

At Los Alamos, I was intent on continuing what I had been doing all of my life; being dedicated and hard working, fulfilling my responsibilities to the full satisfaction of both my employer and those I served. That included not only the Los Alamos National Laboratory and the University of California, but all Americans. American citizens were paying my salary and benefits, and I appreciated it. Without the United States taxpayer, research at the Los Alamos National Laboratory would come to a crashing halt. As with all my other positions, I was committed to fiscal responsibility. Unfortunately, I soon began to realize that not all lab employees were wise stewards of taxpayer dollars. I also was becoming aware that arrogance and apathy had infected some officials at New Mexico's secret-weapons laboratory, thus putting at jeopardy the top secrets I was hired to help guard. I was becoming more and more alarmed.

Contrary to the policing world I came from, as emphasized by Ken Schiffer, S-Division had no FBI-type Uniform Crime Reporting system to illustrate crime statistics. For six weeks I scoured lab policies and regulations. I asked questions of lab personnel in an attempt to locate a unit that could give me a grasp on the lab's theft problems, however, specific and validated information was difficult to find. Finally, OSI inquirer Richard Naranjo suggested that I contact the Business Operations Division (BUS) – specifically, BUS-6, the Business Operations Division unit where Naranjo's wife worked. I soon contacted a BUS-6 manager named Leroy Padilla, a congenial gentleman who had deep knowledge of lab procurement and control policies. Interested in my project, he said he'd forward to me his division's Annual Lost and Stolen Reports for 1999, 2000, and 2001. "The reports will show hundreds of items that had been lost or stolen," Padilla said. That meant that the Business Operations Division, which was responsible for control of these items, had no idea where any of the hundreds of items were.

"We do annual audits," Padilla said, "but we could never find any of these items."

Padilla's reports revealed that government property totaling nearly three million dollars in U.S. taxpayers' money was either lost or stolen between 1999 and 2001. Padilla forwarded another report to me, illustrating that during the first quarter of 2002 nearly $300,000 in government property was either lost or stolen. The 1999-2001 reports included notation of more than 700 pieces of lost or stolen property. Of these 700-plus pieces of property, sixty-six items were listed as stolen, amounting to $148,000 of the nearly three million dollars in total property value. The remaining missing articles were classified as *lost* and never accounted for.

Among the items, the lab had allegedly "lost" were an industrial water tank, a one-ton magnet-lifting unit, research oscillators, trailer vans, hundreds of computers and computer workstations alike.

I couldn't quite hide an under the breath laugh, *Gee honey, I misplaced the one-ton magnet-lifting unit along with our 400 computers... Did you see them lying around somewhere?*

The growing problem, however, was no laughing matter. My review also showed that, each year, approximately 90 percent of the lost items was reported in January, about 5 percent in June, and the remaining 5 percent scattered throughout the year. I e-mailed Padilla and asked him his theory regarding this phenomenon. Padilla responded, "Christmas."

I passed this information and my exchange with Padilla to Falcon, who wasn't at all surprised. "Padilla is right," Falcon said. It is common knowledge that people at the lab *shop for Christmas gifts* in December and *graduation gifts* in May, continued Falcon, and so there is an increase in *lost items* reported in January and June.

Although some of the lab thefts made their way onto inquiry reports prepared by Office of Security Inquiries personnel, the great majority of the crimes were never reported to OSI. In addition, none of the stolen items were reported to the FBI's Uniform Crime Reporting System, nor were they entered into the National Crime Information Center (NCIC) nationwide database.

Interviewing Los Alamos County Deputy Police Chief Marla Brooks, I was told that lab crimes investigated by an Office of Security Inquiries member were never reported to the UCR system because we weren't sure they really had happened. She told me that the inquiries coming out of OSI are not the best.

Brooks apprised, that since OSI reports were so poorly done, her department couldn't tell if they were really factual. Therefore, Brooks continued, we didn't enter them into the national database because we had concerns that, if the information was wrong, the LAPD would be held civilly liable. In other words, if a police department were to enter items into the NCIC system, claiming they were stolen, and the items really weren't stolen, and a police officer took an individual into custody because he or she had those items in his or her possession, that individual would have been able to sue the arresting policing agency and the policing agency that placed the erroneous information into the system for false arrest.

And conversely, since the stolen items were never placed into the National Crime Information Center database, a police officer, for example, stopping a vehicle loaded with stolen lab computers would never know they were stolen since they were not on the nationwide stolen item list.

Telephoning Padilla, I asked who was responsible for determining when an incident would be classified as lost or stolen. Padilla said that the BUS-1 Property Account group makes those decisions, based mainly on the information recorded on the lab's Report of Lost, Damaged or Destroyed Property (RLDD). Padilla said he didn't agree with that policy and offered to send a copy of an RLDD to me, along with clarification on when and how the report is prepared.

Lab policy directed that every time a piece of property was lost, damaged, salvaged, destroyed or stolen, a Report of Lost, Damaged or Destroyed Property had to be prepared and submitted. Each completed RLDD had a unique identification number for tracking purposes. The individual responsible for the property had to identify the property and justify the reason why or how it was damaged, lost, salvaged, destroyed or stolen. As long as the justification was accepted, no matter how flimsy or ludicrous, lab audit reports would reflect a clean record, and if logged as lost, destroyed, salvaged, or damaged, it would never be reported to the Office of Security Inquiries for investigation. And, in hundreds of cases, even if the item was listed as stolen, the theft incident was never reported to the Office of Security Inquiries for investigation.

I decided I needed to speak about this with the S-Division Property Control Officer Ron Eckrote. I outlined the problems, to which he responded, "You're right. It's common lab practice to use the RLDD to clear property records." Eckrote continued, stating that if a certain piece of property cannot be found, you simply prepare an RLDD and list the item as lost, salvaged, destroyed, or some other wording and that cleans the record. You just need a little justi-fication; no matter what it is, it will go through; it just isn't challenged. The justification is accepted as long as it makes a little sense. It is just the way it works at LANL, and that's the way it has been for years, concluded Eckrote.

When I conveyed the magnitude of the problem to Falcon, he agreed with Eckrote's assessment.

There was another acceptable lab term I learned. In addition to salvaged, destroyed, damaged, stolen and lost, the word "retired" was a common classification. When some lab employees retired, the equipment they had been using appeared to have retired along with them, and the record books were cleaned through submission of the RLDD, with the item listed as *retired.*

Many times, after reviewing reports of lost items, I contacted the staffer in the specific division who submitted the report. Often I was told the property was most likely cannibalized – using the parts from one machine to fix another. Every single time, I was told that even though it was a violation of lab policy, division personnel ap-parently *forgot* to complete a separate Salvage Report, in addition to the Report of Lost, Damaged or Destroyed Property, to prove the cannibalization. Therefore, they had no Salvage Reports to show me to prove that the item *was cannibalized even though they said it was cannibalized.* I never did get to see one Salvage Report.

While I began to see a bad pattern developing with regard to certain employees' unwillingness to be forthcoming about the lab's chronic property theft/loss issues, it still didn't appear to me to be epidemic at this stage of my investigation. However, soon, during an interview with Gene Wagner, Security Officer for Johnson Con-trols of Northern New Mexico (JCNNM), more information surfaced which indicated that the lab's problems might be far greater than I had feared. Johnson Controls was a contractor responsible for overall maintenance at the lab. During this interview, Wagner con-firmed that lab thefts occurring in his area of responsibility, involving items valued at $5,000 and above were always referred to OSI for inquiry, but anything that was valued under $5,000 was not reported to OSI. I asked Wagner if there were a significant number of thefts involving government property valued at under $5,000. "There are a lot of thefts within that value amount, and it is mostly all government property," he responded.

I immediately requested theft data on the stolen items valued at under $5,000 that occurred in his area over the last three years. Wagner agreed to provide that information to me, but added, "My bosses would not be happy if they knew I gave you that information. They don't want that information known."

I understood that but continued, is it possible that if someone wanted to confuse authorities, they could list an item that had a value greater than $5,000 as being under $5,000 in value? Wagner agreed it was possible that could happen. I also asked Wagner if he was aware that if any item is stolen, even if it is valued under $5,000, by policy it must be reported to the Office of Security Inquiries for inquiry. Wagner responded, "Yes; but we don't do that."

Although I contacted Wagner multiple times asking for the report, he never gave the information to me.

Lab policy dictated that all lab employees and contractors who received government property (any equipment and material belonging to the U.S. government), accepted the responsibility for that property. That responsibility included the mandate that any property that was lost, damaged, or suspected to have been stolen had to be "immediately" reported to the Office of Security Inquiries and their unit's property administrator, "regardless of the value of the property."

Digging further into the information available to me, I compared the Office of Security Inquiries theft reports for 1999-2001 with the lab's BUS-6 Stolen Reports for 1999-2001. They didn't match. Not even close. Lab policy may have been clearly written out, but it was obvious that a significant number of lab personnel were not complying. The obvious question to me, "Why not?"

As I gathered more and more information, I also concluded

that among many lab managers, there was further trouble with reporting. There were a huge number of thefts, most likely thousands, which were never reported to the Office of Security Inquiries and, consequently, were never placed on the BUS-6 Stolen Property Report. And so, my reasoning went, there apparently was a good deal of property that was written off.

Nevertheless, I felt uplifted that some lab personnel were clearly upset by the rampant theft and loss that was occurring. One of them was Phillip Howe, the manager in the Engineering Sciences and Applications (ESA) Division. He contacted me to complain about the epidemic of thefts in his area. Howe told me he and many other managers had become increasingly agitated that LANL property was being stolen, especially because it affected the operations of their units. He believed that the root of many of the problems was in the "drop-point" system the lab used to distribute incoming parcels. I also believed it was a system that could place the laboratory's contents and secrets in serious jeopardy, especially during these dangerous times when terrorism threats were growing more and more ominous.

The drop-point system was a certifiable mess. When items were delivered to the lab's warehouse for distribution, most items were dropped off at assigned drop points so the recipient could pick them up later. Most of the drop points were located in secluded and unsecured areas. In many cases, the parcel would be missing when the recipient came to pick it up. Obviously, this distribution system was remarkably conducive to significant theft. In the summer of 2002, even the Office of Security Inquiries had over $30,000 worth of items stolen through this appalling distribution system.

Unbelievably, the drop-point system had been in place for years. When I asked OSI inquirer Marty Farley about the system, he stated, that he tried to get the lab to change it, but warehouse personnel said it was too much trouble to have the driver take the package to a person who could sign for it. According to Farley, no one appeared to be concerned about all the thefts that were occurring at the drop points, so OSI just let it be.

To correct this problem I felt I needed to implement something like a UPS system, where a person would have to sign for the item being delivered. But when I approached the distribution center manager, I was, for the most part, blown off. I hired James (Jim) Mullins, a good-looking, shaven head, physically fit, medium-build Texan to assist me. Jim was a former member of the Dallas, Texas Police Department and FBI employee, with an endearing sense of humor. I hired Jim because he was a seasoned police officer with a keen sense for criminal investigation. I assigned Mullins to conduct an in-depth study on the drop-point system, intending to forward the report to a higher-up so that lab leadership could implement obvious necessary changes to the system.

Another major weakness, which I believed contributed to the lab's property control problems, was the purchase card program that had been in place since December 1994. With the use of federal purchase cards, lab employees purchased an average of 45,000 items amounting to $35 million every year. Among the inadequacies of the system were that no accurate list existed of employees who used the cards, no audits were ever performed on the use of the cards, many sensitive items purchased with the cards were not bar-coded as required by regulations which meant the items could never be tracked, and there was no accounting of purchase cards after employees had stopped working at the lab.

Now informed by my analyses of OSI criminal inquiry reports, the annual lost and stolen reports, and my interviews with Wagner, Eckrote, Padilla, Howe, and Falcon, I wrote a report titled *"Analysis of Theft of Property at LANL."* I submitted the report to Madison on March 26, 2002. The report not only outlined aspects of theft and lost property, but also commented on the cavalier approach some lab employees took toward theft and national security measures. It quickly became known throughout lab circles as "Walp's Theft Report."

Some Los Alamos National Laboratory employees were

aghast after reading it, while others were concerned that this information would go public. Many accepted the magnitude of the problem and began to initiate corrective action.

Madison was among those who expressed shock at the findings. He agreed the report indicated significant theft.

Madison directed me to discuss the theft issue with Terry Owens, a University of California security specialist, based in Oakland, California. I made contact with Owens who told me he was not aware there was a major theft problem at LANL but recommended that I contact the person in charge of security at UC's Lawrence Livermore National Laboratory (LLNL) for some guidance. I proceeded to leave several telephone messages over the next few weeks at LLNL's security office, explaining what I was seeking. None of my calls were ever returned.

Los Alamos business managers were concerned about the inordinate amount of government property lost between 1999 and 2001, and that by the spring of 2002, still nobody at the lab had any idea where the property was or what had happened to it. Those responsible for property control were now scrambling to address the issue. Some were afraid of losing their jobs, others were concerned the lab would not receive additional funding by meeting Department of Energy Appendix guidelines, while many feared the University of California contract would be lost. Soon, it would become apparent to me that theft issues were superseded by even more grave problems.

VIII

Doran Comes on Board

After Wismer left, I sorely needed a person with both the ability and desire to help me with the critical issues of criminal inquiry.

Madison, true to his word, allowed me to advertise nation-wide to find a law enforcement official to assist me in professional-izing the Office of Security Inquiries.

In early spring of 2002, Steve Doran received a telephone call from S-Division's Victoria Snelling asking if he'd be interested in a security specialist position at the lab. Snelling gave Steve a rous-ing post-September 11 God-and-Country speech and extolled the virtues of the Office of Security Inquiries' new leader.

Snelling told Doran, all you need to do is pick up a newspa-per and see what a mess LANL is in and how we need people like you to help correct these deficiencies.

Steve, a loyal American and a supremely talented individual, answered the call, and along with many other candidates ventured to Los Alamos for his interview. Of all the candidates interviewed, two rose to the top: Steve Doran and James Mullins. Madison was asked if he would be willing to hire both Doran and Mullins because of their remarkable credentials. Madison agreed and indicated that he would be adding entry-level personnel to the office, as well. Snelling called Doran and Mullins, giving them the nod for the positions of OSI Security Specialists III.

Snelling urged Steve to accept the job, reiterating the God-and-Country speech. There are critical issues facing the Los Alamos National Laboratory that affect national security, she told him, and he'd be able to use all the resources the laboratory and the United States Government has to ensure that the failures currently occurring at the lab comes to an end. You and Glenn, Snelling continued, would complement each other in doing the job that needs to be done. The lab has never seen anything like you guys and it is way past due, concluded Snelling.

Steve, a staunch patriot, believed this would be an excellent opportunity to help protect the United States and keep it secure. Steve returned Victoria's call and verbally accepted the position.

Steven Larry Doran, a tall, handsome man with an impressive physique and military bearing, was no stranger to tough challenges and complex investigations. Doran was born on September 9, 1963, the second and last child of Savannah Coleen and Robert Allen Doran. Robert Doran and his wife separated by the time Steve was two-years-old, and his mother and grandparents, Erleen and Clifford Carl Bertram, raised Steve in Pontiac, Michigan. Savannah remarried when Steve was five, at which point his life became a nightmare. Doran describes his stepfather as an insecure, cruel man.

"My stepfather was a little guy with a Napoleon complex, and a coward. He would only pick on the weak, and he picked on me."

Steve's once peaceful, secure existence became a world of disruption and, at times, violence in the home, on the streets, and in the schools. Conflict became commonplace, mainly because Steve refused to join illegal gangs or to become involved with the drug crowd and the bullying that went on.

Steve found serenity and stability with his grandfather, Clifford Bertram, in the great outdoors. Grandfather and grandson spent countless hours together as Steve learned field craft, hunting, fishing, and tracking. He became a crack rifle and pistol shot at the age of ten. When Steve was not honing his woodsman skills, he was captivated and energized by reading adventure and survival books, identifying with historical role models, such as Daniel Boone, Davy Crocket, and Lewis and Clark. Steve was also enthralled with survival books, especially those written by the father of modern survival techniques, Bradford Anger.

"Losing and laboring taught me how to win and fight smarter, instead of harder. It also taught me how ruthless people can be, and what I needed to do to overcome my adversary. During my whole childhood, I could only think about when I got older, it would be different. I would never allow these types of things to happen as long as I could do anything about it. I still think that way, and have no patience for bullies, cruel or selfish people. The main factors my younger life taught me were that I would never treat anyone the way I was treated, and that I needed the Lord to help me to be patient and understanding."

Faced with the unending mistreatment from his stepfather, Steve realized a drastic change had to be made. At sixteen, he quit school with his mother's approval and enlisted in the United States Army. He was assigned to boot camp at Fort Sill, Oklahoma.

Steve thought he had finally found an environment in which he could excel. But what he found in the Army — at least in his Oklahoma base — were the same things he had wanted to flee in Michigan: commonplace illegal drugs and gang activity. Being a man of quick action, Steve met with his commanding officer and told him of his concerns. The commander patiently listened, and then responded, if you want discipline and really want to be a warrior, you should have joined the Marines. Steve promptly contacted a Marine recruiter, and, within one month, he was honorably discharged from the United States Army and joined the United States Marine Corps.

It was back to boot camp, this time at Parris Island, South Carolina. Soon he was recruited by a superior officer to become a member of the prominent Special Operations Unit Air Naval Gunfire Liaison Company. Because of Steve's extensive knowledge of field craft, his physical stature and strength, and his ability to persevere under the harshest of conditions, he was consistently assigned to classified missions in the United States and abroad. Steve became a highly decorated Marine, receiving, among others, Marine Corps and Army Forces Expeditionary Medals, a Combat Action Medal, Rifle and Pistol Expert Awards, admission into the prestigious Band of Brothers, and an Internal Fellowship Award for going above and beyond the call of duty.

In his last year of service, Steve was named Security Chief at the Pohang Marine Base in South Korea, where he was responsible for directing and conducting critical investigations into security breaches and theft of government property. He developed the first-ever criminal intelligence network at the Pohang base, recruiting locals to provide confidential information.

The nation was in full recession in 1983, so when Steve was honorably discharged from the United States Marine Corps in December, he returned to Pontiac, but couldn't find work. The automotive industry in Detroit was waning and steel mills were closing down.

A friend at the Oakland County Sheriff's Department in Michigan encouraged Steve to apply for an opening as a deputy sheriff. The problem was that there were hundreds of applicants, and Steve wasn't one of the lucky ones. Undaunted, he returned to the sheriff's department on a daily basis to ask for something to do in the hopes it would increase his chances at getting a job there. Department personnel advised him, perhaps out of frustration and/or sympathy, that he could work as a volunteer dispatcher. During one of his volunteer shifts, the sheriff approached him.

"Who are you and what are you doing?"

"I'm a volunteer dispatcher, sir."

"We have no volunteer dispatchers in my department!"

After the sheriff stormed off, Steve figured that was the end of any opportunity with the Pontiac department. Yet just a few months later, a sergeant approached him.

"The sheriff thinks you've got a lot of guts, Steve. Go get a uniform because he just created a law enforcement position for you."

Steve soaked in everything he could, sharpening his investigative skills, reading voraciously, taking notes on the job, and seeking advice and knowledge from his peers. He became particularly skillful in taking on and solving cold cases. In short order, Steve was recruited by the Clare County Prosecutor's Office to supervise investigations into corruption, was asked to initiate a felony task force, and then was hired by the Oakland County Sheriff's Department as the assistant division chief.

He garnered the attention of multiple Fortune 100 and 500 corporations wanting him to assist them with issues regarding security, espionage, theft, and corruption within their organizations. Eventually, he began to run search and rescue operations for missing persons around the globe.

But after seventeen years in Michigan, Steve had a compelling desire to move west. He accepted a position as Chief of Police in Idaho City, Idaho, where city and county officials promptly took note of his investigative abilities. He was quickly assigned to direct a multi-jurisdictional unit investigating drug trafficking and corruption within criminal justice organizations, including one case involving a high-ranking member of a local police department. Steve's unit made more felony arrests in just a few months than all of the other county law enforcement officers had made in the last few years.

Soon after these civic accomplishments, Steve Doran was offered a position as OSI Security Specialist at LANL. Before he'd even worked his first day, Steve was initiated into the corruption problems at Los Alamos.

As part of his job requirements, Steve needed to purchase a pair of steel-toe boots. Come back in six months and we'll give you a new pair, said the Los Alamos vendor employee who sold him the boots.

"I'll never wear these out in six months."

It doesn't matter, the lab doesn't care, the vendor employee proposed, just come back and we'll give you a brand new pair. Everybody does it.

It was Steve's first early shock. It was not his last.

IX

Inklings of a Cover-Up

People were laughing, and they definitely weren't laughing with me.

I was attending one of a series of mandatory lab seminars, during which the issue of theft of government property came up. One instructor joked that each year like clockwork, just prior to elk hunting season, some lab employee purchased — with lab funds — bright orange coveralls, a cap, gloves, boots and socks. Chuckles and snickers resounded.

Well, we know what he's doing, the instructor went on.

I raised my hand. Has anyone, I asked, ever challenged this individual on their actions?

"No, it's just Harry, and he does it every year during hunting season!"

More laughter – this time long, boisterous guffaws from the vast majority of those in the audience that included administrators, scientists, contract employees, and rank and file personnel. I looked around dismayed that this kind of brazen theft, in this case petty, created mirth and/or disdained dismissal.

Sitting next to me, frowning, was Marci Smith of the lab's Office of Public Affairs. Marci told me she was really distressed by the indifference of most of the lab personnel regarding lab thefts. She believed there was a significant amount of lab theft, big and small, and asked me for a copy of the theft report I had just submitted to Madison. After she received the report, she sent me a thank-you e-mail. "I thought the all-managers memo that came out on the theft subject was great," she wrote. "The rescind message wasn't so great. We'll see where lab-wide attention to your report goes."

Smith was referring to an April memorandum distributed by Thomas Palmieri, the Business Operations Division leader, regarding institutional accountability of government property. That memo was immediately rescinded by some higher lab authority whose identity was not known. Palmieri's memo noted the "disturbing negative trend concerning the lab's management of government property and corrective action was needed," because neither the lab nor the Department of Energy could "accept 1.3 million dollars in unaccounted property." He wrote that property classified as "missing" during the 2001 fiscal year nearly tripled that of the previous year, and he said that property listed as missing as early as 1999 was still missing three years later. The upshot, Palmieri wrote, was that the situation would jeopardize the lab's efforts to receive additional Department of Energy funding.

To my amazement, Palmieri suggested that $720,000.00 in missing property — not lost or stolen — could not be found, which was *in addition to* the nearly 3 million dollars I had already reported lost or stolen in the theft report I submitted to Madison in March.

Meanwhile, Ken Schiffer told me he found my theft report sobering and said he thought the FBI would be extremely interested in my analyses, especially those concerning the scope and extent of the thefts. Schiffer proposed there was a strong possibility that RICO (Racketeering Influenced Crime Organization) violations had been committed in the thefts. He suggested I press Falcon on ordering the task force Ken had recommended in our previous meeting, to determine if a link existed with illegal drug activity in northern New Mexico.

Schiffer's task force made sense, especially since I felt it would take qualified investigators associated with the FBI to search for evidence that, in my opinion, would be buried within the lab's Business Office purchase and audit documents. OSI does not have the quantity or quality of personnel necessary to conduct these complicated white-collar inquiries, I told Schiffer.

That isn't all, I added. The more I learn about the lab's theft problems, I continued, the more it seems to me that its culture accepts the thefts as part of daily life, and it appears certain managers and a significant number of rank and file personnel have lost sight that theft is a criminal act. Shaking my head, I observed, that I didn't think it would be easy to change the existing lab culture that accepts stealing as normal, but I assured Ken that I would do everything within my power to make that happen.

Schiffer strongly agreed, stating he felt there was a culture of theft at the lab, and again suggested I put pressure on Falcon to help me with this. Schiffer postulated that theft had been occurring at the lab for a long time, and, until I got there, no one had done anything about it. Unfortunately, said Schiffer, I can't tell Falcon what to do, but maybe you can persuade him to finally do something. Ken then reiterated, with anxious emotion, that he believed national security could be at risk.

Taking Schiffer's advice, I met with Falcon. After I presented my observations, Falcon spoke with unnerving emotion. Bringing an FBI task force into the lab to do theft investigations just won't happen, he blurted out, before going on to explain his reasoning. There were a few moments of silence then he went on, stating that lab officials have an extremely bad taste for the FBI because of the Wen Ho Lee and lost hard drive cases.

Many felt the FBI had abused its powers during the Wen Ho Lee incident by ordering around lab officials and employees and mandating polygraphs, Falcon explained. Falcon continued ominously, that the lab would never put up with that situation again. Falcon then proposed an alarming addendum, stating, that as I pursed these theft incidents, "who knows how high up the management chain it would go?" And, continued Falcon, "that may not be good for the lab or its image."

After hearing Falcon's perspectives, I went into a full-court press. "Matt, there is more than sufficient evidence to warrant a task force proceedings," I said. Falcon responded that convincing top lab officials to bring in an FBI task force would be nearly impossible. But then Falcon quickly backed off, suggesting I write a white paper in an attempt to persuade the unnamed top officials Falcon was talking about, to agree to the task force.

I had the impression that Falcon agreed with me, but he was presenting the feelings of people above him. Interfaced with my reasoning was that I also was being given the proverbial runaround to once again appease me on a hot topic. I also reasoned that Falcon realized that this Walp and his pursuit for truth were not going away.

Taking the offensive, I shot back, stating that I realized I was new around there, but this culture of theft, beyond its being criminal and wrong, causes me great concern for a more threatening issue that involves the jeopardizing of lab secrets. I began to outline my ideas about the criminal mind. It's the same condition as a person involved in an activity such as illegal drugs, prostitution, and gambling, since a lab employee involved in thefts may be identified by an enemy of United States as being vulnerable for espionage, I said. That is, I continued, the enemy may approach the person and tell them they will report them to authorities unless they are given classified information. So in fear of losing their job and reputation, and perhaps risking going to prison, they could succumb to the pressure and release the classified data. This condition, I strongly suggested, has the potential of significantly compromising the lab's systems of safety, security and the protection of our national secrets.

Falcon stared at the ceiling for a moment, smiled — did not

say he disagreed with my position, in fact I perceived he concurred with me — and then told me in a calm voice, "Glenn the meeting is over."

Of course, I was aware it wouldn't be good for the lab's image if high management personnel were involved in the thefts, but I asked myself, "Do you cover that up and hope it just goes away, or do you confront the problems and correct them?"

I told Schiffer about my conversation with Falcon. He was disheartened by the position Falcon had outlined, but urged me to gather as much data as possible to support the white paper I was assigned to write. Schiffer contacted me about every two weeks to see how I was doing, but I had to tell him that the paltering by lab employees hampered the research. "Besides," I said, "if my theft report doesn't contain enough evidence to prove there is major theft going on, I don't know what will convince them." At that point, I wasn't so sure they wanted to be convinced.

A few weeks later, Meredith Brown of S-Division asked me if she could include an article in the lab's *News Bulletin* publication concerning my theft report. That is a great idea, I said, I will present your request to Falcon. But Falcon conveyed to me that he didn't want Meredith to write any articles concerning theft at the lab. Once again he repeated the rationale that it would not be in the best interest of the lab to distribute this type of information.

I wasn't about to give up so easily. Despite the setbacks, by May 1, the new reporting system I had tried to implement previously in February, notwithstanding resistance and apparent subversion, was online and was functioning fairly well as a new standard of professional Office of Security Inquiries reporting. A Department of Energy auditor assigned to the Albuquerque office noted in his late spring 2002 audit of the Office of Security Inquiries that the audit team was impressed with the professional changes that had been made to the Office of Security Inquiries reporting system. These changes, the auditor recorded, were long overdue and showed solid evidence that the Office of Security Inquiries had taken concrete action to correct longstanding reporting problems. A month later, the auditor asked Falcon to produce a document illustrating the specific changes that had occurred since I was hired.

Falcon's report indicated the following: That the OSI office had been restaffed and reorganized; that new policies had upgraded the reporting process; that we had enhanced the effectiveness of criminal inquiries; that inquirers had been sent to receive new training; that we had implemented a program to identify human errors that contribute to security incidents; and that we had instituted a new policy to improve the control, and maintenance of property and evidence brought into custody.

Falcon's document proposed that from the time of my hire in January 2002, the Office of Security Inquiries had shifted from operational ineptness and apathy to a department that had new guidelines for professionalism and expertise. Despite this, I was troubled by what I perceived as inconsistencies between the words and actions. Still, a flurry of positive activity resulted from the release of my theft report.

A few weeks after the report was released, BUS-6 Group Leader Allen Wallace and BUS-6 Project Leader Joe Roybal wrote a memorandum to the Associate Director of Administration, Richard Marquez, regarding major flaws they identified within the purchase card program. They wrote that of the 45,000 annual transactions, about 1,700 of them, valued at 5 million dollars, did not receive bar code tagging as directed by the federal government, the Department of Energy, and in the contract between the Department of Energy and the University of California. Thus, federal property worth 4.3 million dollars that had been purchased in 2001, and should have been barcoded in accordance with federal law, could not be traced.

Bar code tagging was specifically for items that the lab classified as sensitive and/or attractive, in part, because they could be easily converted to personal use or sold and were more susceptible to theft; even more ominous is that these items could be used by spies and terrorists. Items requiring bar code tagging included still cameras, firearms, video camcorders, personal computers (which may have sensitive information), and two-way radios. Who knows what may have been on the computers or into whose hands they fell?

Wallace and Roybal recommended in their memo that sensitive items should not be allowed to be bought with a purchase card because, they wrote, the process was lending itself to possible fraudulent use of government property, abuse of purchase card acquisitions, and potential theft of United States government-owned property.

Commending Roybal for the report, I told him I agreed with his points about flaws in the purchase card system. The lab's systems are inherently fraught with the potential for fraud, corruption, larceny, and, of extreme importance, the compromising of national security, I said grimly.

A few days later, BUS-6 manager Leroy Padilla asked me to review a draft memorandum he authored, titled "Protection of Government Property." The memorandum was commissioned by Joe Roybal, and was to be signed by Richard Marquez before being distributed to all lab employees. The memorandum emphasized that all lab employees were responsible for all U.S. government property, whether or not it was assigned to them, and that all employees were required to comply with all lab policies, one of which required the immediate reporting to their immediate supervisor of any lost, stolen, destroyed, or damaged lab property. Finally, the memo clarified that any acts of theft, illegal possession, unlawful disposition, unlawful appropriation, or misuse of government property are federal offenses subject to criminal prosecution by the U.S. Attorney General or the District Attorney.

Following some minor modifications to the memorandum, I gave the document to Falcon for review and comment. Falcon advised me that Madison would review it and that Falcon would get back to me with any changes Madison recommended, whereupon I could forward the material to Padilla. During the next few weeks,

Joe Roybal frequently e-mailed me, asking if Madison was requesting any changes on the memorandum. When I hadn't heard anything, I contacted Falcon and was informed that Madison had forwarded the memo to lab attorney Jim Mitchell for review but hadn't heard back.

My frustration was growing. The planned memo fell into another lab black hole. Subsequently it was never signed or distributed.

My theft report clearly stated to lab managers that they needed to take immediate action to address the now exposed fault lines. After my report came out, I got a call from Richard (Rich) Gitto, the BUS-6 Deputy Group Leader, who told me he was well aware of the problems I outlined in my theft report, and was extremely interested in working with OSI, and with me specifically, to resolve the problems.

Throughout April, Gitto and I communicated frequently. We saw eye-to-eye on the lab's deficiencies, and we were committed to initiate the appropriate action to correct the shortcomings.

Lab regulations dictate that all loss and theft issues must be reported to the Office of Security Inquiries, and then someone in OSI makes the decision on whether an incident is classified as lost or stolen, not BUS-1, Gitto said. If the Office of Security Inquiries determines the item was stolen, then OSI does a theft report, said Gitto. At that point Gitto informed me that OSI's decision is then to be forwarded to BUS-1 for placement in BUS-5's database – and BUS's Annual Lost and Stolen Report is to be based on that database information. From that point on, we agreed that an Office of Security Inquiries staffer would be making the decision on which incidents would be classified as lost or stolen, not someone in the lab's Business Office. It was logical for us to assume that a significant number of incidents had probably been inappropriately classified as lost rather than stolen. Regardless of whether those incorrect classifications were willful or not, there could be no argument that determinations were being made by people who weren't trained in criminal law classifications or criminal investigation processes.

Returning to my office I issued an edict: all Office of Security Inquiries personnel receiving reports of lost or stolen property from any lab employee, by any means, were to forward that information directly to me. I would determine whether the incident would receive a lost classification or stolen classification.

I heard from various sources that on several occasions, some lab employees actually had followed policy by contacting the Office of Security Inquiries, but OSI personnel did not return their calls. It turned out to be true. Some Office of Security Inquiries personnel had in fact received official complaints on thefts and burglaries but had failed to follow up with an inquiry. When I challenged the Office of Security Inquiries personnel on this issue, their excuses included: "I forgot," "I don't remember," "They are mistaken," and "I was going to get to it."

Certain inquirers, from my view, were less than enthusiastic about preparing investigative reports. Some it seemed preferred sitting in their office chairs, tending to personal affairs, running personal errands, taking a 1 hour breakfast on company time, making personal phone calls, drinking coffee on the back stoop or sitting around jawing about how bad life was. These were administrative issues I needed to address – but more pressing matters consumed my attention.

Soon Rich Gitto invited me to a BUS-6 staff meeting where he wanted me to explain my new ideas on fighting theft. Gitto said he would take the unprecedented step of having me assign an OSI member (Doran) who had recently come on board to participate in the Business Division audit validation process. Then, if the Office of Security Inquiries determined that a theft had occurred, the two groups could work together to resolve the issue. Approximately 20 Business-6 personnel attended, all with extensive experience in the lab's procurement, audit and property control systems. After I completed my presentation, most of the attendees stood up, clapped, and cheered.

Soon after that meeting, auditor Michael Ares, one who'd applauded my efforts, invited Doran to another meeting, to begin Doran's participation in the audit validation program, along with lab employees Mike Trujillo, Julian Sandoval, Dennis Martinez, Connie Lucero, and representatives from the Department of Energy. At the very first meeting, Ares told Doran, that at times when he could not find property, he would talk to the person responsible for the property, and in many instances, year after year, they would tell him to get the hell out of there, and if he didn't, they would commit physical violence against him. I brought this information to our bosses, continued Ares, but no one did anything about it; they just didn't seem to care. There are hundreds of items, which I never found so I just wrote them off, said Ares. The lab has no idea what happened to this property, and I mean expensive government property, concluded Ares.

It looked like we had a solid meeting of the minds in this group. Doran quickly shot off an e-mail to Ares. "We are not afraid to be the bad guys and take the heat," Doran wrote. "That's what we get paid to do. We want our relationship with you and your shop to be a good one, not only for the good information you can provide, but one of trust as well. You know we will…keep all the information you provide us in confidence."

Gitto and Ares were clearly interested in taking appropriate action. Yet elsewhere, others in authority were squashing these attempts.

But, why?

Why were the ones in power rejecting the task force concept and why were they so protective of the lab's image? Why was lab theft so cavalierly shrugged off, as evidenced by my experience in the training seminars? Why did Falcon reject a request to distribute a lab-wide article on lab theft? Why was Marquez's memorandum concerning lab employee's responsibility in protecting government property rejected? Why was Palmieri's memorandum on institutional accountability of government property rescinded? Why would lab leaders allow theft and defunct business practices to exist for so many years without taking strong corrective action?

And, why did lab leaders block attempts by lab managers to correct these failings? Reflecting on my law enforcement experiences, I thought, if a solid citizen had their residence burglarized, they called the police, but people with something to hide didn't.

As more questions and problems surfaced, I mentally reviewed the events of the past few months. From my view, the management systems reeked with disorganization, apathy, and arrogance, and were driven by greed, self-preservation, and narcissism. United States taxpayers were funding the lab to conduct crucial research, but lab management had failed miserably in practicing responsible fiscal and property management. And in the current terroristic turmoil unleashed around the world, such failings could reveal the facility's secrets to those we most needed to keep them from.

Dark thoughts lay scattered in my mind. Major thefts had been occurring at the lab for years. Schiffer had told me those thefts had the potential of affecting national security, and consequently the protection of the lab's secrets. Falcon said lab theft has been making the valley green for years, and some Business Division personnel alleged no one in authority appeared to care about the thefts. Furthermore, multiple lab memorandums referred to critical, long-term deficiencies in the lab's control and accountability of government property.

Didn't anyone in authority see, as Ken Schiffer and I had, the real and present possibilities that such crimes could lead to much more deadly dangers in which the very secrets we were supposed to protect were compromised? Why didn't someone in command take action to correct the problems before now? Had management willfully hidden the facts of theft and mismanagement from the rank and file?

I was beginning to think the evidence Steve and I had been accumulating pointed to a cover-up, and if it did, I was determined to get to the bottom of it and expose it.

X

The Hawk Has Landed

Thefts, petty and significant, were coming to my attention. Even less auspicious ones raised questions of how easily security violations could occur at the lab and brought to my mind continuing questions as to the ways America's security secrets could be breached. On June 24, 2002, two lab employees, James Stewart and Jaret Mc-Donald, sent an e-mail to the FBI's main office in Albuquerque complaining of theft within Los Alamos's Nonproliferation and International Security Division (NIS). Stewart and McDonald, who worked in NIS, claimed that Peter L. Bussolini, Scott Alexander, and possibly another NIS employee (who would eventually become a key FBI informant) had stolen thousands of dollars of government property. Laboratory officials were aware of the thefts, they complained, but had failed to take any action.

Stewart and McDonald alleged they had reported the theft to the Office of Security Inquiries in 2001 *three times*, but the OSI inquirer allegedly told them unless they had photographs of an individual stealing and placing the stolen items into the trunk of his car, there was nothing he could do.

Bussolini was the group leader of Facility Management Unit-75 (FMU-75), which was responsible for building repairs and general maintenance, including Technical Areas 33 and 35 (TA-33 and TA-35). Alexander was the procurement specialist for FMU-75 and Bussolini's next in command. Technical Area-33 was a former explosive testing area and Technical Area-35 was the Antares Laser complex; two important facilities. The Nonproliferation and International Security Division was deemed a *black area* because of the top-secret research conducted there.

Three days earlier, Anna Parks, a former Nonproliferation International Security Division Human Resources employee, called McDonald at Stewart's request. McDonald had wanted to discuss concerns about his experiences at TA-35. When they finally met, McDonald told Parks that Bussolini and Alexander were involved in waste, fraud, and abuse totaling $100,000. McDonald said Bussolini and Alexander were ordering unauthorized items from Mesa Equipment and Supply Company, a laboratory vendor in Albuquerque. McDonald told Parks he had overheard Alexander asking a Mesa employee to change the description of items ordered so it wouldn't raise any lab auditing flags. McDonald suggested that the lab was paying for items Bussolini and Alexander were ordering, such as jackets, knives, sleeping bags, tents, walkie-talkies, barbecue grills, remote control airplanes, rototillers, and ATVs — and he said that some employees in Bussolini's area of responsibility not only were aware of the thefts but laughed about how the items vanished from lab property. Facility Management Unit-75 employees kept mum, according to McDonald, because they were afraid of Bussolini.

McDonald told Parks he had spoken to his supervisors at Johnson Controls of Northern New Mexico (contractor responsible for overall maintenance of the lab) but no action was taken. He also said he had reported the thefts to S-Division's Office of Security Inquiries and even had 200 photographs of improperly ordered items that were delivered to Facility Management Unit-75. However, the OSI staffer, according to McDonald, said that if he didn't have pictures of merchandise actually being removed from a vehicle into Bussolini's garage, there was insufficient evidence to move forward with an inquiry.

McDonald, a former police sergeant with the New Mexico State Police Mounted Patrol, told Parks that he had tried to find someone at the laboratory to act on the information, but alleged no one would do anything, not even the Office of Security Inquiries. This caused him to become so frustrated it was making him physically ill. "I originally wanted to remain anonymous," McDonald said, "but I'm at the point now where I don't care if my name comes out."

Parks asked Michelle Cantu of the lab's Assessments and Audits (A&A) Office if the matter fell within A&A domain. Theft wasn't her department's responsibility, Cantu replied, but if receipts were being deliberately altered so they wouldn't reflect what was being delivered, then that would be of interest to her office. Parks instructed McDonald and Stewart to get in touch with Cantu, and on June 27, Parks forwarded all information she had received from McDonald to Human Resources.

A couple of days earlier, I saw OSI Inquirer Marty Farley anxiously pacing up and down the hallway past my office door, appearing extremely agitated. I couldn't help stepping out into the hall and asking Farley what was wrong. He replied that a few TA-33 employees had complained to the FBI about theft, and FBI Agent Jeff Campbell had followed up by telling Farley that the FBI would be getting involved.

"What's wrong with that?" I asked. "If theft is occurring at TA-33, it would be appropriate for a federal agency to do an investigation."

Farley said he had reported the theft to the FBI in the fall of 2001, but nothing happened. Now it may cause problems for him.

"Why would that cause you problems?"

According to Farley, because nobody did anything about the

thefts at that time. And now, Farley told me, he would have to tell Falcon about the FBI's involvement, and he knew Falcon would not be pleased.

Madison soon ordered Farley to prepare a memorandum explaining his initial involvement in the NIS theft case. Farley wrote that Jaret McDonald had contacted him in 2001 to say he had been watching Bussolini, Alexander, and a third FMU-75 employee stealing the lab blind for months. McDonald could not stand by and do nothing any longer, Farley wrote. McDonald told him some of the items they were stealing were small pull-behind trailers, John Deere rototillers, winches, welder tools, global positioning systems and items from Cabela's sporting catalogue. Farley indicated that the day after that meeting, he had asked Pat McDonnell of the Business-7 Office to pull reports on everything the three suspects had purchased in the fiscal year covering 2000-2001. Farley stated that he saw the reports a week later and immediately concluded there were suspicious purchases. At that point, Farley said, he told Falcon that he needed to contact the FBI about McDonald's claims of theft in NIS—not necessarily because of the thefts, but because so much money was involved. Farley wrote that that was when he got in touch with the FBI's Agent Campbell, who told him he would come to the lab around mid-October to discuss the issue.

Farley had written that he showed Campbell the purchase documents and said the lab had no business buying such things.

Farley said that Campbell told him that he would review the information with his boss to see if they could open a case and that he also wanted to meet with McDonald. But Farley wrote that by the end of October, no arrangements had yet been made, so he tried several times to set up a meeting with Campbell. This was less than two months after the September 11 terrorist attacks, and Campbell begged off due to a heavy workload, stated Farley. Besides, Farley wrote, Campbell said he was having trouble convincing his boss that just because they were buying a lot of stuff, it did not mean it was being stolen.

As McDonald's frustration grew, Farley wrote that he called Campbell to find out what was going on, but it seems that McDonald may have gotten tired of waiting and finally sent the complaint directly to the FBI's office in Albuquerque.

Other than his after-the-fact memorandum, Farley had no written documentation supporting any of his information. "Before you got here," Farley told me, "OSI never kept notes on these types of things."

FBI Santa Fe officials claim Farley never told them about McDonald's complaint.

The same day the FBI officially began investigating the Nonproliferation and International Security Division theft case, Madison told me that UC lawyers were not concerned about the NIS people, like Bussolini, and what happens to them, but they would do whatever is necessary to protect the lab.

For months thereafter, those words would haunt me.

I was also a bit haunted about why I had not been told about the Nonproliferation and International Security Division case in the months before I finally became aware of it. After all, I had met with Falcon on January 25, 2002, specifically to discuss lab thefts when I had first arrived at the lab. And it would be natural to assume that Falcon, whom Farley said he had informed about the NIS theft in the fall of 2001, would at least have mentioned to Ken Schiffer and me what appeared to be a major criminal theft incident. And why wouldn't Agent Mike Lowe, the FBI's Santa Fe supervisor tell me about it when he met with me shortly after arriving at the lab in early 2002? Likewise, why didn't Farley—an acting Office of Security Inquiries supervisor before I arrived—who admitted he spoke directly to McDonald about the thefts in 2001, tell me about the case, especially when he and I had met in February, 2002, specifically to discuss all OSI case issues? Furthermore, it was strange that Falcon would reject my recommended FBI task force, because he said lab officials, still bitter from the Wen Ho Lee and lost hard drive cases, would resist; and yet, here was alleged evidence that Falcon and Farley had given a major theft case directly to the FBI just a few months before I was hired. At least I could get an explanation from Falcon or Farley on why they had failed to mention this major theft case to me.

And then I learned about McDonald's contact with Parks, and Parks' contact with Cantu. Certainly, Parks and Cantu had to have told their bosses, but no one told me, contrary to lab regulations. I found out because I called Farley on his erratic behavior outside my office. Was someone willfully keeping this matter from me? And after McDonald told Parks on June 21, about the thefts, why didn't someone at the lab address his concerns immediately? McDonald had to wait three days before he finally went directly to the FBI. Perhaps, I reasoned, lab officials were hoping the whole matter would just disappear.

In early July, Doug Madison, Ken Schiffer, and Marion M. Shapiro, the chief operating officer of the lab director's office, met with the FBI special agent-in-charge in Albuquerque to work out details of a combined investigation into the Nonproliferation and International Security Division theft case. Another meeting was then set for July 16 so that Madison and I could meet with Brian Richard, the lab's lead attorney, to discuss the case. This was my first meeting with Richard, a tall, impressive man, with distinguished gray hair, and a wearer of crisp business suits—a rare commodity at Los Alamos. I immediately recognized that he was all business. My intuition was to watch and listen carefully. As the meeting progressed, I felt sure that Richard was feeling me out. He chose his words carefully and made his points clearly. It was probably obvious to both of us that we were operating from different agendas; I felt he would toe the company line to protect the lab's interests, and I was there specifically to investigate matters that, if they became widely known, might not be in the lab's best interest.

Shapiro is extremely concerned about the NIS case, mainly because it may cause negative public relations for the lab, which may affect the lab's future contract with DOE, Richard proposed at one point. He proceeded to outline his expectations of my investigation of the theft case: That I was to keep a separate Office of Security Inquiries' file on all activities of the case in addition to the FBI's files; that the OSI file was to include what lab employees were interviewed and what they said; that if there were any documentary evidence, then OSI was to keep a separate copy; that I was to have explicit knowledge when the FBI was planning to visit any lab site; that I was to maintain a pulse on everything that was occurring in the theft case; and that I was to keep a written record of all FBI activity. Richard wanted to be briefed on all FBI activities through either Falcon or Madison. "I will not pull any cowboy deals, I will be straight up with the FBI," Richard said, concluding the meeting, "I just want to know what they're doing."

In my opinion, Richard seemed noticeably apprehensive about the FBI's involvement in the Nonproliferation and International Security Division theft case. Of course, it could not be stopped. The only thing he could try to control was attempting to protect the lab's image and interests by keeping close tabs on the FBI's activities.

XI

The Wind Picks Up

The laboratory had better watch out, because things are going to change, and change for the good, Victoria Snelling had said.

I had been hired to do just that and I promptly assigned Steve Doran to assist the FBI in the Nonproliferation and International Security Division theft case, as well as to participate in the lab's Business Division audit validation project.

Madison, Campbell, Farley, Doran, Gitto, and I attended the first NIS theft case meeting between the FBI and the Office of Security Inquiries trench workers on July 19. Madison kicked off the meeting stating, this is what the people above me want:

> The NIS case is an official FBI investigation and the lab will not interfere with the FBI's investigation. However, I'm placing responsibility on Walp to ensure if, at any point during the investigation it appears there is sufficient evidence to suspend or ter-

minate the suspects, Walp will bring that information to the attention of his superiors, and the lab will take appropriate personnel action. The lab would rather the FBI prosecute civilians than lab employees. I have spoken to Marquez, Gitto's boss. Marquez has directed that Gitto give OSI and the FBI all necessary assistance. If Gitto has any problems, he should contact Walp, Walp would then contact me, and I will resolve the problem. The FBI will give copies of all their investigative reports to Walp. The reason for giving these reports to Walp is because of Walp's extensive background in criminal investigations. Walp may be able to assist Campbell in directing the course of the investigation. Walp is the only person within the lab who will receive and be able to review the FBI reports. The combined efforts between the FBI and the lab will give Marquez the leverage to do what he needs to do to clean up the situation. It should be understood, the situation is a business line for Marquez. Therefore, if it costs $10 million to clean up the case and the stolen items were only valued at $500, it wouldn't be worth the effort. This does not appear to be the situation in this case, however.

Then Madison, saying he had an appointment, excused himself from the meeting.

Rich Gitto spent much of the meeting giving explanations on how the BUS-6 procurement and control processes worked. But when talk turned to the NIS case, the general consensus was that Peter (Pete) Bussolini was the main player, due to his role as the group leader. Records indicated that it was Scott Alexander who ordered most of the suspected stolen items. For 2000 and 2001, purchase records showed that Alexander purchased more than $400,000 of questionable items. Also, based on what McDonald and Stewart had said, a significant amount of improperly purchased property was probably hidden in multiple Nonproliferation and International Security Division bunkers, and would eventually make its way off lab property.

At the lab, Gitto explained, the first method to purchase items such as computers was the Just in Time (JIT) system. If orders couldn't be filled there, then items could be purchased through the Local Vendors Agreement (LVA). But there were supposed to be certain limits of spending imposed on the LVA system. Gitto also said that any lab employee could use their *lab identification badge like a credit card* to go to any of the approximate 160 approved vendors in New Mexico and buy almost anything they wanted. It's the loosest purchasing system the lab has; therefore, it is probably the easiest way to improperly purchase items because it lacks controls, said Gitto.

Agent Campbell learned later that Gitto was right, and that in addition to the misuse of the identification badge purchases per se, the lab failed to keep accurate accounting of these purchases. One division director told Campbell, as an example, that every one of his employees (about 30) could buy a full cart of Craftsman tools everyday with their lab identification badges, and he would have no idea they were being purchased because the lab failed to keep adequate records on these types of purchases.

A congressional body would later determine that in one year more than $800,000 of the lab's money was used to buy shoes of all types including sandals and sneakers through the Local Vender Agreement system.

Talk then turned to the Mesa Equipment and Supply Company that McDonald had identified. We tossed about the name of the sales person at Mesa Equipment and Supply who allegedly was doing business with Bussolini and Alexander. Rather than taking the items to the lab's distribution warehouse center, the salesman supposedly delivered the items directly to the lab site. Gitto noted this was contrary to lab rules.

We also speculated on what was being done with these stolen items. Were they all for personal use or given to family members and friends? Were they sold for cash? Were they somehow connected to the northern New Mexico illegal drug trade, or worse, were they falling into the hands of those who had more sinister purposes?

Because Gitto had confidential access to all lab business records, we agreed that he would be a key player in the investigation. We agreed that after the FBI determined what information they needed, they'd direct their request to me, and I'd forward it to Gitto. Gitto would then give me the information and I would give it to Agent Campbell.

We also agreed that everything discussed at the meeting, or any future Nonproliferation and International Security Division investigative meeting, would not go past the meeting doors. Naturally, I was obligated to inform Madison and Falcon about that rule. Campbell said he would have his FBI supervisors contact Richard and Shapiro and give them the same information. As an aside, Campbell told Doran and me that some members of the FBI asserted previous problems with Richard because he allegedly didn't keep a tight lip on confidential FBI information. Consequently, said Campbell, the FBI already contacted Richard reminding the barrister not to tell anyone about the NIS case unless he received approval from the FBI.

But there was to be, as I was beginning to suspect, an even worse danger lurking. Two hours after the meeting ended, Gitto came to my office and gave me a Business Division organizational chart. He then told me in a stern and concerned voice that he had some real personal concerns about our national security. These guys, continued Gitto, are apparently doing a lot of bad things in NIS, and it could mean "they are involved in spying." I agreed with Gitto, and told him that he could be assured that I would be working very closely with the FBI on this concern in conjunction with the thefts.

As we proceeded with our investigation, we employed typical FBI investigative practices that included record checking, surveillance, interviews, clandestine investigations of NIS bunkers to photograph and secretly mark suspected stolen items, and even dumpster diving. Campbell was the lead investigator, Doran assisted, and I supervised the inquiry from the Office of Security Inquiries perspective. We interviewed several lab employees, most of whom cited alleged repeated unauthorized purchases by Bussolini and Alexander. There were several striking similarities in these interviews, especially in opinions that surfaced regarding Bussolini and Alexander's behaviors toward others, and their relationship with each other. One allegation was that Bussolini was like a "Mafia don," and Alexander could be characterized as his henchman. Some employees stated they both exhibited abusive tendencies toward employees. Several employees referred to radio frequency detectors purchased with lab funds that the two placed on their desks to make sure no one was recording their conversations.

A former Facility Management Unit-75 employee disclosed she had left the unit because of Bussolini's stream of unauthorized purchases. "At first I liked working for Mr. Bussolini," she said, "but as time went on he became more and more of a tyrant." The woman also claimed, "Alexander was the one who placed the big orders after Bussolini told him to." Bussolini and Alexander, she said, were "like enforcer and confidant." According to her, "if Bussolini couldn't get cooperation from an employee he would tell Alexander to get it done." This witness went on to confide that in her opinion, "Alexander would then either try charm or intimidation, to include threats with physical violence. Whatever worked to get the job done for Bussolini, Alexander did it."

One FMU-75 contract employee said the "stealing by Bussolini and Alexander was well known, and Alexander threatened people with violence if they did not do what he or Bussolini said."

More and more employees confided their encounters and what they'd witnessed. One incident after another of questionable purchases and encounters began to surface.

A Nonproliferation and International Security employee —a man I personally know for his truth and veracity—called me and told me that as the investigation went on, Bussolini and Alexander were being kept out of many of the division's classified meetings because someone high in the division didn't trust them anymore. Bussolini and Alexander then generated a scheme, said the employee, to arrange a weekend bogus electrical breaker maintenance operation at Technical Area-33. Technical Area–33 is a highly classified SCIF (Secret Compartmentalized Information Facility) area that holds top-secret information. Their plan, continued the employee, was for Bussolini and Alexander to enter the facility during the bogus operation to check secret files to determine why they were being excluded from the meetings. At the last moment, Bussolini and Alexander backed out, said the employee.

Drawing on our interviews and investigations, Doran submitted an Office of Security Inquiries supplemental report on the Nonproliferation and International Security Division case. This report indicated that Bussolini and Alexander had high-tech lock picking equipment, sophisticated long-distant cameras, and clandestine radio transmitting devices—spy-type equipment—in their possession. Rich Gitto had already told us that Bussolini had control of all the keys and lock cores to the Nonproliferation and International Security Division. We also knew that Bussolini and Alexander held SCIF clearances, one of the lab's highest security clearances. Furthermore, they worked in a top-secret research area. Doran and I worried about leaks and openings for possible spying, and Doran expressed our fears in a supplement report. We wanted to ensure both Falcon and Madison knew of our concern.

When Falcon read Doran's theory on spying dangers, he summoned me to his office, strongly and emotionally objecting to this being included in the report. Falcon then directed me to tell Doran to remove anything about spying from the report.

Steve and I were flabbergasted at Falcon's position. This was S-Division, the division responsible for safeguarding the entire lab and its national nuclear-weapons secrets. Steve and I felt Falcon's mandate simply didn't make reasonable sense. I told Steve I had already expressed my concerns to Falcon about the growing critical potential of serious security breakdown, but Falcon didn't appear to be, at least to me, that concerned, and now he was maintaining his position even in the face of some pretty solid evidence that should, in our opinions, raise some red flags.

In early October, 2002, I finally received my Q-clearance. A few days later, Falcon told me that since I was now cleared, he could tell me why he had to have Doran take the spy information out of his supplemental. We have contractors, said Falcon, who work in NIS, and if they ever got wind that spying may be occurring in NIS they would drop their contracts, and that would not be good for the lab's DOE contract. I had to have Doran remove that information because it's not something we want to let out, concluded Falcon.

As the investigation progressed, we learned that Bussolini and Alexander also had in their possession glass-cutting equipment, approximately 100 keys to NIS doors that provided access to areas that contained classified information concerning national security, and CD-ROMs that explained how to pick locks.

The investigation also yielded telling evidence that nine other lab employees were involved in the Nonproliferation and International Security Division thefts. Six of them had become FBI informants and provided additional evidence that Alexander and Bussolini improperly bought items with government money, which were later found in their homes.

A few of the informants divulged their theories on Bussolini and Alexander's skill in re-identifying items so they wouldn't gain the attention of the lab's audit team. Agent Campbell and Doran confirmed their investigation and evidence on these allegations and immediately followed up with the auditors assigned to the Business Division in an attempt to determine why these purchases weren't caught. The auditors indicated they were not aware of any improper purchases by Bussolini and Alexander. Well, Campbell asked one auditor, what about this item identified as a receiver? What do you think it is? The auditor replied, I really don't know, but I'm sure they can use some type of receiver in NIS. He then became dumbfounded when Campbell asked, do you realize this receiver is actually a remote-controlled airplane controller?

For the next four months, Doran and I were continuously frustrated by some lab officials in our honest attempts to address blatant impropriety, financial abuse, and mismanagement at the lab. We had managed to unearth plenty of dirt.

By August 2002, four investigations were opened by either the FBI or the Department of Energy Inspector General (DOE IG), and, this was only the beginning of the discovery of the dark underbelly of the petty and large crimes, as well as the danger of even greater ones at the Los Alamos National Laboratory.

The FBI's NIS investigation continued throughout October 2002, with search warrants issued on Halloween. Agent Campbell noted in the federal search warrants that Bussolini and Alexander had abused their respective positions by improperly purchasing items with government funds, then removing the items from lab property for their personal use. Lab officials subsequently verified that they could *prove* that Bussolini and Alexander had stolen *only* about $350,000.00 of goods purchased by federal funds. Agent Campbell, Doran and I felt, based on the information we had, it had to be much more – perhaps millions more.

In May 2004, Bussolini and Alexander were indicted by a federal grand jury on 28 counts including 13 felonies. In October 2004, they pleaded guilty to felony charges of conspiracy and mail fraud, and in February 2005, they were sentenced to two separate federal prisons in the State of Colorado.

Bussolini, the alleged mastermind behind the crimes, received a lighter sentence of six months and was incarcerated in a soft prison environment. Alexander received a one-year sentence and was incarcerated in a hard-core prison. Why this disparity? A discretionary decision of a federal judge. Although thefts had been occurring at the lab for decades, it was reported that this was the first time since the beginning of the Manhattan Project that a federal agency arrested, prosecuted, and incarcerated a Los Alamos National Laboratory employee for laboratory theft.

The only reason Bussolini and Alexander were exposed for their egregious crime was McDonald and Stewart's courage in coming forward. But McDonald and Stewart also paid a high price for their stand for truth and justice. Over a two year period after coming forward, Jaret McDonald's life was threatened multiple times, including gun shots fired outside his residence; vehicles driving by his residence with the occupants yelling, "We are going to fucking kill you, you whistleblower;" and threatening telephone calls at his residence at all hours of the day, but especially during the wee hours of the morning. Although these activities were reported to the local police, no arrests were ever made. Most regrettably, some months after telling all to the FBI, James Stewart, God bless his soul, took his own life. Some, including Jaret McDonald and FBI informant John Jennings, felt it was the unbearable pressures of fear and stress that were placed upon this good man for helping to expose the crime and corruption at the Los Alamos National Laboratory that lead to this unfortunate and saddening event.

XII

Interference Begins

Round and round the circuitous path, ferreting out the truth about theft and mismanagement issues led me. In my first seven months at the Los Alamos laboratory, I had encountered apathy, cavalier attitudes, and reluctance to pursue serious problems, which I firmly believed could or was compromising the security of America's top secrets. What we were seeing some would say were surface problems, but the greed evidenced in these chaotic times could lead to profound jeopardizing and pitfalls.

Around that time lab attorney Gayle Rollins walked into my office unannounced and asked for copies of the FBI's NIS reports so that she could take them back to her office and review them. Less than two weeks earlier, at the Nonproliferation and International Security Division theft case meeting, Madison had specifically indicated that I would be the only lab employee to receive and review those reports. I respectfully refused Rollins' request, repeating Madison's mandate: however, Rollins persisted.

"If Richard contacts the FBI, and the FBI agrees to allow me to give you the reports, you can have them," I told Rollins. "However, it is my professional obligation not to let them out of my possession unless directed to do otherwise by the FBI."

Rollins continued to argue with me. She was adamant about getting the reports even though I kept insisting that her request could potentially interfere with a successful FBI investigation. At that point, she snapped. Our job is to determine if there is enough evidence to fire or suspend an employee, not whether we have the evidence to arrest and prosecute. I'm not concerned whether we violate any-one's constitutional rights or interfere with an FBI investigation; our job is to protect our employer, she said.

Finally, I told her, "Gayle, the only way you'll get these re-ports is over my dead body."

Rollins stormed out. I still had the reports and was very much alive.

After conferring with Falcon, I called Agent Campbell to con-firm the FBI's position. He reiterated the FBI did not want confiden-tial investigative information in the hands of people who should not have access to that information and that included attorneys in the lab's legal office. The FBI had even told the lab's top management that I was to be the only lab employee to have access to the con-fidential information, said Campbell. Two things occurred after my exchange with Rollins: first, no lab employee ever demanded those reports from me again; second, Campbell and I agreed that it would be best if I didn't receive any more FBI reports.

Curiously, that same day, Business Operations Division-5 employee Arleen Roybal called Doran to say that a BUS leader had ordered her and her co-worker Eric Martinez to let him review and approve all Business Division records before handing them over to Walp or Doran, and that the Business Division would be controlling all the information the Office of Security Inquiries received from that point on. Roybal was at a loss to explain where the orders were coming from.

Roybal called Doran again that day to tell him that Gayle Rollins was roaming around the BUS-5 area, asking questions and scouring through files in an attempt to obtain information and evidence on FBI and Office of Security Inquiries cases. When I told Falcon about this, stating it looked to me like a clear case of obstruction of justice, Falcon said he'd take care of it. Apparently he did, because later that day, according to Gitto, Rollins was directed by someone to stay out of the Business Division and not to speak to anyone or attempt to get any records concerning any OSI or FBI investigations.

Doran and I found reads on Falcon to be confusing. At times we felt confident of his full support, while at other times we couldn't be sure. Falcon called the two of us into a meeting on August 14 and, in an avuncular manner, revealed to us that he didn't think lab leadership was professional enough. He said that they didn't follow professional protocol and that they didn't adhere to the chain-of-command philosophy. But that's just the way it is, said Falcon, as he shook his head and shrugged his shoulders.

He then proceeded to make a statement that left both of us stunned. "I don't want you two to get in trouble with lab officials," Falcon said, but questioning the leaders' ethics and the way they handle procedures at the lab, especially Richard, could get you in trouble. "The lab is famous for sacrificing their children for the sake of its image;" it has happened many times before and it can happen to you, concluded Falcon.

Falcon then parroted Rollins' words to us: That one of our first responsibilities was to the lab and its management. Our job included looking out for the lab, the lab's image, and the University of California contract. Lab management, Falcon emphasized, consisted of the people who pay our checks.

Falcon turned to me and said that I needed to understand that what I was doing had never been done before. "You've upset the rice bowl Glenn and the lab doesn't know how to handle you," said Falcon.

Steve and I felt Falcon's position was becoming transparent as he discussed the involvement of the FBI and the Department of Energy Inspector General investigators in the Office of Security Inquiries cases.

You don't want to have to deal with the FBI or the Inspector General here at the lab because of their arrogance, said Falcon, and they'll tell you to get out of your offices, swear at you, tell you they are in charge, take over all your cases, and will not let you be involved. It won't be good if we allow the FBI or the Inspector General to come in and investigate our cases, Falcon continued.

We didn't know it then, but the lab's Audits and Assessments Unit was now becoming a major player in the investigations. That began to become clear in late August at a meeting Richard called, ostensibly to introduce Barbara Flynn of the PriceWaterhouseCoopers (PWC) purchase card audit unit. Richard told me he wanted to discuss Flynn's auditing responsibilities and her need to review lab audit documents.

Right before that meeting started, Rich Gitto intercepted Doran in his office. Be careful Steve, Gitto said, because Richard is going to take the meeting into a different direction then what he told Glenn. Gitto then recommended Doran give all investigative information the Office of Security Inquiries was working on to either FBI or DOE IG investigators, because it appears Richard and Shapiro plan to turn everything over to the Audits and Assessments Office, and that will not be good, Gitto said.

Richard began the meeting by saying he originally wanted to talk about audit documents, but then went on to say that we have other issues to discuss.

Richard turned the session over to Flynn, who immediately starting asking Doran and me about our policing experience and education. Then, abruptly, she asked us to give her all the information we had on Office of Security Inquiries investigations and the FBI's investigations. "I want to know everything," Flynn continued, about every inquiry and investigation OSI is involved in, how OSI got to where they are in their inquiries, where OSI is planning to go with their inquiries, and everything you know about the FBI investigations. At that point Richard interrupted and turned to Steve and me. Glenn and Steve, said Richard, "everything is open and on the table." You are to be candid with her, because Barbara needs to know everything, everyone in this room must know everything; everything must be placed on the table for everyone's knowledge, said Richard.

I stared at the ceiling for a moment recalling that I had been made aware Richard had been specifically directed by the FBI not to mention anything to anyone other than the OSI inquirers, Campbell, Shapiro, Richard, Marquez, Madison, Falcon, and Gitto regarding the NIS theft case. In addition, no one was to provide information to anyone from A&A because one of the FBI's suspected Nonproliferation and International Security Division thieves was known to work in Audits and Assessments. Yet Marcellaa Zambrea, who we later learned was the head of A&A, had been invited to this meeting. Now Richard was prodding Doran and me into telling everyone in the room all that we knew about our inquiries and FBI investigations.

Flynn may have been asking for specifics, but it was clear she already had detailed information, particularly about the Nonproliferation and International Security Division case. Doran and I tiptoed through our presentations, but Flynn began to zero in on more and more specifics. As Doran and I talked, Flynn frequently interrupted, saying, "I already know that," including that Bussolini and Alexander are suspects in the NIS case.

I was greatly disturbed by hearing all this. Flynn and others in the room should not have known this information, now or before. And yet they did. There was no question that this could potentially damage the FBI's investigations. We need to be careful what information is revealed and who gains knowledge of that information so it will not interfere with an OSI inquiry or, more importantly, an FBI investigation, I said. In fact, this discussion is crossing into areas "that may border on obstruction of justice," I continued.

89

Richard's naturally ruddy complexion turned bright red as he lunged across the conference table, posturing himself directly in front of Doran and me. "Let's not go there, boys," he bellowed. Remember who you work for, your boss is the lab, not the FBI, and you will tell everyone in this room everything you know about these cases, because that's the way it is, said Richard. We look out for the lab first, not FBI investigations, Richard concluded.

As Richard retreated to his chair, Doran cleared his throat and said the FBI would be interviewing a witness in the NIS case today.

"I want to sit in on the interview," Flynn said.

"I'll ask Agent Campbell," I responded, "but I don't think he'll agree to it." In my opinion, I continued, it would be improper for you to be there, but perhaps we can arrange for you to interview the witness after the FBI conducts its interview.

The FBI interviewed the witness for more than three hours. Barbara Flynn and Vickie Murphy, an aid to Richard who was to assist Flynn and also attended the meeting, got tired of waiting and left before the interview had concluded.

Doran and I doubled back with Agent Campbell and James Mullins after the interview was completed, and Campbell expressed outrage over a number of issues. He absolutely did not want Zambrea to know anything about his investigations, especially the Nonproliferation and International Security Division theft case. He also appeared to be extremely bitter that Richard had coerced Doran and me to give investigation details to Zambrea, Flynn, and Murphy. Campbell said he would ask his supervisor to tell Shapiro of Richard's actions and said that he didn't want it to happen again because it had the potential of blowing the FBI's cases.

After talking to his supervisor, Campbell decided to talk to Zambrea directly, rather than going through Richard. Using my office telephone, Campbell then called Zambrea and advised her not to tell anyone what she now knew about the FBI's investigations, particularly the NIS theft case. I understand, Zambrea told Campbell; I won't say anything to anyone.

Things were getting intense, not to mention curiouser and curiouser. Within the hour, Richard called me up to apologize about having to meet me under less-than-desirable circumstances earlier that day. I regret you and I haven't met before, Richard said to me.

I wondered if he had forgotten our meeting in July. Moreover, what exactly was he apologizing for?

Nevertheless, I took the opportunity to tell Richard that I thought it would be important for him to remind Zambrea, Flynn, and Murphy not to divulge any knowledge of the FBI investigations to anyone. If the Audits and Assessments Unit FBI suspect knew about the NIS theft case, it could jeopardize the FBI's investigation.

Richard said he understood, and he would take care of it immediately.

Next I met with Falcon and told him that Campbell and I were extremely upset with Richard's actions at our meeting. Falcon became visibly upset and told me he'd get back to me. When he did, later that day, he said he had spoken with Madison and that both of them agreed that Richard had been totally out of line. I spoke with Richard about the issue, and he told me Flynn would not be involved in any OSI or FBI investigations, said Falcon. She'll stay within the confines of her audit related to the lab's purchase card system, Falcon concluded.

Falcon then told me that if anything like that ever happened again, I was not to yield to pressure and that I was not to allow Flynn or anyone else, including Richard, to interfere with an Office of Security Inquiries inquiry or FBI investigation.

Later that day, Campbell, Mullins, Doran, and I had a telephone conversation with Gitto. Flynn should not have gone into the areas she did, questioning you on your inquiries or FBI investigations, Gitto told us. That was not her charge, Gitto continued, and OSI must make it clear to Flynn that she has nothing to do with your inquiries. Richard knew that, Gitto said, but he told her to ask the questions, but it isn't Richard's order that is now keeping Flynn out of your inquiries and investigations, that's coming from Shapiro.

Does Flynn understand this? I asked Gitto. Is someone with high authority ensuring she understands that she must stay out of our business, so I don't have to deal with her on a daily basis?

That would be nice, Gitto responded, but I don't think it's going to happen.

A few days later Flynn called a meeting with her assistant Bill Horn, Gitto, Doran, and me to allegedly discuss her audit procedures. Only a few minutes into the meeting Flynn started to ask for details of our inquiries and FBI investigations. I had to shut her down. "Barbara, I refuse to discuss anything about OSI or FBI cases, period," I said firmly.

Flynn's face reddened. She appeared shaken, but she didn't pursue the matter any further.

That was just one very minor victory in a campaign heavily weighted against our investigations. That the lab was tenaciously determined to prevent the Office of Security Inquiries and the FBI from objectively pursuing the facts became crystal clear when Agent Campbell asked me to get information as soon as possible on a lab employee who was a suspect in the NIS theft case. I asked Doran to get in touch with Gitto for the specific information, and Gitto replied with an answer neither of us wanted to hear.

"Richard changed the process of giving information to OSI and the FBI," Gitto told Doran and me. Gitto concluded that Richard has directed that any request must go directly to him, and he'll decide what information, if any, will be passed on.

So much for Madison's mandate of July 19, when he specifically directed that all FBI requests for information on the Non-proliferation and International Security Division theft case would go through me, then to Gitto, who would secure the information and give it to me, and then I'd pass it on to the FBI. Richard had just given himself total control.

I told Gitto he should try to get the information Agent Campbell wanted from Richard because it was extremely important to their case. Gitto told Steve and me a few hours later that he gave Richard the message, but, according to Campbell, Richard failed to pass the requested information to the FBI. Campbell told Steve and me that when the FBI asked Richard in October why he hadn't complied with their request, Richard, with Shapiro present, said he didn't remember Gitto's request. At that point, said Campbell, Shapiro verbally chastised Richard, not just for not following through with the FBI's request, but for implementing the revised procedure that gave Richard complete control of the information release.

Gitto called me at home to tell me that Richard wanted to get into the TA-33 bunkers to view NIS theft evidence, and, that he wanted Campbell, Doran, and Gitto there when he entered the bunkers. The next morning, Agent Campbell appeared stunned by the request. "You've got to be kidding," he said. "That's all the suspects need to see, someone they're familiar with, like Richard — especially from lab counsel — looking at the stolen items. It could destroy the whole case." Campbell said he'd try to get his supervisor to call Shapiro, or even Richard, to tell them to stay out of the FBI's business. "How can Richard not see the problems with his request," asked Campbell.

I told Doran to tell Gitto that the FBI wouldn't give Richard access to the Bunkers. I'll tell Richard, Gitto said, but I know he won't be happy.

And he wasn't. Gitto called Steve and me back and stated that Richard had said, "Doran and Walp fucked us."

"He's blaming this on you two," Gitto said. And, continued Gitto, every time Richard wants to blame someone for causing him problems he levels his blame on you, Glenn.

XIII

The Evidence

I wanted Thanh Nguyen to join my mission at the Office of Security Inquiries as soon as I learned about his background. A graduate of New York's John Jay College of Criminal Justice, Nguyen was among the few specialists selected by the FBI to work as a civilian within its nationwide Violent Criminal Apprehension Program. When he came on board, I met with him, was impressed, and immediately assigned him to work with me on correcting the blatant deficiencies within OSI's property evidence control system. To my amazement, when I arrived at the Office of Security Inquiries I found criminal investigative evidence in unlocked desk drawers and filing cabinets, stacked against office walls, and sitting on unsecured office shelves. Except for some items locked in an outside container, evidence security was nearly nonexistent. Some inquirers had no clue about, or apparently no interest in, how to maintain pure evidentiary chain of custody control, which is essential to successful criminal prosecution.

I wanted Nguyen to create, with my guidance, a professional

property control system, which I felt would become critical as we gathered potential evidence on the criminal cases the FBI, Doran, Mullins, and I were encountering.

Soon FBI Agent Campbell came by my office with Doran and expressed his appreciation for the work Steve, Jim, and I were doing. You guys don't realize the difference you've made, Campbell said. Before you got here, continued Campbell, we never got the support of LANL, and it's not that there weren't any crimes here; it's just that they didn't involve us and didn't want us here. The FBI, said Campbell, except for the Lee and hard drive cases, was not involved in one criminal case between January 1999 and May 2002, but since June, 02 four major criminal cases had come under FBI scrutiny, and you three are the reason for the change. Think what it will be like if you guys can stay here for a couple years; we could clean up the mess that has littered this lab for a long time, concluded Campbell.

Campbell then made an ominous comment. "We [FBI agents in the Santa Fe District Office] have some serious concerns that the lab is not going to let you guys stay around. This is not how they normally conduct business, and you guys have upset the apple cart."

In one FBI investigation reams of evidence were confiscated from a lab site. That there might be important information contained in the items confiscated was confirmed when we learned that Richard's legal assistant, Vickie Murphy, would visit the Office of Security Inquiries in early September to review some of the confiscated material. Murphy was to be accompanied by Barbara Flynn, the lab's on-site administrator for PriceWaterhouseCoopers. This made me uncomfortable because their review could interfere with the FBI's investigation. However, I agreed to allow them access to the evidence within certain guidelines. Nguyen would monitor the review. Nguyen would then return the evidence to the evidence container for storage. "All appropriate chain of custody procedures will be followed," I told them, "thereby ensuring the chain of custody link is not broken."

The first review occurred on September 4 with Flynn and

her assistant, Bill Horn. As they reviewed portions of the evidence, Nguyen watched over the proceedings to make sure the chain of custody was maintained. That same day, Falcon told me that Richard was ordering me to allow George Bellstrum, a personal friend of the employee under investigation, and Murphy, on Flynn's behalf, to review all the evidence. I told Falcon I didn't have any problem with lab attorney Murphy, as long as she followed the same procedure that Flynn and Horn had followed. But I told Falcon that having Murphy review the evidence was totally different than having Bellstrum review it. Allowing Bellstrum to review the evidence is improper and borders on obstruction of justice because his access to the evidence had the potential of tainting the evidence per se, and destroying the chain of custody, I told Falcon. My reasoning Matt? It was reported to me that Bellstrum had been heard in various lab locations telling people he was attempting to review the evidence to get information that would help the employee under investigation, and giving Bellstrum access was not a sound decision, I said.

Falcon's response was that Richard was ordering it; therefore, Bellstrum would be allowed to review the evidence in the Harry Moss case, and would be allowed to do so in private.

Murphy called me on September 9 to say she would come to OSI later in the day to take some of the evidence back to Richard's office in Los Alamos for review. I told Falcon I would assign Nguyen to assist Murphy, using the same procedures I used when Flynn and Horn reviewed the evidence. For whatever reason, Murphy never showed up to conduct the review.

Bellstrum also called me that day. He said he needed to get into the evidence to clean up some records he needed for an upcoming audit. Based on Falcon's previous mandate, I told Bellstrum to contact me later in the week, and I would give him a date when he could review the evidence. I was stalling for time, hoping the FBI would first review the evidence. Meanwhile, Doran called Arleen Roybal to get her perspective on Bellstrum's request. The audit is valid, but Bellstrum doesn't need those records, because we have duplicate records that he can use, she said. Bellstrum knows we have duplicate records, and I feel his attempt to get into the evidence is a sham; in my opinion he is just trying to get information that he feels may help the employee, continued Roybal.

Campbell was furious about this latest series of events. He didn't want Bellstrum going through the evidence before the FBI did, especially in private, and said he'd try to get his supervisor to stop Richard from interfering. But plenty of interference attempts were already happening; Campbell had learned that on several occasions since August 20, someone from Richard's office had contacted the FBI asking to review the evidence in order to establish a human resources case. The FBI, Campbell said, was becoming increasingly frustrated with Richard's attempts to get into the evidence before the FBI did, and the bureau was thinking about getting a search warrant to confiscate all of the evidence and take it into its custody. "If the search warrant isn't issued," Campbell told me, "I may ask your personnel to review the evidence in this Harry Moss incident, on my behalf to determine if there is any evidence that would be relevant to the FBI case." Any found evidence could be secured by OSI, and the remaining items that are irrelevant to our investigation could be turned over to Richard, said Campbell.

As it turned out, a search warrant was not going to be issued, on orders from the U.S. Attorney. Campbell then told me he would probably be contacting me in the near future to have Office of Security Inquiries members review the evidence on behalf of the FBI and their official investigation.

Shortly thereafter, I received a copy of a letter addressed to Richard, written by Gregory Calles, an FBI supervisor. This letter made it clear from my perspective that Campbell would have to give his approval before any of the evidence was reviewed by any lab official. Agent Campbell contacted me the same day I received the letter and directed me to assign an OSI member to review the evidence on their behalf.

I assigned Mullins and Nguyen to that task at 7:30 a.m. the

next day, and at 7:35 I received a call from Falcon. He told me that at 9 a.m., high-ranking PriceWaterhouseCoopers personnel would be at the Office of Security Inquiries to take all the evidence.

What about the FBI letter indicating Campbell had to approve such a transaction? Falcon responded to Steve and me that since the FBI had not served a search warrant on the boxes, he saw no problem with PriceWaterhouseCoopers personnel reviewing all the evidence or taking the evidence away from OSI. I told Falcon I had assigned Mullins and Nguyen, on Campbell's direction, to review the evidence first.

I asked Falcon if we couldn't get PWC to hold off until Mullins and Nguyen completed their review. The review wouldn't take long, and I was concerned that moving the evidence was contrary to an FBI directive and could be construed as potentially obstructing justice.

No, Falcon said with emphasis. You need to work with me on this, "because this is what Richard wants," Falcon continued.

I told Falcon I'd assign Nguyen to assist PriceWaterhouseCoopers people, and then I advised everybody at OSI that anybody who came to review or take the evidence was to ask for Nguyen because I would be at a lab training session in the nearby town of White Rock. Privately, I told Mullins and Nguyen that they were to give the PWC people all of the evidence if they wanted it. The only stipulation; whoever took the evidence must sign out for it. I told Mullins to make Campbell aware of what was now occurring.

As soon as I got to White Rock, Mullins paged me. He told me Campbell said the FBI was tired of fighting this battle with Richard because it just isn't worth it. Mullins told me that Campbell said Richard can do what he wants, but that he'd attempt to contact the Department of Energy Inspector General's office in Albuquerque because the Inspector General may have a different position on what was occurring. I reiterated to Mullins that if PriceWaterhouseCoopers personnel showed up for the evidence, they still needed to sign out for it, in accordance with Office of Security Inquiries policy.

"If the PWC detail takes the evidence into their custody and then return it," I said, "there is no need to reseal it, because the chain of evidence will be broken."

A half-hour after I returned to my class, Mullins paged me again to tell me Campbell recontacted him and told him he couldn't make contact with anyone at the Inspector General's office, and that a PriceWaterhouseCoopers representative had come to the Office of Security Inquiries and was extremely arrogant. The representative, it turned out, was a former inspector general for a federal department. Mullins said the representative boasted how much experience he had in law enforcement; therefore, he knew what he was doing and I didn't. Mullins felt the representative was claiming that all of the items confiscated were not evidence and that's why they were taking it. Mullins told me he and the representative had engaged in a heated argument. The main reason I'm calling you, Mullins went on, is because it appears the representative was at OSI simply to be argumentative because when he was told he could take all the evidence, he never did; he just left even though a lab employee came with him with a truck to pick the evidence up.

I returned from training in the early afternoon to learn that Falcon had scheduled meetings that day. The first one would be between Falcon and Moe Shapiro, the Lab's Deputy Director. The second one was to be with Falcon, Shapiro, Madison, Doran, and me. The reason for the second meeting was "to discuss OSI's lack of cooperation concerning the evidence."

I told Falcon about the exchange earlier that day between the PriceWaterhouseCoopers representative and Mullins. At no time was anyone uncooperative, I said to Falcon. The representative actually was given full authority to take the evidence if he wanted, I said, and all he had to do was sign out for it, but for some reason he didn't take it, even though a driver with a truck was standing by to load it. I went on to say Mullins and Nguyen had both told me they believed the representative was sent to the Office of Security Inquiries just to make it appear as if we were uncooperative. Finally, I couldn't hold back any longer. Based on a range of recent events, I told Falcon, that it seemed OSI was being undermined. "Could Richard be a major player in this situation?" I asked myself.

Falcon seemed clearly upset when I clarified that Mullins and Nguyen had felt the PWC representative was being extraordinarily and unreasonably arrogant. He told me he wanted to hear Doran's, Mullins' and Nguyen's version first-hand. Within ten minutes, Doran, Nguyen and Mullins were in Falcon's office. Nguyen and Mullins told Falcon they both believed that someone had sent the representative to the Office of Security Inquiries specifically to make it look as though OSI was being uncooperative. Then I told Falcon how frustrated I was about certain lab officials being more concerned with the lab's image, rather than doing the right thing. Doran chimed in, "I don't understand why there is such a big ado. These lab officials are completely overreacting over peons being investigated for thefts."

Doran, Mullins, Nguyen, and I pondered whether Richard was involved. Was there an attempt at a cover-up, we asked ourselves. I told Falcon that in my opinion, Richard could appear deceptive. I reminded him about the press release the lab distributed in August, about thefts at the lab. Richard had intentionally authored a vague press release so that the media would not get all the details of an alleged lab theft. When the media caught him in his deception, it was reported that Shapiro came down on him. Richard then telephoned me and tried to get me to say that I authored the release. I told him bluntly, "No way, Brian, that was your idea." In a later telephone conversation with Falcon, which Madison and I overheard on Falcon's speakerphone, Richard admitted to Falcon that he tried to sucker me into taking the heat for him.

Richard may be retaliating against me or OSI for doing what we were hired to do; to conduct inquiries on theft, I said, and now that these theft issues are going public I don't think the lab likes it. Falcon asked me to elaborate. I repeated my complaint that Richard and others were probably concerned about losing their jobs. If details about these theft activities became public, the lab could be in danger of losing its contract, and if the University of California lost the contract, their employment could go away. I told Falcon that it appeared management was emphasizing the protection of the contract over everything else. "Perhaps," I told Falcon, "this should go before a congressional body for review."

That comment clearly upset Falcon. Glenn, said Falcon, I can't believe you would make a statement about "dropping a nickel on some political committee." Alarmed and clearly agitated, Falcon then said, this meeting is over.

Ten minutes later, Falcon called to tell me about a meeting he had just scheduled for 3 p.m. in which he and I, along with Richard and three PriceWaterhouseCoopers staffers would "kiss and make up." The meeting would also be attended by the PWC representative who appeared at the Office of Security Inquiries earlier that day; former Department of Energy Inspector General John Layton; and Donald Kintzer, PWC's off-site administrator. Richard told us that Shapiro had hired Layton and the representative, at about $450 an hour each, to oversee PriceWaterhouseCoopers' audit inquiry. At one point, Richard said, jokingly, that the last U.S. Attorney during the Wen Ho Lee case had attempted to accuse him of obstruction of justice but nothing ever came of it because he didn't have any evidence. The meeting was mainly for Layton to clarify what the team's audit responsibilities were and how the audit would proceed. Most likely, Layton said, the audit team would be contacting OSI for assistance on such matters as a lab employee who allegedly purchased personal diamond jewelry with a federal credit card. It seemed to me that someone was determined to smooth our mutual relationships, and as an offshoot, it was probably in the back of their mind that by having us kiss and make up, that I'd forget the idea about trying to get a congressional body to review what was going on at the lab. During the time the meeting was taking place, all the evidence was being picked up and transferred to Richard's office.

On September 23, Bellstrum called me again, requesting a review of the evidence. I told Bellstrum to contact Brian Richard - he had the evidence.

XIV

The Sleeping Dog Awakens

I felt only the tip of the iceberg had been uncovered, and that beneath the ominous object were many dark ventures, which could wreak even more havoc in this treacherous climate of potential terrorist threats. Nevertheless, at least our revelation and disclosures of the criminal cases apparently caused a stir within the Department of Energy's Inspector General's Office in Albuquerque. Previously, on August 29, the lab's Arleen Roybal was informed by a memo from Department of Energy Assistant Special Agent-in-Charge Adrian Gallegos that his Albuquerque office was investigating purchase card fraud at the lab. Gallegos identified nine lab cardholders who had *questionable purchases* in 2000 and 2001. Some of questionable purchases that amounted to thousands of dollars were made at Stairmaster Medical Supply, Par Golf Supply, and Name It Golf. Agent Gallegos then contacted me requesting a meeting with FBI Agent Campbell, Doran, Mullins, and me on September 10. Gallegos and fellow agents Rosemarie Peterson and Brandon Curry represented the Department of Energy Inspector General's office.

For years we have been attempting to get sufficient evidence against LANL on their mismanagement and cover-up practices, Peterson said. Perhaps the information you four have will give us the evidence we need to move forward, she continued.

Gallegos voiced his concerns. It's well known that LANL has difficulty maintaining control of property and has a well-established reputation for theft, he said. Gallegos went on to say that the Inspector General's office supported our efforts in uncovering mismanagement, thefts, and the cover-up of the thefts. He then asked if we were familiar with DOE Orders 221.1 and 221.2, which dealt with reporting fraud, waste, and abuse to his office. The orders state that any DOE employee or contractor who has information about any fraud, waste, abuse, misuse, corruption, criminal acts, or mismanagement relating to DOE programs is required to notify an "appropriate authority," which includes someone within the Department of Energy Inspector General's office; not just a lab employee, said Gallegos. Therefore, if you have any information like that, you don't have to get approval from anyone, including your superiors, to contact us directly, and we can go from there, Gallegos said.

Gallegos ended the meeting by repeating the difficulties his office had experienced with Los Alamos management attempting to block their investigations. He said he would appeal to Shapiro and Richard in an attempt to get them to support our efforts. But there was an addendum. I'll do the best I can, he said, but you need to understand I can only go so far, "because *I'm controlled by politics.*"

I went to Falcon the next day and told him about Gallegos' talk and the DOE orders. You show me the orders, Glenn. They don't exist, Falcon retorted. I'm telling you, said Falcon, that if you have any information like that you cannot go directly to the IG first; you must first come to me, and then Richard will determine what happens with that information. You show me the orders, Falcon concluded.

Falcon continued, explaining that the way it works at LANL, is that we refer all matters to Richard, who then determines what, if anything, should be done. If Richard feels it should go further, he will contact the DOE in Washington, and if the DOE thinks it should go further, they would contact the FBI, DOE IG, or whoever, said Falcon. However, we do not, you do not, contact the FBI or the DOE IG or any other police department directly on any cases OSI is working on.

I followed up this dialogue by making copies of the orders dated March 22, 2001 and which were to expire exactly four years later. I forwarded them to Falcon by internal mail and I added a note: "These are the orders Gallegos was referring to. They confirm what Gallegos said. Please review, and then I would like to discuss them with you."

Falcon never responded to my request.

XV

Fall Guys

Fall began early in 2002 – on September 18 at 3:20 p.m., to be exact. That's when Falcon called me into a meeting, which I was told would include Madison. We then would have another meeting with Doran immediately following.

The Madison meeting began like many others. He reminded me how important it was for the lab to maintain its DOE contract. Then came a rehashing of the lab's bitter feelings toward the FBI and the U.S. Attorney as a result of the Wen Ho Lee and lost hard drive cases. The Wen Ho Lee case didn't go well for the lab, and Richard blamed the FBI and the U.S. Attorney, and the FBI and the U.S. Attorney blamed the lab, and Richard was now desperately trying to repair those relationships, Madison said. Richard is a great guy who has a lot of responsibility, Madison continued, and he's attempting to balance issues and keep everybody happy by trying to manage the PriceWaterhouseCoopers team, me, Falcon, OSI, and you.

Yes, me. The meeting was definitely about me. I feel badly that you perceive Richard from a negative view, Madison said. I have never known Richard to be the type of individual who would try to willfully attempt to get rid of an employee, but if Brian felt you were getting in his way, like interfering with his relationship with the U.S. Attorney or the FBI, Brian would *put both barrels on you and level you,* said Madison.

Of course, that was Madison's opinion, but I felt both barrels on me. I don't think you are on Brian's hit list either way, Madison said, but Richard isn't trying to get you, but you're not popular with Richard either.

Madison changed the subject and the focus turned to Doran. Didn't Doran have more than a few conversations with Richard? questioned Madison. Maybe Steve misled Brian, Madison said. You know, continued Madison, he has to be careful what he tells the FBI; I mean, instead of saying, "Let's say no to Brian about getting into the bunker..."

"That didn't happen, Doug," I said, interrupting.

I know that didn't happen, I'm not saying it happened, Madison said, appearing irritated. I'm suggesting, continued Madison, rather than saying that, say something like, hey, how can we make this happen? How can we make this work for Brian? Then it was back to me. Why do you think Richard may be out to get you? Madison asked.

Because I had challenged Richard on August 28 when he attempted to force Doran and me to reveal confidential OSI and FBI information to those who should not have known, I said. But there are more obvious, damning examples, I continued, such as Rich Gitto's September 11 phone call telling Doran and me how Richard had tried to get Gitto to agree that I was uncooperative in ongoing investigations, with Gitto stating that he felt Richard was putting his sights on me. And that statement, Doug, I said, is similar to your comment that Richard is capable of leveling me with both barrels. Then there was the Gitto-Doran phone call on September 11 when Gitto recounted how Richard had expressed extreme anger because the FBI denied him access to the TA-33 bunkers, I added. Gitto said Richard blamed the FBI's refusal on Doran and me, I continued, and said that Richard said Doran and Walp fucked us. I provided several more examples, including the September 17 call Doran and I received from Gitto when Gitto said Richard was trying to blame OSI for incorrect chronology in an investigative case. Gitto said concerning that issue that it appeared that Richard was trying to deflect his failure to establish a case against the employee so that he wouldn't look bad in front of Shapiro. I feel these are sufficient indicators to lead a reasonable and prudent person to opine that Richard may be attempting, as you say, to level me with both barrels, I concluded.

Madison and Falcon looked like they were zapped with a Tazer.

I guess that with your place in life, Glenn, you can be a bit more forceful in the way you can present things, Madison said.

Apparently, he was referring to my age and career accomplishments, and that I was already receiving retirement benefits from the Pennsylvania State Police.

We're getting to that place in life, too, Madison said, motioning to Falcon.

A pause.

You and Steve need to understand, said Madison, who it is you work for, and that's the lab. I know you both came from backgrounds where your job was to go out and get people and arrest people, but its different here; that's not your job here, said Madison. Law enforcement is not your job anymore, Madison continued. Yes, you are to help the FBI, but that's not your only job; one of your jobs is to look out for the lab, concluded Madison.

Doran was then summoned to the meeting. I continued with the previous conversation. That doesn't mean we throw the ethics of a professional police officer to the wind, I told Madison. We know we are no longer police officers, but I will assure you that Steve and

I will maintain our police professionalism, and that means we will be honest and forthright in all that we do with our job responsibilities, I continued.

Madison turned to Doran and threw down the gauntlet, stating that Steve needed to ensure that Richard has a good relationship with the FBI and U.S. Attorney. If Brian thinks you are getting in the way of his relationship with either of them, "you'll be fired," said Madison. One of your jobs, like Glenn's, is to look out for the lab, concluded Madison.

End of meeting.

Doran and I left to collect our thoughts. As we talked, our conclusions solidified. The gist of what we concluded was this: We were hired to conduct, in part, inquiries on theft. Some people, Richard appearing to be the most prominent, and probably others, were apparently upset that the theft and mismanagement problems were becoming public knowledge. That was hurting the lab's image and placing its future in jeopardy. Therefore, the work we were doing was hurting the lab, and because the lab was employing us, our job was no longer the same as we thought it would be when we were hired. One of our jobs, according to our employers, was to protect the lab. The consequences of not performing those duties were painfully clear — and clearly painful to us as lifelong police officers.

The morning after our meeting with Madison, I was in the lab's gymnasium at 5:30 a.m., just finishing my first set of squats, when Falcon paged me. He said he needed to see me as soon as I got back to the office.

I rushed my exercise routine and arrived at the lab an hour before my usual start time. In Falcon's office was another S-Division employee, there to discuss a security incident. Within minutes, Richard called Falcon, who did not use the speakerphone as he normally did. At the end of the call, Falcon told me Richard wanted Doran and me to once again review the timelines in an investigation by 1 p.m., at which point we'd be meeting with Richard, Falcon, Flynn, Horn, and a Shapiro aide named Tom Gunnerston. The meeting is being held to review the timelines, to ensure they are correct, Falcon said, and if any changes are needed, they can be made at the meeting.

Then Falcon dropped his bombshell, stating that he just had a call from Richard, and Richard may be zeroing in on Doran "to be the fall guy." At that point, Madison walked in, and Falcon told him the same thing. Then Madison told me he thought Richard would be trying to make me a fall guy as well.

"This is getting personal, Steve," I said to Doran when I got back to my office. "Surely they are trying to frame us in order to get rid of us."

Despite the pressure, Doran and I poured over the investigative data to prepare for the meeting. In the middle of our task, Falcon called to summon me to a meeting with him and Madison. I just had another telephone conversation with Richard and it sounds like he's ready to declare defeat on the Harry Moss case, and blame S-Division for its failure, Falcon said.

I think they have enough to fire Harry if they want to, Madison said.

"If they want to," Falcon responded. That's the key, continued Falcon; it just seems to me that Brian is getting cold feet about firing him – period.

An hour later, Falcon came into my office and told Doran and me that he was concerned about what we would say at the 1 p.m. meeting, and that we shouldn't be concerned about Richard's apparent intent to make us the fall guys.

Well, we'll be professional about it, I said, but if it looks like someone is going to go after us and try to frame us, we're not just going to just sit there and accept it; we'll defend ourselves.

I'm telling you, don't be defensive, Falcon responded.

"That bothers me, Matt," I said. Steve and I are conscientious lab employees doing our job, doing the right thing, I said, and Madison and you tell us a few hours ago that the lab's chief counsel may be attempting to set us up as fall guys, and then you say we shouldn't be concerned?

Just don't be defensive, Falcon said, and left my office.

This much seemed clear to Steve and me; Falcon and perhaps Madison didn't want Richard to know they had warned us about his intent to lay the blame on us. If Richard found out, then they'd be toast, too.

It was nearly 1 p.m. as we hurried to the meeting. We began by reviewing the timelines. Richard and Flynn then asked Doran to clarify every piece of evidence he had on Moss. Doran presented the evidence in explicit detail, making sure to point out at the end of his presentation, that thus far, it was strictly a circumstantial case with no smoking gun, and that further investigation needed to be done before any final conclusions could be made. The meeting ended with Richard and Flynn announcing that, as far as they were concerned, there was more than sufficient evidence to fire Moss.

Later that day, Rich Gitto called Doran and me to inform us that earlier that morning Shapiro had chewed out Richard, threatening to replace him. Doran then recounted all of the day's events to Gitto, including Falcon's statement that Richard may be zeroing in on us, along with the information that Richard and Flynn agreed there was more than enough evidence to fire Moss.

Now it all makes sense, Gitto said. Gitto then laid out his theory:

> This morning, Richard was beside himself attempting to get sufficient evidence to fire the employee. If Richard felt he didn't have enough information to fire the employee, I think he would attempt to switch blame and try to make OSI the fall guys by saying they didn't give him enough information. Richard had gone out on a limb by pushing to place the employee on investigative leave so the lab wouldn't look bad. Richard didn't plan ahead on how much evidence, or what evidence there was, and now he

was scrambling to try to find the evidence that Shapiro would accept as sufficient to fire the employee. Richard probably told Shapiro he might not have the evidence to fire the person, and Shapiro probably unloaded on Richard. If Richard felt he didn't have enough evidence to fire Moss, he may have blamed it on OSI, using the ploy that they did not give him accurate or enough information. There is no way Richard would accept that responsibility.

Yes, it did make sense. Madison had already told us the lab would prefer the FBI to prosecute civilians over lab employees. And when the case first materialized, Richard stated he wanted the employee on investigative leave before the FBI took action so it would not be as embarrassing for the lab. We figured Richard might have changed his perspective on seeking a fall guy because he determined at the 1 p.m. meeting that there was enough evidence to fire Moss. That would take Richard off the hook with Shapiro.

But the hook was still hanging there, waiting to snare someone. Later that afternoon, Campbell told Doran that the assistant U.S. Attorney was extremely upset that the FBI had supplied information to Richard regarding several investigations. He said, said Campbell, don't you know Richard's job is to defend lab employees, and here we are giving information to Richard? As a result, continued Campbell, the attorney was directing the FBI not to give Richard anymore confidential criminal investigative information, and that he would call Richard that afternoon to tell him.

We wondered how that conversation would affect us. Madison, after all, had just told us that I would be leveled with both barrels and Doran would be fired if either one of us got in the way of a positive relationship between Richard and the FBI and/or the U.S. Attorney. Maybe Richard would blame us, as he did, according to Gitto, in the bunker issue.

About a week later, my wife and I hosted a party at our residence in Santa Fe for all new OSI employees, including Doran and his girlfriend, Mullins and his wife, and Thanh Nyugen. We also invited Rich Gitto and his significant other. Nyugen and I were talking to Gitto when he looked at me and said in a friendly manner, Glenn, you have a good job, you are paid well; you don't have to do anything if you really don't want to. You could easily float, continued Gitto, and get your salary and not have to put up with the troubles you're now encountering, so why don't you just relax and cool it and things would go much better for you and the lab.

Gitto obviously didn't know me that well. "I didn't come to LANL to sit around and collect a check," I replied. "That's not who I am, or what I represent, I will do the job I'm being paid to do. Apparently the lab didn't do their homework on me, because it is clear they don't know me."

Gitto smiled and nodded, indicating he understood. I couldn't help wondering if those were Gitto's opinions alone, or had someone suggested he say those things to me, hoping that I'd back off.

XVI

Forgery Too

The numerous incidents of theft, some admittedly petty, were setting off serious questions in the minds of Mullins, Doran, and me about the safety and security of Los Alamos secrets.

It had taken about a month for James Mullins, the former Dallas police officer and FBI employee, to realize that lab procedures were more than somewhat askew. Mullins' first assignment had been to evaluate the drop-point distribution system and then provide recommendations on how this system — that, in my opinion, and soon his, practically begged for thefts to occur — could be corrected. Mullins' second assignment had helped solidify the suspicion in our minds how deep corruption and cover-ups were flooding the Los Alamos National Laboratory.

In late September I received a phone call from Ken Leivo of Human Resources. Leivo called to say an alleged crime, misappropriation of federal funds by an employee who forged a government check, appeared to have been committed within the Nonproliferation and International Security Division. The crime, however, had been committed about two weeks prior, said Leivo.

I assigned Mullins to the case, but within a few hours, we learned that the employee had already confessed to the crime, was fired by his supervisor and allowed to make restitution without the crime being investigated by an investigative authority, as required by federal law.

"Glenn, is this how the lab handles federal crimes?" asked Mullins.

I immediately called Falcon to discuss the issue, and he deferred a meeting with Mullins and me until the following day, September 24. Falcon outlined what he knew about the forgery case, and he was conspicuously disturbed. They've failed to notify us of a federal crime they knew about, and they're telling us they settled it on their own, said Falcon. It's wrong, continued Falcon, and what they have done is a crime, in addition to the forgery crime.

It certainly looked as though complicity involving other lab employees seemed to have existed, in our opinions, in the case. I know Tony Ling, said Falcon, one of the NIS Division supervisors, knew about this Friday, because he talked to me about it on Friday, so if there is complicity, that would be a felony too, and that also must be addressed as a federal crime, emphasized Falcon to Jim and I.

Falcon ordered Mullins and me to interview Ling and the employee's immediate supervisor, Katie Farber, back to back. The Miranda law – that individuals be advised of their legal rights before they are interrogated by a law enforcement official – was a concern. We all agreed we did not want to create a situation where a court challenge would negate a criminal prosecution based on a technicality of the law. After all, it could be interpreted that an Office of Security Inquiries member was an extension of the law enforcement arm. We decided that Mullins and I would interview the employee and leader without warnings, but allow them the latitude, as in all lab inquiries, not to talk to the inquirers if they did not want to. Falcon said if our inquiry established a suspect, or suspects, then we'd refer any following interrogation to an appropriate law enforcement agency.

It was obvious to me that Ling was expecting my call. On the speakerphone, with Mullins listening in, he said he was the one who directed Farber to accept the employee's restitution check, and that it was his decision to fire the employee. I told Ling that Mullins and I would be interviewing him and Farber that afternoon. I also told him Farber wasn't required to speak with us because the incident may involve a federal felony.

"What do you mean a federal felony?"

I explained aspects of the law that could make the incident a federal crime. Ling became upset. You are not blaming Katie, my employee, or anyone else for this, because I did it, it was my decision, Ling said.

The man's anger was mounting. Do you know, said Ling, I just came from a meeting this morning with Brian Richard and Falcon, and Richard said there was no problem with what I did? Richard said restitution is part of the process, said I could do it, and I could do anything I wanted, and let her go and just let her pay back the restitution without telling anyone, said Ling. Richard told me, continued Ling, I did everything right, telling me the only thing I had to do was keep a copy of the check and everything would be okay.

At that point, it became clear that we needed to talk about this with Falcon before our interviews. Ling agreed, and we hung up.

With Mullins listening on the speakerphone, I telephoned Falcon. Matt, Ling told me about the meeting Richard, he, and you had this morning, and Ling may have just confessed to complicity in a federal crime, and he may have implicated Richard.

There was dead silence on the line - long moments of silence.

Yes, Glenn, said Falcon, Brian did give directions telling him it was okay to let the employee pay the restitution and then let her go.

"Matt, why didn't you tell Mullins and me about the meeting?"

I can't tell you everything Glenn, said Falcon. Look, *they have now also implicated me as well,* continued Falcon.

Falcon then said he had to call Richard immediately.

Five minutes later, Falcon called back, and while on the speakerphone said, *"They're circling the wagons."* Falcon continued, stating that Richard wants to have a meeting with all of us tomorrow where we can talk this situation through and work it all out. Richard *is now saying,* said Falcon, he will probably turn the case over to the DOE Inspector General. According to Richard, it doesn't fall under FBI jurisdiction because they won't accept any case under $100,000, continued Falcon.

"Matt, that's not true." I said. "The FBI would certainly accept cases under $100,000."

Then more dead silence — much longer than before. It was clear to Jim and me that Matt was searching for words, but they were difficult to find.

Glenn, I know the FBI can accept a case, "even over a dollar," said Falcon.

"Matt," I said strongly, "I won't be involved in any shenanigans for anybody at this lab. You'd better report this crime to an appropriate police agency according to federal law if you don't want me to blow the whistle."

"Please, Glenn, don't do that."

"Matt, the right thing has to be done. I'll do the right thing if others won't."

Falcon told us not to do anything until we heard back from him.

Shortly after 2 p.m., Falcon came to my office. He told Mullins and me that he was concerned about when the case was brought to the Nonproliferation and International Security Division's attention, and when the Nonproliferation and International Security Division's Human Resources started its inquiry, because lab policy stated they had to report this incident to the Office of Security Inquiries immediately. Falcon asked Mullins for specifics because Mullins was initially assigned to the case. Falcon said he'd be meeting with Richard the following day to try to *persuade Richard to do the right thing* by turning the case over to the Department of Energy Inspector General, as it should have been done right from the beginning. But how can anyone arrest her now for a crime she confessed to after they already cut a deal with her, said Falcon?

"Exactly my point Matt," I said, because it appears that until *their deal* was challenged, they had no plans of telling anyone, and that is why they are now scrambling, and is the reason you said yesterday, they are circling the wagons.

By the way, said Falcon, OSI is now off the case. I'd rather an investigator come in from the outside to interview the involved people to determine exactly what happened, so you guys are out of it, continued Falcon.

Falcon initially asked Mullins and me to attend the meeting with Richard, but I told him I didn't think it would be appropriate if it was later learned that there was some type of conspiracy involving Human Resources and/or the legal office. Falcon agreed with that, but stressed that he wanted all the information we had in order to help his case with Richard.

What a difference a day makes indeed. Early the next day, after Falcon had his meeting with Richard and perhaps whomever else, he *stormed* into my office with fire in his eyes. He said he was upset with me because the day before I made comments in front of Mullins about Richard possibly being involved in the case.

I told Falcon, as you know Matt, Mullins was fully aware of all aspects of the case, Mullins was in the same meeting with you and me; what are you talking about?

Falcon didn't pursue the matter, but once again, he was approaching something differently than he had before, and it was clear to me he was building a foundation for something else.

I offered my steel-edged opinion, "Matt, I think you're setting us up."

I reminded him that he had never told Mullins or me about his meeting with Richard and Ling before he had met with us, instead ordering us to find out what was going on when he already knew what was going on. If we're working as a team on security and criminal issues, it certainly would be nice if my supervisor would tell me about these issues before sending me off on a path that involves possible federal felonies while not giving me all the facts, I barked. You put us in a difficult position. We should have been armed with information about possible complicity before we pursued the interview with Ling, but you failed to tell us, I said.

Again, Falcon said, "Glenn, I can't tell you everything."

I reminded Falcon of what had transpired. We had agreed on September 24 that it was possible that a federal crime had been committed and that somebody in the lab may have directed an in-house settlement of the crime, which also may be a crime. We had also talked about Miranda rights so there would be no interference with a possible future criminal prosecution. Then you directed Mullins and me to meet with Ling and Farber without telling us you had just walked out of a meeting with Ling and Richard, knowing everything Richard had said about the deal, but, you didn't tell us, and that is why Mullins and I feel you set us up, I said.

Falcon looked perturbed, but said softly, "I didn't think you needed that information."

In the middle of what was becoming a heated dialogue, Falcon asked what I would do if the District Attorney did this. What would you do, said Falcon, if he made the same decision?

There's a big difference, Matt, I replied. If I believed the District Attorney may be committing a crime, not just making a legal decision, I would go to the Attorney General, I responded, but here I have no one to go to but you, and then you tell me they're circling the wagons and they possibly have implicated you; Matt, you put me in a very precarious situation.

I don't know what you're getting all upset about, said Matt, the money that was taken by the employee *"is not federal money, it is not taxpayer money, it belongs to UC."* Once the DOE gives the money to the University of California, continued Falcon, it now belongs to the university, not the government. Brian Richard then, on behalf of the lab, said Falcon, has the authority to do whatever he wants with this case. He can make any deal he wants on these decisions, it's his call; he doesn't have to call law enforcement if he doesn't want to; he can make any deal he wants because it's not taxpayer money, concluded Falcon.

Was he saying that all lab property that is stolen from the lab, including money, doesn't involve taxpayer funds? And that's why Richard can do anything he wants, because there is no victim?

Yes, that's right; that's the way it is, Falcon said.

"You are saying that is the law Matt?"

Yes, Glenn. "That's the law."

Within my mind I was thinking. "This guy must really think I'm an idiot. Does he really think I am going to buy his absurd reasoning?"

Let me get this straight, I said. In the future, if OSI determines from facts we've gathered that there is a criminal suspect, that it might not be reported to law enforcement even if it involves a federal felony because Richard says lab property belongs to UC, and not to the United States taxpayer? And you support this? I asked.

That's right, Falcon said. In any future OSI cases involving a crime, continued Falcon, that has a suspect, it must be first sent up to Brian, and Brian will decide what happens to it, because S-Division and OSI do not have the latitude of making that decision. Richard can have people resign or not resign, pay restitution or not pay restitution, not take it to a law enforcement agency, whatever, because whatever Brian says, that's the way it is, that's the way it goes, Falcon snapped.

And once again, I was reminded I was not a policeman. I was reminded who paid my salary; that I worked for the lab, not the FBI.

I couldn't help but protest. If an OSI inquirer determines a suspect may have committed a crime, federal law mandates that the crime must be reported to an appropriate law enforcement agency, whether it is the LAPD, FBI, DOE IG, or whoever, I said. They do their own investigation, and if they confirm there is a suspect, they would take that information to an appropriate judicial body, such as a United States Attorney, and the United States Attorney would determine what should be done in the case; not Brian Richard, I said strongly.

No, Glenn, that's not the way it will be done, said Falcon, Brian will make all the decisions in these matters.

Again, I was reminded how important the Department of Energy contract was to the lab. That statement was really becoming nauseating to me.

I understand the sensitivity of the issue, I said, but personally Matt, I really don't give a damn who has the contract, nor in my opinion, should any OSI member be concerned about that. If any OSI conclusions or decisions are based on a fear of losing the DOE contract, then, in my opinion, I said forcefully, that person should not be working in OSI. That is totally unethical and unprofessional, and I, as the Office Leader, will never allow OSI personnel to operate under that context. Madison told Steve, Jim and me that OSI members were to be the black hats – meaning we must take a stand for truth, justice and what is right, regardless of anyone else's position, including Richard, I continued. I thought that is what the DOE mandated of the lab, so tell me if I am wrong, Matt! If anyone at this lab doesn't like that, so be it — I will do my job for the American taxpayer regardless of any personal consequences, I concluded.

The lines in the sand were about to be drawn more clearly and distinctly than ever before.

Glenn, your work ethics is impeccable, Falcon began, but you're having a difficult time acclimating to the LANL way, to the lab's corporate philosophy. It's different at LANL.

"It certainly is," I said.

"Is it different here than wherever you worked before?"

"Absolutely," I replied, without skipping a beat. "Doran, Mullins, and I feel the LANL world is totally different than what we have ever experienced."

You need to understand you're going to be involved in taking directions from Richard on a daily basis, Falcon said.

It's not a matter of Brian giving directions and following those directions, that's not the problem, I said, but I believe when lab managers attempt to cover up crimes, mismanage, and violate DOE and/or lab regulations because they're afraid of bad public relations and/or losing the DOE contract, that's just plain wrong if not illegal. As I see it, the lab's major concern is covering their butts, and doing the right thing is not paramount here, as it should be; you just have to be one of the boys or girls and blend with the LANL program or the lab feels you don't belong here, you are not liked. In my opinion, LANL is more concerned about their image than righteousness, I retorted.

Glenn, have you ever worked for a corporation before? Falcon responded. It's much different working for a corporation than it is for a government or for a governor, continued Falcon. The lab has a certain *corporate philosophy* and certain *corporate rules* that the employee must abide by, said Falcon.

I asked Falcon to outline the corporate philosophy and rules for me.

He explained that what it means for me is that I am not a policeman, and that one of my jobs is to look out for the lab, the lab contract, and the lab's image, and if I felt that I couldn't do something because it was unethical or illegal then I needed to tell Doug or him. Every day, they get directions from Brian, and must abide by his directions, said Falcon, and if I couldn't do that, then I probably wouldn't make it here.

There's nothing wrong with supporting your employer and being dedicated to them, but there is a line you can't cross, the same line Enron executives crossed, I said. "Matt, a person can become so blinded by their loyalty to their bosses that they lose sight of what is legal, ethical, and right, and it becomes a battle between integrity and loyalty, and I choose integrity Matt," I said. "How about you?"

I took a deep breath, and then went on.

Since we have such a disagreement, Matt, do you really want me here? I asked.

What it amounts to is this, Falcon said in reply, if you feel you can't work here then you need to tell me.

"Well, if I wanted to leave here, would you help in the process?"

Falcon looked at me and smiled. "Yes, I would." As he was about to leave my office, his smile vanished. Then he returned and called back over his shoulder, "Glenn, this is not over, this is not over."

Within a nanosecond, Doran, whose office was directly across the hallway from mine, burst into my office. "I heard everything Falcon said, Glenn. I can't believe it", said Doran. "These people are unbelievable. But at least Falcon is being honest about his part."

The Whistleblower Hotline, part of the Government Accountability Project, is a non-profit, nonpartisan entity that advocates occupational free speech. It focuses on government and corporate accountability related to, among other concerns, nuclear weapons oversight, corporate accountability, and environmental protection. I had previously considered contacting Whistleblowers, but hoped my differences with the lab would work themselves out. I did everything possible to work within the system to make the corrections that had to be made, but that was not working. After the events of the last few days, however, it was obvious the time for serious action had arrived. On September 26, I contacted the Albuquerque Whistleblowers Hotline, saying I wanted to place a complaint on the record. I outlined several circumstances concerning cover-up, mismanagement, and the possibility of criminality by lab officials, giving names and dates. Doran contacted the hotline the next day and made the same complaint.

Now I had to contact the Department of Energy Inspector General, Special Agent Adrian Gallegos regarding the latest case of employee theft. I called Gallegos on September 30 and specifically referred to DOE Orders 221.1 and 221.2, as Gallegos had explained them to us three weeks earlier. I asked Gallegos if he could meet to discuss this recent case involving a federal felony. We agreed it was best not to meet on lab property, and so we arranged to convene at Starbucks in downtown Los Alamos. Doran, Mullins, and I met Gallegos and John Solomon, another Inspector General agent, and we began to discuss in detail the forgery case. I gave Gallegos documentation that would support my position, and the conversation drifted to lab management philosophies. We have problems at all the national laboratories, but LANL is unique, Gallegos said. No other lab compares to the problems we have at LANL.

We definitely were of the same opinion on that one.

Breaking up the tension I said, "The Los Alamos lab reminds me of the movie *Invasion of the Body Snatchers*. Certainly there must be pods around here somewhere." Mullins chimed in, "LANL reminds me of an old movie, *The Stepford Wives*," he said. "People around here, especially the managers, walk around like they have a computer chip behind their ear directing them what to do, complying like robots to all the wishes of the lab's leadership."

Law enforcement is serious business that places significant strain upon those who have chosen to wear the badge. A police officer must be careful not to over invest or over identify with the job, or the very job they love can be their nemesis. Thus, a sense of humor is critical in keeping life in its proper perspective and in balance.

As I sat there, an old memory popped into my mind. *As chief of police in Bullhead City, Arizona, in the late 1990s, I had attended a free breakfast program for underprivileged children at a local elementary school as part of a community outreach program. I arrived in full ceremonial uniform, consisting of dress blue trousers, jacket and hat, trimmed in deep gold, my graying hair visible from beneath the hat. Two young boys eyed me intently, not unlike the* way I observed those Pennsylvania State Troopers so many years earlier. With a gesture of trepidation and an expressionless face, one of the boys cautiously motioned with his hand for me to come to his table. I approached and asked how they were doing. The boy who had beckoned me hesitated, then cautiously queried if he could ask me a question.

"Why sure, what is it?"

Sheepish at first, the boy then blurted out with great determination: "Are you … Are you … Are you Captain Crunch?" Out of the mouths of babes, indeed.

My funny memory quickly ended when, as if on cue, Gayle Rollins of the lab's legal office walked in, giving us a long, hard stare. Instead of getting in line to order, Rollins walked to a corner in the back of the café, pulled out her cell phone and made a call. A few minutes later, as we were leaving, Richard pulled his car into the parking lot, got out, entered the shop, and met with Rollins. We guessed Rollins probably did not know who Gallegos and Solomon were, and called Richard to have him come down to see if he could identify the individuals and perhaps get a grasp on what the conclave may concern.

Later, as I sat in my armchair at home reviewing the day's events, my mind drifted back to my conversation with Falcon. There was no question that Doran's, Mullins', and my policing philosophies did not mesh with our lab jobs, at least as our bosses wanted us to perform them. The necessity of police officers to stand up for truth as they perform their jobs, regardless of the price or circumstances, is drilled into the mind of every police cadet. I was now of the opinion the lab didn't want a police officer, because it didn't want truth; it wanted good PR so that it could maintain the Department of Energy contract. The lab's management philosophy of skirting the truth for the sake of its image was totally foreign to our training and way of thinking. In the past, all three of us had risked our lives to maintain professional policing codes. By this time, we realized that at Los Alamos, because of our findings, exposures, and questions about how these impinged on national security, trouble was coming.

XVII

Appendix O

Wen Ho Lee worked as a scientist at the Los Alamos National Laboratory within the lab's Weapons Design Division. In 1999, the FBI arrested Lee for allegedly giving military secrets to China. A federal grand jury indicted Lee on 59 counts, resulting in Lee's incarceration for 9 months. Much to the embarrassment of the Los Alamos National Laboratory and the federal government, the U.S. Department of Justice failed to establish their case against Lee. Lee however, would eventually plead guilty to one count of mishandling sensitive material. Lee accused the government of violating privacy laws by releasing personal information to the press before charges were filed. In 2006, Lee settled an invasion of privacy lawsuit against the U.S. government and five media organizations for $1.65 million. Federal Judge James A. Parker apologized to Lee on behalf of the American people for government misconduct.

In 2000, during the time of the Cerro Grande forest fire that endangered the Los Alamos Laboratory, two lab computer hard drives containing top-secret classified nuclear secrets were lost for nearly three weeks. Information on the hard drives included data needed to render a nuclear device safe as well as secret information on Russia's nuclear weapons programs. It was never determined who had the hard drives or what happened to the secret information during these three weeks. The hard drives were wiped clean of any fingerprints.

The Wen Ho Lee incident, coupled with the lost hard drive case, spurred the Department of Energy to initiate a new contract with the University of California. It placed new accountability requirements regarding the University of California's management of both the Los Alamos and Lawrence Livermore National Laboratories. Program performance initiatives were established for the Los Alamos National Laboratory S-Division, under a section of the contract known as Appendix O. The lab needed to meet these new performance initiatives in order to earn a particularly prized aspect of the Department of Energy budget known as the annual at-risk fee, which provided additional research funding for lab collaborations. For the Los Alamos lab, that amounted to about five million dollars a year. For the Lawrence Livermore National Laboratory, it meant nearly four million dollars per year.

The University of California's retention of the Los Alamos National Laboratory contract was of particular interest to some New Mexico federal and state legislators, and for good reason. The state, especially northern New Mexico, enjoyed greater financial stability because of the association. And the at-risk fund was vitally important because it paid for, in part, joint research ventures between the lab and the University of New Mexico, New Mexico State University, and New Mexico's technical universities.

The University of California was more than willing to share the wealth for political backing that would help them retain the Department of Energy contract. But the lab could only keep the contract by meeting those new performance initiatives.

Safeguards and Security Management, the goal as stated in

one section of Appendix O, was suppose to instill public confidence in both labs' safeguards and security programs. One specific initiative in this section mandated that employees hired into certain line management functions, including my position, the Office of Security Inquiries Office Leader, had to possess the experience, knowledge, skills, and abilities necessary to fulfill the responsibilities of that position. As Madison had told me on January 25, 2002, Falcon and he were very careful in their selection process and believed they had chosen the right person to do the job.

Developing an S-Division communications plan that would solicit employee feedback was another aspect of Appendix O. It was required, in part, to ensure continued top-down leadership and bottom-up workforce participation.

The initiative also stipulated specific objectives and action plans, one of which was that a qualified Office of Security Inquiries Office Leader be hired no later than January 31, 2002. It didn't take me long to surmise that it was a good guess that one of the reasons I was hired — and why I received a $10,000 bonus if I arrived at the lab before the end of January — was to help the University of California qualify to receive the extra nine million dollars in funding.

Specific performance standards that had to be met were dealt with in Appendix F of the new Department of Energy contract in order for the university to receive the nine million dollars. In his April 2002 memorandum, Thomas Palmieri, the division leader of the Business Operations Division, expressed great concern about not meeting Appendix F mandates as it related to property control. The memo was partly in response to my theft report, with Palmieri indicating that if the condition of missing property continues it would negatively impact the lab's Appendix F rating. That, in turn, could adversely affect efforts to receive additional Department of Energy funding. The mismanagement I detailed in my theft report also threatened the lab's meeting the O and F requirements.

Clearly, I felt, I was meeting all the requirements. I also had fulfilled the associated responsibilities of providing feedback to my supervisors, which included informing them of the interference I believed I was receiving from lab leadership. Of course, in my opinion, it turned out that certain superiors did not seem to want to hear that kind of feedback.

Nevertheless, when I received my performance evaluation on October 3, 2002, Madison and Falcon both praised me for my management performance. "He studied hard and applied Integrated Safeguards and Security Management principles and practices within OSI with specific emphasis regarding 'hands-on' leadership and management." My performance evaluation read, in part, "A proactive and caring leader, he has promoted employee feedback...A strong and professional manager who has the potential and aspirations to have a positive and *lasting impact on the laboratory.*"

Madison had given Doran and me lab-sponsored monetary awards for our performance excellence in conducting four major lab criminal inquiries. In addition, Madison presented me with an S-Division Outstanding Achievement Award for my management performance.

Los Alamos laboratory management appeared confident they had completed all Appendix O requirements. They submitted the required reports to the National Nuclear Security Administration (NNSA), and the administration quickly approved it, on October 11, 2002.

Of course, the Palmieri memo that had been rescinded after being distributed —the one I believed provided a solid perspective on how the lab was in total disarray concerning security and safeguard matters and therefore was failing to meet Appendix F and O requirements —was never produced in the course of the NNSA's approval process. Congress would eventually question how it was possible for the National Nuclear Security Administration to approve Appendix O when it had been explicitly expressed to them that severe management security and property control problems existed at the Los Alamos National Laboratory.

However, as the days of October passed, no such objections were raised.

XVIII

Ostracized

In late October, Shapiro and Richard were becoming rambunctious. They forced an October 24 meeting between the U.S. Attorney, who had top responsibility for two major lab investigations, and representatives of the Albuquerque and Santa Fe FBI. Agent Campbell told Steve and me that the meeting had turned into a heated verbal confrontation as Shapiro and Richard relentlessly attempted to coerce quick movement on the cases, all for the purpose of protecting the lab's good image. The U.S. Attorney did relent, throwing one case back to Shapiro and Richard. The FBI's investigation, and concomitantly, the inquiry into the incident by the Office of Security Inquiries had come to an abrupt end.

As a result of the meeting, Madison summoned me to his office. An FBI official told Shapiro and Richard that the criminal cases coming out of the lab are just the tip of the iceberg, Madison told me. Shapiro and Richard, Madison continued, were extremely upset by that comment because it was no longer a question that the

FBI believed there were many more crimes occurring at the lab, it was now a fact.

According to Madison the FBI was hoping to get more evidence in one case to bring charges, but changed their mind and placed the case back in the hands of the lab. And now Richard has ordered him to get more incriminating evidence on the employee from me, so he can direct the firing of the suspect Harry Moss, said Madison.

We have to work with Richard to give him everything OSI has to ensure they are able to get rid of him, Madison said, almost apologetically. I need you and Steve, he continued, to go through the whole case again to make sure we gave Richard everything. I reminded Madison that Richard already had everything OSI had, and that Richard had stated, along with everyone else in the September meeting, that they felt there was sufficient evidence to fire the employee, even though it was a circumstantial case. However, Doran warned them, and the FBI agreed that more investigation needed to be done before any conclusions could be made.

Now Madison delivered the *bombshell.*

You need to be careful on how you take this, Glenn, he said, but you and Steve are not allowed to be involved in the NIS case anymore. He continued, I know this isn't right because you and Steve worked so hard, but that's how it's going to be. I know they're not treating you right, Madison stated with clear disgust, but I can't do anything about it.

"The reason?" I inquired.

Madison explained it was fallout from the run-in I had had with Richard a few weeks earlier concerning the forged check and misappropriation of funds in the Nonproliferation and International Security Division and my threat to blow the whistle if he didn't follow federal law. "I know you feel Brian's an asshole," Madison said. "Well, he thinks you're an asshole, and this is Brian's payback."

At that very moment, Doran and Campbell were out in the field working on the NIS case. I asked Madison if I should pull Doran off right now. Madison replied, no wait. In fact, continued Madison, don't tell Doran anything about this until I have one more chance to review it overnight and perhaps I can get it changed. Then Madison admonished me to stand up and deal with these changes. We're the older people here, and we can take the brunt of this, Madison said. Madison tried to mollify me somewhat, recounting an incident that occurred at the lab's museum several years ago in which Shapiro allegedly *had it out* for an employee and had him fired.

That's how Shapiro operates, Madison said, your case is not unique.

Madison continued, stating that I needed to assign another OSI staffer to assist the FBI with the NIS case.

"Mullins is your only option, Doug," I said.

Head spinning, I returned to my office. The Nonproliferation and International Security case was nearly done. It may involve espionage, and if, as Madison said, Shapiro and Richard were removing Doran and me from any further responsibilities, I felt it had now become a personal, not a professional matter. I believed there was absolutely no logic in such leadership. But I felt more intensely every day that it was just part of the overall pattern, which made the situation at the Los Alamos National Laboratory so filled with peril for our country's top secrets.

The next morning, Doran and I reported to Madison for more of the same. Actually, it was now worse. Doran and I were no longer allowed to *talk to the FBI about any Office of Security Inquiries cases at all.* You cannot have any communications with the FBI about anything within OSI or any lab operations, Madison ordered.

Doran protested after hearing that this order was a direct by-product of the forgery case. "It's not right," Doran said. "Neither Glenn nor I did anything wrong. We were just doing our jobs. And for that, we're being punished?"

I know that Steve, said Madison. What's happening isn't right and we really owe you two guys, but we'll take care of you, because both of you have been doing a great job, continued Madison.

Doran told Madison he was in the process of investigating another criminal incident with the FBI. A former lab intern was telling Australian authorities that terrorists were after him. Should Doran continue? Tell Campbell he has to go through me, and I'll handle it, Madison said, ending the meeting.

FBI Agent Campbell was livid when he heard that. "I'm going to go straight to the lab director," he told Doran.

Doran asked Campbell not to do that.

Campbell then gave us his theory of why he thought Shapiro and Richard were now taking over control and unleashing their venom on us. He had been at the meeting the day before. The U.S. Attorney was hoping to prosecute the Moss case if we could tie up all the loose ends, but Campbell felt Shapiro and Richard were incredibly arrogant. They were demanding the FBI and U.S. Attorney concede to their demands on the case and bring it to a quick conclusion because they wanted to get rid of the employee. The U.S. Attorney said, according to Campbell, that at that point they didn't have enough evidence to establish a solid case. It got so heated that the U.S. Attorney threw it back in the lab's lap, in Campbell's opinion, because of Shapiro and Richard's arrogant demands.

Campbell then called Madison, asking him to put Steve and me back on the NIS case. He said that it is extremely important that we be involved since it was critical to the FBI's investigation. Madison, said Campbell, replied that he was just following orders.

Falcon returned to work on October 29, and I filled him in on what was happening. "That's the most juvenile thing I have ever heard of," he said with disgust, offering his apologies to Doran and me.

Meanwhile, Richard was setting up a meeting among all law enforcement agencies involved in criminal investigations at the lab to discuss some new policy. Soon Falcon called Doran, Mullins, and me into a meeting to affirm the new rules as dictated by Richard. Glenn and Steve are off the NIS case, he said. Neither Steve nor Glenn is allowed to communicate with the FBI on anything, said

Falcon. If the FBI calls on the NIS theft case, the FBI is only allowed to talk to Richard, and then Richard will call either Madison or me and then we'll call Mullins, continued Falcon. If the Department of Energy Inspector General calls on any cases, then the Office of Security Inquiries must tell them they need to contact Richard first, concluded Falcon.

"Does this mean that neither Steve nor I are allowed in on anything with the FBI or DOE, even if it involves national security, *to include terrorism*?" I asked Falcon.

"Yes." It was all Mullins now.

Doran began to make the transfer of information to Mullins that day and submitted Office of Security Inquiries Assignment Report, Event Number – 0446-02, concerning the Australian case. Doran placed the following paragraph in the report: "Because of another situation I was advised that I was no longer to work with Agent Campbell on any assignments, and discontinue any that were currently being performed."

When Falcon received the report, he returned it to Doran and ordered him to delete the paragraph.

At the same time this mayhem was occurring, Campbell informed us that Richard had told the FBI it had forty-eight hours to complete its Nonproliferation and International Security Division theft case or the lab would place all suspects on investigative leave. "That could blow the case," said Campbell. Apparently, Falcon said, responding to Steve and me about Richard's position with the FBI, Richard wanted to place the NIS suspects on leave because of a spying issue. Supposedly, lab officials didn't want to keep two suspects in the Nonproliferation and International Security Division environment any longer, said Falcon, because they had spy-type equipment in their possession, in a top-secret area – and they feared raising concern and criticism if that information became public.

The lab's director Otto Harmon and the Nonproliferation and International Security Division leader had actually taken Bussolini on a tour of NIS just to see what he had access to because they were concerned about Bussolini having access to all classified areas, said Falcon. They said they were happy to see he could not get into all areas, continued Falcon. I later heard from FBI informant John Jennings that after the tour was over, Bussolini told his staff he wanted the keys to the areas he couldn't get into because he wanted to see what was occurring in those places.

The furor inside, and soon to burst outside the facility, was heating up.

XIX

Halloween Assault

Most people agreed that the Los Alamos National Laboratory was the best job around, especially in northern New Mexico. The lab paid the highest salaries and gave more lucrative benefits than any other employer in that part of the state. In fact, the joke at Los Alamos was, the next best job was washing cars in Santa Fe. The high salaries and benefits helped the lab maintain control over some employees. As long as they remained faithful to the lab's corporate philosophy, they'd have a job for life. There was no question in my mind that many employees were aware of corruption and cover-up, but they kept their mouths shut lest they lose their jobs and lucrative salaries.

Falcon had told me several times that as I conducted inquiries, I should be careful to whom I talked and what I said because most employees at the lab were either related or close friends with each other. According to Falcon, the theory that blood was thicker than water held unequivocally true here.

At one point in my investigations, I tested this idea by telling a few people that OSI would be placing hidden cameras in certain office areas that were being hit by a rash of office thefts. The thefts came to an abrupt halt. I soon learned that Falcon hadn't been exaggerating. Whatever you told one lab employee would quickly spread through the lab grapevine.

On October 31, FBI Agent Jeff Campbell signed search warrants on Bussolini's home, his recreational vehicle, Alexander's home, and on Gallegos Motors Used Car Lot in Chamita, New Mexico. The warrants alleged that the Los Alamos National Laboratory had maintained a blanket purchase order contract with Mesa Equipment and Supply, but the contract limited purchases to air compressors, vacuum systems, material handling equipment, machine tools, machine shop supplies, and other items allowed specifically for lab business.

The warrant alleged that Scott Alexander, Bussolini's assistant, had made improper purchases that were contrary to blanket purchase procedures.

After serving the warrants, Bussolini and Alexander were interrogated, and the FBI hauled away two large truckloads of stolen lab property. Another suspect, who worked in the Audits and Assessments unit, also confessed after admitting he received stolen property from Bussolini. Among the items the FBI confiscated was a ring containing 25 keys from Bussolini, and another ring of keys holding 75 keys from Alexander. Many of these keys unlocked doors and gates to some of the lab's most secret areas.

Less than a week later, Madison called an emergency meeting that included Falcon, Mullins, and other Office of Security Inquiries employees. Mullins told Steve and me later, that during the meeting Madison had said, thanks to Mr. Walp and Mr. Doran having such a freaking good relationship with the FBI, we were not given notice of the service of these search warrants. Madison said, continued Mullins, that the only reason the FBI was able to serve the warrants, was because Glenn and Steve gave them the evidence on a silver platter.

During the searches, Falcon had directed Mullins and Jeff Dy, another OSI staffer, to assist the FBI. The FBI wanted to secure the offices of Bussolini and Alexander. Mullins and Dy, along with Aaron Stephens of the Nonproliferation and International Security Division, directed the lab's lock shop to re-core the locks on Bussolini and Alexander's offices, three entry gates, and several bunkers at Technical Area-33. A total of ten locks were changed and re-keyed, and the lock shop, at Mullins' request, made only two keys per lock. Mullins took both keys for each lock and told Falcon. The FBI then sealed both offices.

"Nearly every day, Falcon called me," said Mullins, "and asked who had the keys. One time, he specifically asked, how do you think we could go about getting into Bussolini's and Alexander's offices?"

There is no way, Mullins told Falcon. Campbell's specific directions were that nobody could enter those sites without his consent.

Stephens came in with a strange request in early November, Mullins said, when he called and asked, rather frantically, when he thought someone from NIS could get into Bussolini's and Alexander's offices? Even though Mullins replied firmly that this would not happen, Stephens contacted Mullins again twice, both times nervously and tensely. As mid-month approached, said Mullins, Falcon kept on trying; insisting that Richard's legal department needed access to the two offices. Mullins said, I told Falcon that nobody, including the Office of Security Inquiries, could enter Bussolini or Alexander's offices without Agent Campbell's consent.

Yes, you're right, we need to keep out of the sites, Falcon said. But do you still have the two keys for each lock?

"Yes, I do," said Mullins.

"In my opinion, Falcon was being pressured by someone," said Mullins. "It appeared somebody at the lab wanted to get into those offices before the FBI was able to conduct their search." Mullins relayed his concerns to Campbell, at which point he told Mullins he'd be coming by immediately to take one of the two new keys Mullins was holding for each office. Several days later at a meeting with Department of Energy Inspector General personnel, Mullins gave the other key to Agent Gallegos. The very next day, said Mullins, Falcon called me to ask if I still had the keys, at which time I told him that now Campbell had one and Gallegos the other.

Mullins said, "I could hear heavy sighing on the other end of the phone. 'So, we no longer have any keys to the offices?' Falcon asked me. 'That's correct,' I said. Falcon didn't sound pleased, to say the least", Mullins concluded.

But there was an interesting twist that neither Mullins nor the FBI knew about. According to FBI informant John Jennings, after the FBI sealed Bussolini and Alexander's offices, another FBI informant who helped gather evidence on the two men, had broken into Bussolini's office. He had gotten the key from someone at the lab. And the reason he broke in? He wanted to retrieve college transcripts he had forged and left in Bussolini's office. Allegedly he had forged the transcripts, because his grades were not good enough for him to continue receiving lab scholarship funds, and Bussolini was aware of the forgery, and used that against the person, concluded Jennings, in order to get him to cover for him.

Less than two weeks after warrants were served on Bussolini's and Alexander's homes, the FBI served new warrants on their offices at the lab.

According to Mullins, Falcon was extremely upset about those office warrants because, allegedly, nobody had told him about them. Falcon, according to Mullins, dealt with Mullins in the same strong-arm way he had dealt with Doran and me. "I felt Falcon asked me to come over to his office to discuss some issues," Mullins said, "which not surprisingly had to do with going along with the corporate philosophy of looking out for the lab's image, and that one of my jobs was to look out for the lab. I felt Falcon was testing me to see if I would go along with their corporate philosophy program, just like he did with you, Glenn."

One wall of Bussolini's office had a large poster of Marlon

Brando in his *Godfather* role with a little man sitting on his knee. The word Godfather was inscribed in bold at the top of the poster; at the bottom was an inscription in ink: "To Don, from the FMU family." Bussolini was known by some NIS employees for giving *presents* that, investigations confirmed, were purchased with lab funds. The Audits and Assessments suspect the FBI was investigating had confessed to the FBI that he had taken presents from Bussolini, but he claimed he wasn't really a thief, because he only took a car trunk full of items.

Reflecting on the poster, and Bussolini's reputation for gifts, I realized it reminded me of a Mafia figure I investigated in Pennsylvania. This man was loved by the locals because of his philanthropic contributions to the community, even though he was able to afford to make his lavish gifts from the money he made through his involvements in prostitution, illegal drug and gun trafficking, and illegal gambling.

Falcon remained upset about the office warrants, saying to me that he didn't feel they were necessary. I disagreed, telling Falcon the FBI could easily find evidence that would help its case. "You know, Matt," I said, "this is a major case based on the evidence we have thus far, and it's likely the FBI can prove around a half a million in stolen items."

Glenn, even if it is a half-million, that doesn't make it a major case, Falcon replied. Besides, at this point it's only $50,000, and anyway, a half a million is not much when you consider how big the lab's budget is, continued Falcon.

I felt Falcon had an odd attitude toward theft; after all, he was the guy responsible for lab security. I asked myself how many millions of dollars was stolen from the lab through the decades and was unaccounted for? Where would scientific research be if those millions of dollars were funneled into research efforts, rather than being thrown down a rat hole? Maybe for new technologies to fight terrorism or find a cure for cancer? Instead, tax dollars, regardless of the amount, had definitely been squandered, because, in my opinion, some lab leaders were focused on maintaining a contract that would ensure their robust salaries and prestigious positions. Certain laboratory leadership, Doran, Mullins, and I opined, was so concerned about keeping their jobs that it resulted in malignant crime and corruption.

Meanwhile, Mullins, now in Doran's old role, was helping Campbell find items stolen and stored by Bussolini and Alexander. A close relative of Alexander, under questioning from Campbell, admitted he had received quite a few items from Alexander. The relative gave those items to Campbell for FBI evidence on November 6, and Campbell asked Mullins to store them in his office until the next day, when Campbell would drive a larger vehicle to the lab so he could transport the property to FBI evidence control. The transfer didn't occur the following day because Campbell was called away on another matter.

"Glenn, you're not going to believe this," Mullins told me on November 12, "but someone stole two knives from the FBI evidence I had locked in my office. Only two people knew I had those items, and both worked in OSI."

We immediately went to Falcon. I told him in no uncertain terms that this incident needed to be investigated by a law-enforcement agency right away. "I will not rest until we find out who stole the knives," I said.

What we had here was evidence in an FBI federal felony stored behind a security fence controlled by a card key and palm-print locking system, situated inside of a building with a card key and palm-print locking system, and then further situated inside of a locked office. It was theoretically as secure and impenetrable as a police station. "If someone is able to steal that item," I said to Falcon, "you know you have a real problem with crime."

Falcon told us the following day that Agent Gallegos would investigate on behalf of the Department of Energy Inspector General. I immediately contacted Gallegos and asked that he request every Office of Security Inquiries employee to take a polygraph test.

I knew no one could be forced to take such a test, and I wasn't saying that it was an Office of Security Inquiries employee, but it was the most logical way to begin. I volunteered to be the first person to take the test. "I want to find out who did this, and I will push for prosecution," I told Falcon.

I told all staff on November 14 about the test. "I'll be the first one up to the plate," I said. "Mullins and Doran will be numbers 2 and 3."

The Department of Energy Inspector General never prosecuted anyone on that theft. It's quite possible that someone at the lab, perhaps in the Security and Safeguards Division, who is responsible for the theft, is still employed there. What other possible weapons have been stolen by a *trusted* employee on the inside, and for what future purposes?

XX

Deep Cover Informant

In many criminal investigations an inside informant will come forward to assist law enforcement in their efforts. "He made the old man get down on his knees. He put the shotgun to the back of his head and pulled the trigger, shooting him like a rabbit." These were the words of a confidential informant (CI) in a cold, bloody murder I investigated in western Pennsylvania during the 1970s.

People become informants for multiple reasons. At times, they want to make a deal for self-preservation, other times they are pressured by loved ones to tell the truth, and sometimes they are fed up with what they have seen and know. That was the case at the Los Alamos National Laboratory when John Jennings, a 10-year employee under Pete Bussolini, agreed to go undercover for the FBI because he had had enough of his boss's stealing, manipulations and deception.

In 2001, no one at Los Alamos would listen to McDonald and Stewart when they told them that Bussolini and Alexander were walking away with the farm, so in 2002, they went directly to the FBI.

During our July 19 investigative planning meeting, we learned that McDonald and Stewart believed Jennings might have been involved in the thefts. The reasons were that he was so close to Bussolini, and that they had heard rumors that Jennings may have been delivering stolen goods to Bussolini's residence in his personal pickup truck. Because of Jennings' personality characteristics, McDonald and Stewart believed Jennings might confess if he was caught holding incriminating evidence.

After gathering the paper trail data, our plan was to establish probable cause for a traffic stop on Jennings pickup, hoping to find evidence in the open-backed bed. This may force Jennings to turn state's evidence that hopefully, would be followed up by the issuing of search warrants for Bussolini's and Alexander's homes, lab offices and other points of interest.

After further evaluation by FBI Agent Campbell, Doran, and me, we decided to abandon the traffic stop concept. We had received additional information leading us to believe that Jennings was not personally involved in the thefts, but that he could have information regarding them. Because of Jennings' close working relationship with Bussolini, and his insider position, we thought he might be able to help our investigation, if it were proven he was clean, by going undercover.

We knew bringing Jennings into the investigation was a risky gamble. To help alleviate that risk, Campbell and Doran conducted extensive undercover surveillance on Jennings, while checking avenue after avenue of his possible involvement. We eventually concluded that he was clean and was merely being used by Bussolini and Alexander in their criminal enterprise.

Once satisfied that Jennings was not directly involved, Campbell and Doran arranged a secret meeting with Jennings in Santa Fe on the pretense of wanting to interview him regarding some fabricated reasoning.

The policing world teaches cops that when dealing with

a potential informant, it's important to create a comfortable environment to ensure that the potential CI feels safe, secure, and at ease. This increased the chance of success. Doran found out that Jennings had a weakness for donuts, so the meeting location, of course, involved donuts and coffee. Within our circle, we labeled Jennings *The Donut Informant*.

After a few minutes of pleasantries and a couple of donuts, Jennings admitted that he had delivered about eight truckloads of items, including furniture, tools, a generator and compressor to Bussolini's residence. Bussolini, said Jennings, had told him he purchased the items under a personal account and at discount from Mesa Equipment, and then had Mesa Equipment deliver the items to the lab so he could avoid delivery charges to his house. Bussolini told me that his truck was undergoing repairs, said Jennings, and that was the reason he asked Jennings to deliver the stuff to his house.

"I always did what Pete told me to do, but after a few times I got the feeling, although I didn't want to believe it, that Pete and Scott may be stealing," Jennings said. "I later found out that Pete's truck really wasn't broken so I think he just didn't want to haul it himself, and got me to do it for him. Because of my gut feeling, I did some snooping into the purchase files and saw some items that just didn't make sense as to why we would be purchasing them, such as hunting and camping gear. Pete did tell me it was for his personal use, but then I thought, why would he buy so many of the same types of items? At times, I saw the items in Pete or Scott's possession, or it just turned up missing from lab property, which increased my suspicion. The last straw was when Pete asked me to deliver some stuff to his home in late 2001, and while I was unloading it, his young daughter said, 'So you're stealing for my Daddy.' "

Jennings told us that lab audit personnel knew he was looking into NIS purchasing files. Then the auditing people called Bussolini and told him what I was doing, said Jennings. "I knew Pete was getting suspicious of me checking his purchasing files," Jennings stated, "so Pete told me and others that he thought I was mentally disturbed; something the lab has done for years when they want to shut you up and keep people from believing you. Pete, as my boss, then ordered me to undergo medical and psychological testing. After my tests, he told everyone not to believe anything I said because I was mentally ill."

Jennings said he wanted to tell his suspicions to someone at the lab with authority, so early in 2002, he went to the lab's Human Resources Office and the Audits and Assessments Unit, but no one would listen to him. "It was clear to me they were told I was mentally ill and just wrote me off as crazy," Jennings said. "I also went to the lab's Homeland Security supervisor and told him of my suspicions because I was also concerned about national security." Pete, proposed Jennings, had keys to just about every door in NIS, including personal desks and files, and had secret pass codes. He always wants to know what everyone is doing and saying, even the scientists — and he has the most sensitive clearance anyone can get, giving him open access to most everything, continued Jennings. When I told the Homeland Security supervisor of my suspicions, I could just tell he was warned that I was crazy, so he called Pete and told him I was there before I even got back to my office, and that is Pete's way of keeping me under control; telling people I have mental problems, said Jennings.

At the next clandestine meeting over more donuts and coffee Jeff asked Jennings the piercing question: John, would you be willing to take on the role of an undercover informant for the FBI?

Giving information was one thing, but going undercover for the FBI was a totally different proposition. After some soul searching, Jennings finally agreed to work with the FBI, and thus began his secret mission.

Jennings had complete access to all purchase records because he had the necessary federal clearances. He was able to enter computerized financial records, allowing him to look up purchased items and identify suspect purchases. He knew Bussolini would get increasingly suspicious of him, but he was willing to take that chance.

Jennings explained how clever Bussolini was in protecting himself from being discovered. Bussolini at one time was the acting division director, had approximately 1,000 employees working for him, and wrote the security plans for the secret Technical Area-33 area and other classified areas, said Jennings. Everybody thinks Pete is just in charge of maintenance and those types of things, but he really is powerful, Jennings continued. He has been here a long time; has the highest clearance you can get; he knows most everyone, and many of them are beholding to him because of his *gift giving;* and that he has stuff on them, continued Jennings. Scott and Pete are threatening characters, and some of us are afraid of them to the point of being scared for our lives, said Jennings. According to Jennings, Bussolini convinced his superiors that Protection Technologies of Los Alamos, the lab's security force, should not be trusted, so they were not allowed into many areas. Then Bussolini would limit and control the people who could get into those areas; that was one of Bussolini's ways of controlling his activities without interference or observation by others, explained Jennings.

Jennings' duties included safety functions, so he was able to get keys to NIS storage areas by claiming he had to conduct safety checks. It was within these secret storage areas that John found small warehouses filled with questionable items. He painstakingly recorded what he found, then checked purchase records and identified items he figured had been purchased by Bussolini and Alexander to later convert to their own use.

Campbell would call Jennings most every day on his cell phone as Jennings drove home from work, and they would pass information. At times, they would meet at a secret location in the Pojoaque Valley to review and pass documents.

As Jennings dug deeper into Bussolini's and Alexander's methodologies, he stated that he learned that Bussolini had convinced a Mesa Equipment salesman that some of the items he was purchasing may be off the wall; items such as model airplanes and fishing waders, but he had to purchase these items because they were being used for some type of secret project related to keeping spies out of the lab, proposed Jennings. Consequently, according to Jennings, Pete told the salesman that it had to be kept secret because national security is at risk. As part of the charade, said Jennings, he had the salesman change the wording on purchase documents, such as listing plasma TVs as computer terminals.

Jennings took the next step into the dark world of a deep cover informant and, after initially refusing, agreed to wear a hidden body device that would record conversations. Giving information was scary enough, but having a bug hidden on his body for the FBI was something else. There was a strict rule to the process however. The wire could not be used in any secure areas of the laboratory, only areas that allowed this type of activity as mandated by federal law. That is, for example, no one was allowed to take a cellular telephone, camera, or recording device into a lab location identified as secure. But Jennings had concerns. Will the device be seen, will it make a noise, and will he be found out? After agreeing, he began to attach the device to his person on a daily basis before heading to work. For nearly two months, Jennings worked side by side with Bussolini and Alexander, doing his normal tasks as a fellow worker and friend, while at the same time gathering crucial information for the FBI that would eventually help place them into a federal prison.

Jennings had been a loyal lab worker for 28 years. For 10 of those years, he worked for Bussolini, whom he perceived as a mentor and father figure.

Bussolini took advantage of the situation, said Jennings, facetiously calling me his son, and at times praising me and then immediately turning around and chastising me. Other NIS employees said that Bussolini played upon Jennings' weakness and manipulated him into doing his bidding while constantly ridiculing him for his weight and threatening his job. One employee said Bussolini poured a full can of Coca-Cola over John's office desk while he was sitting there, walked away, then turned around and said to Jennings,

"You're a great employee."

It was clear that Jennings had extremely low self-esteem and that he craved to be liked by everyone, especially by his boss and father figure. One of Jennings' closest lab friends confirmed that Jennings abhorred confrontation, even refusing to take a malfunctioning personal appliance he had just purchased back to the vendor because he didn't want to face the conflict it would bring.

Other lab employees agreed that Bussolini employed mind-control tactics on many employees by using threats and intimidation. Many of Bussolini's employees fell prey to these Stockholm syndrome tactics – perhaps none more than John Jennings.

Jennings said that Scott Alexander had a famous line of threat that he used on many NIS employees, not only him. "Scott would say," said Jennings, 'Nobody ever better fuck with me, or I will throw them up on the table and fuck their ass, and their mother's ass and their family's ass.' Scott had a name for it, which I think he got from an old TV program, calling it *Pooh-Goo*, and he used that threat a lot, and I was scared, and so were others; it wasn't as if he said it in a funny way. Then Bussolini would say, 'Don't fuck with me, you know what Scott just told you.' I mean, how could you say something horrible like that in a funny way, especially when referring to your mother and family? And there was no sense telling anyone at the lab, because if they didn't believe you when you told them major theft was occurring, why would they do anything about that?"

Jennings' mousing for the FBI included searching for items Bussolini or Alexander may have hidden for later removal. He eventually found expensive equipment such as welding machines and air tools secreted in high weeds along remote lab roadways. After logging the items in his little black book, Jennings was directed by the FBI to take the information back to Bussolini to see how he would react. Bussolini fell headlong into the trap, still thinking Jennings was a *family* member. According to Jennings, Bussolini said, between the two of us, John, we will find out if anyone is stealing the government's money.

There was a caveat. Jennings said Bussolini told him not to tell anyone but him what he found, because Bussolini was secretly working with security, so he didn't want any of this to leak out, because it may involve spies. In Bussolini's eyes, said Jennings, I was his faithful patsy, but little did he realize I was working with the FBI to nail him.

In early October, Bussolini's intuition that something was up went into overdrive. He had many lab friends, said Jennings, to whom he gave many taxpayer-purchased presents through the years, and this ensured Bussolini of their allegiance while securing his power and command. It got so bad, Jennings continued, that one Christmas an office staff member in a division administrative office *ordered* a pair of gloves from Pete. The staff member later called and complained that they were the wrong size and needed them replaced because he was giving them to someone as a Christmas gift, said Jennings.

So it was not a surprise when word leaked out that the lab director's office was secretly sending someone to talk to Jennings, but Bussolini would not be told for what. Bussolini told me, said Jennings, to meet with the interviewer in the NIS conference room. "It was well known that conversations taking place in the ladies' room adjacent to the conference room could be overheard," continued Jennings, "and because of this, Bussolini, many years before had a folding tripod sign made up indicating the restroom was closed; he also placed a stepladder in the ladies' room." Continuing, Jennings said that when Bussolini wanted to hear what people in the conference room were saying, he would put up the sign, get on the ladder, remove some ceiling tiles and listen in, and he would also assign Alexander to crouch beneath a window on the outside of the building to listen, and they would later compare notes. Bussolini told me to meet in the conference room specifically so he and Alexander could listen, said Jennings, and Pete told me to tell them that nothing, absolutely nothing, was wrong, and warned me that he would be listening in.

Jennings did as he was ordered and the interviewer was sent away with nothing; but little did they all know that Jennings was passing information to the FBI on a daily basis.

A few days after the restroom caper, Bussolini, apparently believing that I was still under his spell, e-mailed me, said Jennings, and it said, "I need you to be the Rock of Gibraltar right now for me; you are still my son, so don't worry and be happy." Bussolini followed up, continued Jennings, by walking into my office and saying, "Look me in the eye and tell me nothing is wrong, John." I played my role said Jennings, and replied, "Pete, nothing is wrong." Bussolini then left the building and I followed a few minutes later retching my guts outside the door, concluded Jennings. Jennings knew his *father* was guilty as sin, but he still felt he was betraying the man he loved, and it hurt.

Because of the daily stress, Jennings gained 40 pounds to an already large body. "I used eating to comfort my feelings and hide what I knew," Jennings said. "I was really afraid for my life because I knew how vicious Scott and Pete could get, especially if anyone went up against them."

Jennings's undercover duties became even more intense on October 31, when Bussolini hung up his phone after being told by the Nonproliferation and International Security Division Director that Alexander and he had to report immediately to the director's office. Bussolini turned to me and said, I hope to God you had nothing to do with him calling me, said Jennings.

When Bussolini and Alexander were nabbed that Halloween day, Jennings experienced sadness and joy. His confidential informant days were over because the matter was now out in the open and that brought relief. But the person he had respected and been so loyal to for nearly a decade was plucked from the lab. It hit home for Jennings that what he had done during his stealth FBI assignment could place Bussolini into the custody of federal authorities. "It hurts, but it also feels good because I am no longer Pete's fool," Jennings told Doran. "He played me for years, but now he is dancing for me."

Even though Jennings was a crucial player in helping the FBI bring justice to the lab, his life thereafter, proposed Jennings, was fraught with stress, anxiety, and attacks at the hands of none other than several lab officials. Here was a man who stood up for truth under extremely trying personal circumstances. He reported perceived illegal activities to the lab's Human Resources Staff Relations, Audits and Assessments, and the Office of Homeland Security long before the FBI became involved. However, that stand could bring embarrassment to the lab and its image, and help place the lab contract in jeopardy. Consequently, for his efforts, Jennings was exiled to the outer limits of the Los Alamos laboratory. After numerous legal entanglements, an outside arbiter ruled in favor of Jennings, giving Jennings back a meaningful job and cleansing his personnel file.

Jennings retired from the Los Alamos lab in 2006. Regrettably, he still suffers from the stress and anxiety he encountered in helping to bring one of the lab's theft empires to ruin, but even more so, said Jennings, from the relentless pursuit by certain lab officials. Jennings said he refused to comply with the lab's corporate philosophy, and for that he paid dearly. It was a stinging lesson Steve and I shared along with, unfortunately, many other lab employees.

XXI

Bull's Eye: Los Alamos

On November 5, *The Energy Daily*, a newspaper based in Washington, D.C., printed an article headlined, "Criminal Activity Alleged at Top-Secret Los Alamos Unit." The article stated in part:

> An unknown source has released information that events are unfolding at the Los Alamos National Laboratory in Los Alamos, New Mexico, regarding major criminal activity, administrative mismanagement and high-level corruption. The leaders of the laboratory are attempting to hide these events and activities from the public, DOE, federal law enforcement agencies, political oversight groups, and especially the media for fear that if the truth is known, it will have a negative affect on their upcoming contract. These leaders are afraid that if these events become known to the public, their contract will be

lost and they will lose their jobs, salaries, benefits, and retirement from the University of California program. Lab officials had successfully hidden other cases of credit card fraud by referring them to Los Alamos' Internal Fraud Unit and then having perpetrators reimburse stolen monies and resign from the lab – all without informing law enforcement.

A buzz stirred that Steve and I were the anonymous source in that report, though it was neither Doran nor I. I don't know for sure, but I don't believe laboratory leaders knew that Steve and I had already told the Whistleblower Hotline everything. But we did know we had initiated a drop of truth into a raging flood of lies.

Yes, in fact, we did take our jobs personally.

As soon as that article got out, Adrian Gallegos from the Department of Energy asked to discuss the contents with Doran, Mullins, DOE Agent John Solomon, and me. *"The Energy Daily* article," Gallegos said as he held it up, has grabbed the attention of people in Washington, and I have received orders direct from Washington to address the matters that were contained within the article. Gallegos continued *"We're trying to develop an obstruction of justice case against Brian Richard."* Gallegos asked for copies of any documents showing that any of our superiors, including Falcon, Madison, and Richard, had interfered with any of our cases. We've had information on Richard in the past, but we could never make a case against him, Gallegos said, and if Madison and Falcon want to go down with him, that's their call.

Gallegos told us he and Solomon would be interviewing Falcon and Madison soon. Gallegos then demanded that we give him all the documentary evidence we had on alleged interference by lab officials. Doran immediately gave Gallegos copies of personal memos and notes, and I told him I would gather my material and present it to him by November 11.

Gallegos made it clear that Doran, Mullins, and I had to cooperate fully with his office, and that we were forbidden from conversing with anyone about what we discussed in the meeting or there would be consequences. He also said that he had told Shapiro and Richard that he'd be having this meeting with us. I followed up by telling Falcon in an e-mail that we had just met with Inspector General Agent Gallegos, and Gallegos had ordered us not to disclose what we had discussed in the meeting.

In a few hours, I was ordered into Falcon's office. Madison was there. "Glenn," Madison said, "did the IG give you your constitutional rights?"

"No."

"Did they tell you that you had to get out of your offices or anything like that?"

"No."

Neither Madison nor Falcon pushed for anything that was discussed in the meeting.

Madison looked at me and said S-Division is having some credibility problems. You know we don't want our bosses coming down and saying they have lost confidence in us, and you know if they do they are probably going to come down and blame this on me, said Madison. You, Matt, and I are really under a cloud of suspicion for these things, and all three of us could be blamed; we're having real credibility problems, Madison repeated.

Madison and Falcon seemed to me to be succumbing to a cloud of fear. I remembered that Victoria Snelling had told Doran, Mullins, and me, more than once, that after the Wen Ho Lee and lost hard drive cases, that Madison and Falcon would never survive another security fiasco. They were definitely hearing approaching trouble now. And that was ironic. When they hired me, they kept telling me that they had hired the right person. Now they were unable to control an angry outside authority getting angrier by the day. I felt that they knew how to do the right thing and wanted to do the right thing, but they seemed, in my opinion, paralyzed by trying to maintain a balance between right and wrongs of others in leadership positions above them. I felt they wanted to support us, but that support appeared to be waning. I could see how worried they were about what Mullins, Doran, and I may have told the Department of Energy investigators. And, I felt, they knew they'd be anguished if *they didn't obey the lab's corporate philosophy.*

As I saw it, the rock was here, the hard place was there, and Madison and Falcon were cemented right in the middle.

As more and more people got wind of *The Energy Daily* report, a firestorm of political, media, and public concern heatedly rose. Media sources all across America contacted politicians, political groups, and lab officials clamoring to know if the accusations by the anonymous source were true. Was major crime occurring at LANL? Was there mismanagement? Was there high-level corruption? Were some lab officials involved in cover-up? Were the FBI investigations being interfered with? And, most important, *Was national security at risk?*

After Notra Trulock, a reporter for *NewsMax.com*, interviewed Doug Belden of the FBI Albuquerque field office, he wrote that Belden spoke artfully about interference with FBI investigations. The bureau, Trulock quoted Belden as saying, had "encountered no interference that impeded the investigation in any significant way."

Those skilled at reading between the lines could see there was, in fact, trouble at the Los Alamos National Laboratory.

Soon members of Congress began to express worry about *The Energy Daily's* report. Iowa Senator Charles Grassley, the ranking Republican on the Senate Finance Committee, said he was interested in knowing if the suspected misappropriations were indicative of a broader management problem. Heidi Tringe, a spokeswoman for the House Committee on Science, said the committee would likely be holding oversight hearings on the Department of Energy in the coming spring to discuss the overall management of all national laboratories. With regard to LANL, Tringe said, "It remains to be seen the extent of the impact this will have (on the Department of Energy's contract with the University of California), but it is certainly something we will be looking at closely."

University of California officials reacted at the same time, not surprisingly by defending themselves. "The university is always concerned about the quality of the work, both scientific and operational," said UC spokesman Jeff Garberson. "We believe the university has done a good job over the years, and we intend to keep meeting the terms of the contract."

At the same time the news heated up, Rich Gitto asked me to discuss my techniques in investigating lab crimes with the lab's National Property Manager's Association group. During my speech, I clarified the problems the lab faced concerning property control and theft, and how the Office of Security Inquiries and the Business Division could work together to resolve the problems. My talk illustrated the lab's fault lines concerning property management and control, the pervasive culture of theft within the lab, how these thefts and mismanagement could jeopardize our national secrets, and how these failings could be corrected. I supported my statements with hard statistical evidence.

Glenn, you did an outstanding job, Gitto called me to say afterward; my people are in love with you. Gitto said the group was so impressed that Joe Roybal had asked me to present similar comments to the New Mexico National Property Managers Association — which included Sandia National Laboratory staff members — on November 7.

But Gitto's commendation changed to displeasure within a week. First, he told Doran that he was incensed with my November 7 talk and admonished both of us to be cool and to check with him before we made any statements about the lab's Business Division operations. Then he chastised me in an e-mail for talking about the lost and stolen items listed in Padilla's 1999-2001 Lost and Stolen Reports. I responded by e-mail, saying everything I said was factual and based on official records. He never replied, and we haven't communicated since. Regrettably, our once-friendly relationship ended abruptly. I really liked Richard Gitto, and still do, and could only theorize Gitto was receiving tremendous pressure from someone, causing him trepidation for his job.

The theft report I released in March did not become general public knowledge until November 17, when the *Albuquerque Journal North*, in Santa Fe broke this headline: "$3 Million in Lab Items Lost." Staff reporter, Adam Rankin wrote, "Nearly $3 million in items ranging from computers to video cameras to a forklift disappeared from the Los Alamos National Laboratory over three years....", while "A lab contract worker charged about $2,500 at a gas station and at Big Rock Casino in Espanola on a lab credit card, according to receipts." The official report, said Rankin, proposes that the LANL system used to report lost items is conducive to covering up for items that are actually stolen. According to Rankin, lab officials refused to comment on his report, but said a lab spokeswoman stated that the lab had a rigorous accounting system and could account for more than 99 percent of the items considered sensitive/attractive. It could successfully account, said the spokeswoman, for all items valued at more than $5,000, and all sensitive/attractive items were bar-coded for easy tracking. The lab spokeswoman did not comment on items identified as lost but were not classified as sensitive/attractive, or whose value was less than $5,000. Nor did she comment on Allen Wallace and Joe Roybal's memorandum in April, which indicated that the lab failed to bar code more than 80 percent of sensitive/attractive items.

Congressional interest began to peak by mid-November. Pennsylvania Republican Representative James C. Greenwood, the chairman of the Oversight and Investigation Subcommittee of the House Energy and Commerce Committee, requested from University of California President Richard C. Atkinson dozens of records relating to allegations of illegal procurement practices, and theft and misuse of government funds at Los Alamos. Greenwood told Atkinson that recent events had raised serious questions about LANL's procurement policies and oversight practices, and gave Atkinson until December 9 to provide the requested information.

The Department of Energy Inspector General was equally interested. Inspector General Gregory H. Friedman directed that a team of investigators go to Los Alamos on November 18 to begin an inquiry that would look into allegations, "that the management of the laboratory was attempting to cover up security breaches, and hide illegal activities from the public, the Department of Energy, federal law enforcement agencies, and political oversight groups." Friedman also directed that the team investigate the nearly three million dollars in lost or stolen equipment between 1999 and 2001.

A large chunk of those three million dollars was ostensibly paid for computers. Now the question was "*Did any of those computers contain security information*, which could be sensitive and could have been leaked?"

Chris Mechels, a former technical staff member and computer engineer at the Los Alamos laboratory, was among the first of current or former lab employees to sound off publicly against laboratory management. He told reporters on November 20 that LANL's current problems were hardly new. Mechels said the lab's response to security problems since the Wen Ho Lee case amounted to concealment. He felt the intent was to keep security breaches out of the public eye in the hope that the problems would just go away. "We don't know about security problems at Los Alamos anymore," Mechels said. "The reason we don't know is they shut off public access to security problems in October 1999."

A year earlier, Mechels said, the lab had actually taken a positive step by beginning to post its security violations on the Internet. That year, six violations were reported. In 1999, at the peak of the Wen Ho Lee investigation, the lab reported twenty-six violations. In nine of those twenty-six cases, classified information was compromised, and in seven other cases, the incidents were identified as potentially compromising classified information. After that, the lab stopped posting that information online.

The relentless hammering of media pressure and employee unrest compelled Otto Harmon, the lab's director and CEO, to distribute a lab-wide e-mail on November 22 that attempted to extinguish the flames now licking his heels. "Sometimes people salvage old equipment and property without informing their property management representatives," Harmon wrote rather delicately as he addressed theft cases. "Theft is always a possibility and we investigate those allegations." Unfortunately for Harmon, he inadvertently exposed his ignorance of Security and Safeguards Division procedures when he wrote, "If theft is determined, we turn the case over to law enforcement for prosecution." It was obvious he didn't know that no theft was ever turned over to a law enforcement agency unless the Office of Security Inquiries first developed a suspect, and then only after receiving approval from Richard; that in the last decade, S-Division had not identified one criminal suspect that ended up in prosecution and punishment; that not all thefts were being reported to the Office of Security Inquiries for inquiry; and that many of the thefts that were reported to OSI were never investigated.

Struggling to bring the lab and his administration into balance, Harmon ended his e-mail with a plea. "If there are improprieties in your workplace, you have an obligation to report them. I will ensure that there are no reprisals for reporting such matters to us." Harmon sent another e-mail a few weeks later; his third lab-wide e-mail in less than a month. This time he demanded that all personnel promptly report to him, any suspected activity involving waste, fraud, abuse, and theft.

The University of California's President Atkinson was finally roused from his lethargy on November 21, when he directed a team of UC administrators to visit the lab in four days to find out just how bad the situation was. Just a few days earlier, the university's vice president of laboratory management, John McTague, abruptly resigned for personal reasons. McTague had been the first lab management VP, a position created as part of the agreement between the University of California and the Department of Energy to tighten up the Los Alamos National Laboratory management and security failures in the wake of the Wen Ho Lee and lost hard drive debacles.

The agreement included the same Appendix O mandates that precipitated my hiring. The position was responsible for the lab operations that were now coming under fire. Atkinson quickly replaced McTague with his long-time friend, Senior Vice President of University Affairs Bruce Darling.

Atkinson's decision to send a team to Los Alamos apparently created terror throughout the lab's administration building. During the same time Harmon learned Darling and staff would be coming to town, Bussolini and Alexander, who were busted a month earlier, were suddenly placed on investigative leave.

Atkinson explained his position publicly on November 23. "We are very concerned about the recent allegations," he said in a press conference. "The university will not tolerate theft or mismanagement at Los Alamos or in any other part of the university. We intend to find out what occurred, correct any deficiencies, and discipline anyone who has engaged in improper activity."

Stubbornly, Los Alamos officials continued on their same path without giving ground. Harmon downplayed the lab's intensifying problems. He sent a lab-wide e-mail attempting to put the allegations into an imprudent perspective as Falcon did with me. That is, that the three million dollars worth of lost or stolen government property paled in comparison to the lab's one billion dollar inventory; therefore, the reader was to conclude, it wasn't that big of a deal.

Meanwhile, other lab officials repeated the diversionary claim that the lab could account for more than 99 percent of its sensitive/attractive items and items valued at more than $5,000; never mind that lab employees had direct control over the bar-coding system, and that hundreds if not thousands of items were not being properly bar-coded. Los Alamos officials also adamantly denied that missing computers contained classified information, proposing that it was an impossibility because of the lab's strict controls and audit procedures on computers that processed classified information.

Peter Stockton of the Project on Government Oversight (POGO) group in Washington, D.C., said it was unbelievable that the lab was claiming that no computers containing sensitive information were lost. "How do they know that?" he asked. "There is a hell of a lot of computers missing from some pretty sensitive areas."

Colonel Glenn A. Walp, Commissioner of the Pennsylvania State Police
- Photo courtesy of the Pennsylvania State Police -

Chief of Police Steven L. Doran, Idaho City, Idaho

Los Alamos National Laboratory, Los Alamos, New Mexico
- Photo taken by an employee of the United States Department of Energy
during the course of their official duties, and is in the public domain -

From left, General Leslie R. Groves (leader of the Manhattan Project)
and J. Robert Oppenheimer
(first Los Alamos National Laboratory Director)
- Photo courtesy of the United States Department of Energy
Photo Gallery, and is in the public domain -

From left, Steven L. Doran and Glenn A. Walp,
in Walp's living room in Santa Fe, New Mexico,
three days after their terminations
- Photo by AP/Wide World Photos, Boston,
MA-AP/ Photographer Jake Schoellkopf -

From left, Glenn A. Walp, Steven L. Doran and Jaret McDonald, first three witnesses at the Los Alamos National Laboratory congressional hearing in Washington, D.C., February 26, 2003 - Photo by AP/Wide World Photos, Boston, MA-AP/Photographer Susan Walsh -

Chief Investigator Steven L. Doran on a manhunt while assigned
to the Clare County, Michigan Felony Task Force

173

Colonel Glenn A. Walp, Commissioner of the Pennsylvania State Police,
addressing a Pennsylvania State Police Special
Emergency Response Team
- Photo courtesy of the Pennsylvania State Police -

From left, Major Paul Woodring, Assistant Task Force Commander to Colonel Walp; Joseph Peters, Executive Attorney General for the Commonwealth of Pennsylvania; and Colonel Glenn A. Walp, Task Force Commander of the Camp Hill Prison Riot of 1989

"I saw him (Colonel Walp) firsthand, under very difficult circumstances, during the Camp Hill Prison Disturbance of 1989, he was right there inside the wall as the Task Force Commander, this is a hands-on police officer who understands the business of law enforcement."
– Robert P. Casey –
Governor of the Commonwealth of Pennsylvania, April 1991

Los Alamos National Laboratory employee John Jennings –
Undercover FBI Informant

Charles (Chuck) Montano, Los Alamos National Laboratory auditor who uncovered major laboratory auditing improprieties

Cartoon courtesy of Jonathan (Jon) Richards, Santa Fe, New Mexico, as appearing in the Albuquerque Journal North, Santa Fe, newspaper

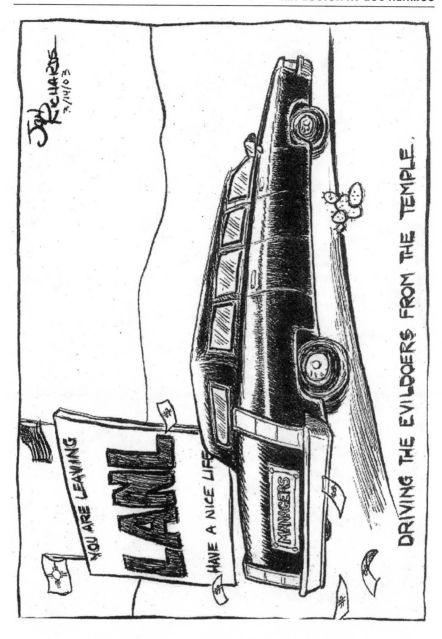

Cartoon courtesy of Jonathan (Jon) Richards, Santa Fe, New Mexico, as appearing in the Albuquerque Journal North, Santa Fe, newspaper

Cartoon by John Trever, Editorial Cartoonist for the
Albuquerque Journal newspaper, Albuquerque, New Mexico

Cartoon by John Trever, Editorial Cartoonist for the
Albuquerque Journal newspaper, Albuquerque, New Mexico

GLENN A. WALP, Ph.D.

home

Performance Summary Review

Employee's name: WALP GLENN A
Division: S
Manager's name:

Review Period
From: 8/1/2001
To: 7/31/2002

Performance Summary:

1. Implement ISSM- A 100% effort was effectuated into this objective. Considerable planning and process development were accomplished in meeting the required metrics. For example, security infractions have been reduced; new policies were placed into effect that produced more professional reports; and a more efficient reporting process was initiated to meet DOE reporting guidelines. A special effort was placed in establishing a root cause analysis program that will go on line within this FY. 2. Safety Performance- A 100% effort. That is, an OSI nested safety committee has been formed that involves all OSI personnel. This process has resulted in the identification of multiple safety factors that have been appropriately addressed through the efforts of OSI employees and the support of S-Division leadership. 3. Human Capital- 100% effort. All hiring goals have been completed. Between 1-02 and 8-02 the OSI complement has been increased by four personnel, meeting all OSI hiring expectations. Within the new hire group one individual is a female and two are minorities. 4. Walkarounds- Over 100% accomplishment- Each quarter OSI has far exceeded the mandated MWA goals. 5. Employee Communications- Over 100% accomplishment. There is daily communications between OSI personnel and the Office Leader and OSI personnel in general. This is accomplished through daily meetings; management by walking around; and daily interaction between OSI personnel and the office leader wherein personal and employment issues are discussed and resolved. All concerns are immediately addressed, perhaps not to the complete satisfaction of the employee, but nonetheless addressed. 6. Effective cost and schedule management- 100% attainment. All available management tools are being used to maintain management control on all major projects. The OSI budget, according to personnel assigned to the S-Division BUS unit, is right on target with no overrun costs anticipated. 7. Financial Management- 100% accomplishment. Deliverables have been determined, resources have been identify, and management of unpredicted costs are balanced within the framework of the OSI budget allocation. Strict guidelines have been implemented to ensure there is avoidance of any unallowable costs. OSI assigned vehicles are properly utilized and maintained. 8. Time Management- The Office Leader is visible to all OSI personnel on a daily bases. The OSI philosophy consists of an open forum wherein the input of all personnel is coveted, asked for and received. This input has lead to multiple OSI policy change that has positively affected the productivity and professionalism of that office. At least 20% of the leaders time is reserved for effective communications with staff, such as in the MWA and group meeting processes. 100 % attainment has been accomplished in these required metrics. Summary: Mr. Walp hit the ground running and has not faltered. His attention to detail has improved the quality and timeliness of "reports of a security concern". The number of significant infractions/violations has diminished with no repeat security infractions within the Office of Security Inquiries (OSI). He studied hard and applied Integrated Safeguards and Security Management principles and practices with OSI with specific emphasis regarding "hands-on leadership and

management". Safety has been the by-word in OSI with no reportable accidents to-date. Implementing a strong nested safety and security committee; he and his people have taken a pro-active approach to both safety and security with no violations of procedures or sound safety practices. He has worked hard to hire quality people with experience and professionalism paramount while at the same time striving for diversity in the hiring process. He is mentoring a new entry-level employee with good results. All mandatory training has been completed in a timely manner and he obtained inquiry officer certtification to better inform himself regarding the process. His safety and security walkarounds are thorough. A pro-active and caring leader, he has promoted employee feedback and is conscious of the tensions and stresses within OSI. He has managed costs and properly projected the OSI budget to include additional staffing requirements. Mr. Walp faces a formable challenge to adapt his professional skills to the corporate structure of the Laboratory. I'm confident he can attain this goal and serve the Laboratory in a commendable fashion. A strong and professional manager who has the potential and aspirations to have a positive and lasting impact on the Laboratory --- very effective performer

Note: You will have an opportunity to enter any comments you may have.

Continued Performance Evaluation for Glenn A. Walp, July 2002

GLENN A. WALP, Ph.D.

Los Alamos
NATIONAL LABORATORY

Security and Safeguards Division
P.O. Box 1663, MS-G729
Los Alamos, New Mexico 87545   Date: November 25, 2002
(505) 667-5911 ph/ (505) 667-5-3810   Refer To: S-DO: 02-254

Mr. Glenn A. Walp
15 Elk Circle, Tierra De Oro
Santa Fe, NM 87506

Subject: Termination Of Employment During New Employee Evaluation Period

Dear Mr. Walp:

Your position as a Laboratory employee in "S" Division will end effective December 10, 2002. The reason for this action is that we have determined, during your new employee evaluation period, that you are not a suitable fit for the requirements of your position.

I have determined that it is in the best interest of the Laboratory that you be provided payment in lieu of the 15 days' notice as specified in AM 103.11. This means that your last day of active work will be today, Monday, November 25, 2002. You will be paid for the period between today and December 10, 2002. Please return all Laboratory property, including keys, credit cards, phone cards, crypto cards, pagers and all Laboratory documents immediately. We will provide assistance to you in this process.

If you have any questions regarding benefits, please contact the Benefits Office at 7-1806.

I have read, understand and acknowledge receipt of this memorandum.

REFUSED TO SIGN $\circleddash\oslash\mathcal{B}$ _[initials]_
_____
Name   Date

Yours truly,

[signature]

Director of Security

Cy: Staff Relations, P126
       LC, A183
       Personnel Security, S-6, B236
       Personnel Records, P235
       S-DO File

Termination Memorandum of Glenn A. Walp, November 2002

Mary V. Walp, Executive Book Secretary,
SunGlow Word Processing, Camp Hill, Pennsylvania

Jon Rochmis, Executive Book Editor, San Francisco, California

XXII

Going Down Slow

Seven investigations were now being conducted regarding lab operations: the FBI's investigation of the Nonproliferation and International Security Division theft case, and another alleged theft incident; Albuquerque Department of Energy Inspector General Office investigations of three alleged criminal cases, to include the forgery investigation and a case where a lab contract employee was utilizing a government credit card at a local casino for gambling; the Department of Energy Inspector General Washington Office's inquiry on allegations of mismanagement and cover-up; and PriceWaterhouseCooper's investigative review of the lab's purchase card system.

"The lab is a case study on why institutions should not be allowed to police themselves."

These were among the first comments that Doran made to Peter Schleck, a special advisor to the United States Department of Energy's Inspector General, on November 18. Schleck had come from Washington with Garrett Westfall, another DOE special agent based in Albuquerque, to interview lab personnel regarding allegations of corruption and cover-up by Los Alamos officials. Schleck interviewed Steve Doran first because Doran had plans to return to his Detroit home later that day to testify in court on a matter not related to the lab. After Doran, Schleck would interview fellow OSI inquirers Jim Mullins, Jeff Dy, Marty Farley, and me.

Doran gave Schleck and Westfall an earful; giving them his perspectives on the improprieties of lab leadership and saying, he believed the lab was incapable of handling its own security. Because Protection Technologies of Los Alamos had a sixty-three million dollar contract with the lab to provide security, it was beholden to lab management, said Doran. For example, Doran proposed, if a PTLA employee raises a concern, he must report that concern to his superior, and that superior looks bad if a problem is brought up, thus, the lab security force should consist of sworn federal police officers who are supervised by the federal government, not lab management; the way it operates now, it is a definite conflict of interest.

Doran stressed that just because the Department of Energy and the Department of Energy Inspector General provided oversight, that didn't mean the lab had federal supervision. That's a hollow view, Doran said; the security force, including the supervisors, should be federal, gun-toting officers.

Later that day, after Doran left for Detroit. Madison and Falcon *burst* into my office.

"Where's Doran?" Madison asked sharply.

"He had to go back to Detroit, and he won't be back until Monday," I replied.

Madison gave a blank stare, then turned to Falcon and stated, "Well, I guess we can't do that now," with both of them quickly exiting my office.

Two days later, just moments before my interview with Schleck was to begin, Doug Madison asked my office administrator for all Office of Security Inquiries travel records from August 1 through August 20. She told me the one they were most interested in concerned when Richard Naranjo, an inquirer at the time, went to Albuquerque to investigate an on-going case. Instantly, I concluded that lab management might assert I improperly allowed Naranjo to rent a vehicle, stay overnight in Albuquerque, and follow the suspect as part of his inquiry. Those thoughts were on my mind as I entered the lab's Badge Office conference room for my meeting with Schleck and Westfall.

Schleck told me to start wherever I wanted to, so I began at the beginning with my hiring. Soon after I started working, I told them, I perceived there might be improper activity occurring at the lab. With more than thirty-five years of law-enforcement experience, I knew I would need to take abundant notes, and I had many of my transcribed notes with me. Schleck asked for a copy, but I politely refused. "Unless you have a subpoena for my personal notes, I will not give them to you," I said. "Quite frankly, I'm not sure whom to trust in these matters." Nevertheless, I decided to reveal what I'd found and read large portions of my notes to them, verbatim, after which Schleck and Westfall asked me a wide variety of questions. Like Doran, I also expressed my opinion that the lab was totally unfit to handle its own security, and that a federal agency not indebted to the lab for their jobs – such as Homeland Security or the Department of Defense – should be in charge of the security force. I made it clear to Schleck and Westfall, that when I referred to the need of an outside security force, that outside force was not only needed to protect the laboratory facility, but also to do investigations into all security matters related to lost/missing computers, mishandling/loss of classified information and the like. It is my position, I said, that allowing a laboratory employee, including a laboratory contract employee, to have any part in security functions at a federal nuclear weapons laboratory, creates a fertile field for corruption and cover-up.

Before the interview concluded, I told Schleck and Westfall of Madison's request to my assistant regarding travel records. I want to place in the record, I continued, that before I rented the vehicle and directed Naranjo and other OSI personnel to follow the suspect, I asked Falcon for permission, and he said I could and should do it. I also asked Madison about following the suspect and Madison said, how the hell else are you going to find out? Yeah, go ahead and do it.

The reason I was telling this to Schleck and Westfall had to do with my growing concerns that Doran and I were being set up as fall guys. Someone may be trying to find fault with us just to fire us because they're afraid we're going to expose them, I told Schleck and Westfall.

If anything like that happens, Schleck said, handing me his cell phone number, "get a hold of me."

Falcon appeared quite busy during the time Schleck was in town. At one point, he came to my office, unannounced, and asked excitedly if the FBI had failed to notify the lab when they served their Halloween Day search warrants on Bussolini and Alexander. The FBI didn't let me know about the search warrants as they said they would, Falcon said, so what do you know about that?

"Can I bring Mullins in here?" I asked Falcon. "He was the one assigned to help the FBI, and I really don't know anything about it because, as you know, Madison and you took me off the case."

I summoned Mullins. "Matt says the FBI didn't tell him when they were going to serve the search warrants," I told Mullins when he arrived.

Campbell contacted me in the early morning, and I immediately contacted you, Matt, Mullins said, looking at Falcon, and I also heard that Campbell called you after he called me.

Falcon said, you did tell me, and Campbell called me, but he said he was just gathering information to serve the search warrants, but never said he was *going to* serve them.

That's all I need, Falcon announced as he quickly left my office.

"Matt's not telling the truth" Mullins said to me. He knew very well the FBI was serving the warrants, and I told Matt and so did

Campbell. It sounds like he's in trouble with someone over this and he is trying to place the blame on someone else to get himself off the hot seat, continued Mullins.

After a few moments, Mullins' rolled his eyes as if he had just thought of something. Besides, why did he come to you? He took you off the case and now he expects you to know what happened? It looks to me, continued Mullins, like he could be trying to find fault with you, blaming you and making you the bad guy, and it's obvious he's getting pressure from someone. Glenn, I don't think they like you, and may be trying to get rid of you, concluded Mullins.

And it was clear that pressure was creating a great deal of anxiety. Madison, Falcon, and other lab officials being on the firing line with higher-ups was not uncommon.

In July, Shapiro called me in, along with Marquez, Richard, Madison, and James Holt, the associate director of operations, for a spur-of-the-moment meeting late in the afternoon to discuss cases the FBI and the Office of Security Inquiries were working on. I had never met Shapiro, but some people called him pompous, and others bombastic, terms often strung together. One could see the tension chiseled into the faces of Richard, Marquez, and Madison as meeting time approached. It soon became apparent that no one told Shapiro what to do or how to do it. If one were planning to present an idea to him, he had better tread lightly. Even if the planner took a meek and submissive approach and the idea was good, he'd best be prepared to be shot down with caustic retribution whether deserved or not. It was apparent to me Shapiro was the alpha male here.

Shapiro was quite concerned that the Project on Government Oversight group would find out about the cases. Shapiro said that Peter Stockton and Congressman John Dingle are enemies of the lab, and if either of them got wind of these cases they would go public, and that would not be good for the lab's PR and the lab's contract with the DOE.

At another impromptu meeting that Shapiro called two days

later, he reiterated his concerns. On this occasion, we met in his plush office, on the fourth floor of the lab's administration building. Richard, Marquez, Madison, and I attended. Shapiro explained that we all needed to understand the major issue here; it is the bad PR that will come to the lab because of these investigations, not necessarily the crimes that are occurring. Shapiro continued that if Ralph Erickson (the National Nuclear Security Administration manager at the Los Alamos site office) finds out today, he'll tell DOE in Washington, and POGO will find out about it by next Wednesday, and if POGO knows, it will not be good, Shapiro concluded.

At this point, I actually liked Shapiro. He was overbearing and pretentious to be sure, but I was used to those traits in commanders and politicians. Shapiro had been a police officer and prosecutor, and he was not shy in letting everyone know how much he knew about the fundamentals of criminal investigation. Shapiro barked out orders on how the investigation should proceed.

Being a former police officer and prosecutor, Shapiro's perceptions illustrated fundamentals of criminal inquiry, and they, in fact, were on my checklist. Although Shapiro had a dictatorial air, at least someone at the lab understood the basics of criminal investigation and was concerned that all the investigative T's were crossed. I watched Richard, Madison, and Marquez grow more and more visibly uncomfortable as Shapiro threw his verbal punches, which, they knew could send any of them out walking the streets.

Watching the pummeling Shapiro administered to his top staff, I was reminded of how quickly loyalty could transform to disloyalty within the criminal society. Thugs may appear to be as tight as brothers before an arrest, but once the handcuffs clicked, those alliances could end in seconds. Men about to be jailed would turn on each other, doing whatever was necessary to save their own necks. Likewise, some of the lab's top managers were scrambling, individually and in groups, attempting to quickly rectify major faults they may have been aware of for years but did nothing to correct. Looking around I decided this prestigious lab *was on a course for implosion*, and everyone in the meeting knew it.

After the excruciating meeting, Richard went cowering to his office while Madison, Marquez, and I rode the elevator down to the first floor. "A few more meetings like this and my ass will disappear," Marquez observed.

XXIII

'Not Suitably Fit'

Before 6 a.m. on the morning of November 25, I reported to work. Though thoughts of the turmoil at Los Alamos were constantly revolving in my mind, I had no thought that I was about to feel the consequences personally. After spending two hours cleaning up unfinished tasks left over from the week before, I grabbed the keys to the OSI white SUV and drove to the Otowi Building where I was going to meet with a Human Resource member to discuss a personnel matter. As I was about to enter the meeting room, Madison's office administrator paged me to tell me that Doug needed to see me as soon as possible.

I told her where I was and that the meeting would only take about fifteen minutes. Less than two minutes later, she paged me again.

Glenn, Doug needs to see you right now, she said.

Canceling my meeting, I returned to S-Division headquarters. His assistant, seeming anxious, was already outside, holding the door open for me. For Madison to call an emergency meeting – probably to deal with a major security incident – was not unusual. But his assistant's worried look caused me immediate concern.

They're waiting for you in the Chief of Staff's office, she said, somberly.

This was also odd, I thought, because she was always up-beat, and there was something disturbing about meeting in the chief's office. There must be a major security matter afoot, I reasoned.

Silently she escorted me down the hall and opened the door to reveal Madison, S-Division Chief of Staff Vicki McCabe, Associate Director of Operations James Holt, and Bill Starkovich, an armed security officer. Time stood still as I paused in the doorway. Madison was looking at papers heaped in front of him, McCabe was looking at a wall, Holt was looking down at his lap, and Starkovich was staring at his clasped hands on the table in front of him. The atmosphere was thick as swamp fog. Finally, Madison said, come on in Glenn and have a seat, I have something I need to discuss with you.

Madison introduced me to Holt, whom I actually had met before. "Why was he in this meeting?" I asked myself. Holt was Madison's immediate supervisor, but I had rarely interacted with him. Madison, Falcon, and I had always dealt directly with Richard and Shapiro.

"Hi, how are you doing?" I said, shaking hands with him.

"I'm fine," Holt replied.

Madison interrupted. Glenn, I'll get right to the point, he said. Your employment at the lab is being terminated. I will read your Letter of Termination. If you have any questions after that, you can ask me, said Madison.

Suddenly, without warning, I was hit head-on with termination for the first time in my life.

After Madison read the memorandum of termination, the only parts which stuck in my mind were, "Your position as a laboratory employee in S-Division will end effective December 10, 2002... We have determined during your new employee evaluation period that *you are not suitably fit* …. This means that your last day of active work will be today, Monday, November 25, 2002....You have until December 10, to resign on your own."

After gaining composure, I asked Doug if I could read the letter. I tried, but I was fixated on the words, "not suitably fit."

"Doug, what does it mean I didn't fit," I asked.

"I don't know," Madison replied, but you are terminated.

Perhaps the character of Senator Charles Meachum in the 2007, movie *Shooter,* was on target when he stated, "There is always a confused soul that thinks that one man can make a difference. And you have to kill him to convince him otherwise. That's the hassle of democracy."

I felt Madison's verbal blast, but I had been shot at before. Suddenly my mind flashed back to an early childhood memory that I periodically found myself revisiting:

> *I had just put my head down to sleep for the night when a bullet whizzed past, shattering a window in the Walp farmhouse. Since a telephone was an unheard-of luxury in our household, my father raced to a neighbor's house to call the police. Two Pennsylvania State Troopers answered the call, parking in the family driveway next to our home. This was the first time I had ever seen a trooper up close, and the images of a four-year-old's awe remain clear decades later: strong, serious men wearing commanding uniforms of gray, burnished riding boots, rigid Stetsons, and Sam Browns adorned with incandescent chrome captured in the rays of a glistening sunrise. What I remember most clearly is sleepily peering out of my parents' second-story bedroom window at the two troopers and their ghost-gray patrol car, feeling safe and assured from the power and authority these two Troopers emanated.*

197

The Troopers stayed there throughout the night, guarding my family until morning.

Within a few days, the Pennsylvania State Police arrested two young thugs for the dastardly deed of getting triple-vision drunk before deciding to use the light bulbs of several residences throughout Pennsylvania's pastoral Conyngham Valley as target practice.

But Madison's detonating action wasn't as odd as the timing. After all, on October 2, less than two months ago, I had received a 100-percent performance evaluation from Madison and Falcon along with a $5,000 dollar raise. Madison had written and signed my evaluation, which read in part, "Mr. Walp hit the ground running and has not faltered. His attention to detail has improved the quality and timeliness of reports of a security concern. The number of significant infractions/violations has diminished with no repeat security infractions within the Office of Security Inquiries. He has worked hard to hire quality people with experience and professionalism paramount, while at the same time striving for diversity in the hiring process. His safety and security walk-arounds are thorough. He has managed costs, and properly projected the OSI budget to include additional staffing requirements; a strong and professional manager who has the potential and aspirations to have a positive and lasting impact on the laboratory - very effective performer." In these crushing moments of time I thought, "A*nd now he is saying I don't fit? What is wrong with* this picture?"

As I mentally reviewed Madison's performance evaluation, now with trenchant thought, I now realized what he meant by his aside comment in the last paragraph of my evaluation. That is, Madison ended my evaluation by stating, "Mr. Walp faces a formidable challenge to adapt his professional skills to the *corporate structures* of the laboratory. I'm confident he can attain this goal and serve the laboratory in a commendable fashion."

198

Doug, it just doesn't make sense, I shook my head. I want to make sure I understand this. You're saying you don't have any idea what "not suitably fit" means; is that correct?

"Yes."

I told him I didn't have any other questions, and Madison told me that Starkovich would escort me to my office and that I would have thirty minutes to clean out my personal items.

There were quite a few personal items and memorabilia in my office, and it would be next to impossible to have them all removed in a half-hour. In addition, I needed to call my wife, Mary, to come to the lab and help me because my car wasn't big enough to transport everything home.

Starkovich escorted me down the hallway into a room with two other armed, uniformed PTLA officers, Terrance Hogan and Pete Peterson. I called my wife and explained what was happening and that I needed her assistance. I told her not to be nervous or upset. "Just drive safely to the lab and park in the parking lot next to the OSI office," I said.

With Starkovich watching everything, I began to separate all lab property from my personal belongings. Starkovich and I scrutinized each piece of paper to make sure all lab property stayed at the lab. I'm sorry for what I have to do, but I am just obeying orders, Starkovich said. I told him I understood. He was being extremely kind, helping me pack and carry boxes to my car and my wife's car. He let me park both vehicles inside the security fence to shorten the lugging distance.

I didn't know it at the time, but Doran was also being fired. As I was packing up, I saw Steve walking through the back door, escorted by three other armed PTLA guards.

Our eyes met. Doran asked his guard if we could speak. "No," the man responded, sternly.

Later I learned Doran was a bit feisty during his firing. After Madison had given Doran his copy of the termination letter, Madison said, Steve, if you know what is good for you, you will resign.

The next time you hear from me, Doug, it will be a letter from my attorney, Doran replied, I'm not taking this lightly. I came here, continued Doran, and did what I was hired to do, and now I am being terminated; my attorney will be in touch.

They didn't know it, but I was aware that Doran's philosophy included, *"Losing and laboring taught me how to win and fight smarter, instead of harder. It also taught me how ruthless people can be, and what I needed to do to overcome my adversary. During my whole childhood, I could only think about when I got older, it would be different. I would never allow these types of things to happen as long as I could do anything about it. I still think that way, and have no patience for bullies, cruel or selfish people."*

Doran didn't have much personal property in his office, so he was finished packing up well within the thirty-minute period. It took me a bit more time. In fact, Starkovich received three calls on his cell phone while I packed. Each time, Starkovich replied in his phone, it looks like we'll be here for another ten-twenty minutes. When both cars were finally packed, I looked over to see Jim Mullins consoling my wife, Mary, who was visibly upset. I walked over and gave her a long hug when a Protection Technologies of Los Alamos patrol vehicle with four guards inside drove up. "You need to leave lab property right now," the one guard commanded sternly.

And so we did, driving straight to Doran's home in Los Alamos.

As we all sat together in his living room, Doran and I spoke of how we were amazed at how incongruous, contradictory, and ironic, the entire saga had been. Just the way real criminals, or possible criminals at Los Alamos were handled compared with the ignominious way our departures had been staged, to us was unbelievable. We were the good guys! Bussolini and Alexander, who stole hundreds of thousands of dollars of taxpayer property — and were eventually confined in federal prison for their crimes — were escorted off lab property by non-uniformed, unarmed lab personnel. At the time of our terminations, neither of them had been fired and both were still collecting their full salaries and benefits.

But Doran and I, who were the ones instrumental in helping to uncover their crimes, were summarily fired, escorted by armed guards to our offices, given a half-hour to remove all of our belongings, and strongly told to get off lab property. We were also informed our salaries and benefits would end shortly – a few weeks before Christmas.

"We have two choices, Steve," I said. "We can both take the deal and resign to keep our records clean – and, of course, that's what they want us to do; or we can fight."

Looking at each other, we didn't even have to say another word. We already knew each other's combative spirit in the face of wrongdoings. We were going to fight.

XXIV

Media Exoneration

"I am going home to make some phones calls," I told Doran. Steve and I embraced and said a prayer. "Stand by Steve," I said. "I'll get back to you." He nodded, knowing I would do just that.

Later that day, said Mullins, Snelling told me that after Steve and I were fired, her division supervisor told all S-Division managers they were prohibited from communicating with Steve or me about anything, even personal matters. Steve and I were totally off limits. Someone at the lab, it seemed to us, was out to ensure that Doran and I would be meted the full wrath of their displeasure.

Perhaps POGO, which was perceived by some as an enemy of the lab, could help us. The Project on Government Oversight had been established in 1981 as the Project on Military Procurement. The organization's founder, Dina Rasor, initially focused on governmental waste within the Department of Defense. In 1990, the project expanded its purview to include systemic waste, fraud, and abuse in all federal agencies and at that time changed its name to its present one. POGO became an extremely powerful and valiant watchdog, saving billions of American dollars. The organization's efforts included helping improve policymaking and accountability at the Department of Defense, the Department of Energy, the Environmental Protection Agency, the Federal Election Commission, the Department of Health and Human Services, the Department of Interior, the Department of Transportation, and the United States Congress. In recent years POGO has given vigilant oversight of the multi-billion dollar government bailout of corporations and Wall Street, and in September, 2009 uncovered the alarming security failures by certain employees of Wackenhut Services, Inc., at the American Embassy in Kabul, Afghanistan. In August 2009, POGO was awarded the coveted *National Sunshine Award*, by the Society of Professional Journalists, for their important contributions in the area of open government.

I was particularly impressed that POGO had a proven track record of verifying data through investigations, and then working through a bipartisan network of contacts in Congress, federal agencies, the media, and public-interest groups. Danielle Brian became president and executive director in 1993, and when the media got wind of our firings, she was widely quoted as saying, "All signs indicate that leaders at Los Alamos were motivated in the firings by a desire to silence these and other individuals who are uncovering widespread corruption."

POGO's senior investigator is Peter Stockton, a former security advisor to Secretary of Energy Bill Richardson, soon to become governor of New Mexico. Falcon told me at one point, that "Shapiro regarded Stockton as poison."

In fact, in mid-November when media and government attention increased as a result of *The Energy Daily* report, Stockton expressed his cynicism at the lab's weak claims that the anonymous sources had "a hidden agenda."

Stockton was widely quoted in media reports. "The whistleblower, whoever he or she may be, is extraordinarily credible since all of their allegations thus far have been correct. Although the whistleblower apparently believes they had gone through proper channels, they apparently felt that lab's upper management was trying to cover up the problems. LANL is well known for harsh treatment of whistleblowers, which forces people to put out information anonymously. There are horror stories all over the place where whistleblowers have all kinds of protections, allegedly, but man do they get creamed. Very few come out the other end half together, and that's why this whistleblower is hiding their identity."

I picked up and dialed the POGO number.

"POGO, can I help you?" a deep male voice answered.

"Is Peter Stockton there?" I asked.

"This is Peter Stockton speaking. Can I be of some help?"

I smiled, "I hope so," I replied.

I began to tell him what had happened. Along the way, Stockton provided me with a list of legal firms he thought would be skilled in handling our wrongful termination case. We believed we were fired in retaliation for our disclosures of illegalities, gross waste of government monies, and gross abuse of management authority resulting in security problems at the Los Alamos National Laboratory. After considerable research, in mid-December, Doran and I settled on the Washington D.C. law firm of Bernabei and Katz, which was recognized as one of the premier employment-law firms in United States. The agency specialized in providing legal advice and representation to individuals and organizations about employment law, civil rights and civil liberties matters, and, of critical importance, whistleblower law. Lynne Bernabei took the lead counsel position, with assistance from Debra Katz and Allen Kabat.

The Project on Government Oversight group became an instant rock for us. Within hours of speaking to Stockton, Doran and I were barraged with telephone calls from news media throughout the United States and abroad. The frenzy escalated with each hour. Within two days, Doran and I had our first major television interviews, appearing on *CBS Nightly News with Dan Rather*, interviewed by correspondent Sharyl Attkisson.

We were extremely happy CBS put Attkisson on the story. We knew she had received the coveted 2002 Emmy Award for Outstanding Investigative Journalism. Her background included reporting on theft; fraud, and mismanagement at Firestone, Enron, and the Red Cross, among others. She would report on the Los Alamos National Laboratory's corruption, mismanagement, and security failures on more than a dozen occasions for CBS.

In introducing Attkisson, Rather first referred to her work on the security and spy investigations evolving from the Wen Ho Lee case four years earlier: "This time," he went on, "there are allegations the lab has bungled and covered up a new investigation by punishing the very people who turned up wrongdoing."

That night, Attkisson developed this hard-hitting theme: "Investigators Glenn Walp and Steven Doran were hired by the Los Alamos weapons lab earlier this year in part to make sure equipment and research, which could help America's enemies, didn't just walk out the door. They quickly uncovered stunning security lapses. They uncovered millions of dollars in stolen and missing items. They began working with the FBI. But the more Walp and Doran uncovered, the more lab managers tried to cover up, worried more about keeping the security problems quiet. Walp and Doran say there is no telling how many people have committed crimes or how long it's gone on. That's what they were working to find out. The Energy Department and FBI continue investigating, but now without the help of the two investigative insiders who may have been able to uncover the most."

As promised, CBS stayed on the story and filed another report on December 6. "CBS News has been looking into security breaches at the nation's top nuclear-weapons research facility," Rather related. He added, "Sharyl Attkisson has been doing some more digging."

Attkisson began her next report with news that federal investigators were looking at two managers at the lab. "The first is the lab's top attorney, Brian Richard. Sources say Richard undercut two lab investigators who were helping the FBI to probe widespread abuse. Investigators are also looking at the lab division run by Marcellaa Zambrea - and whether Zambrea used her position to bury problems instead of exposing them, all to protect the University of California."

Our second major media appearance occurred three days after our terminations when Bill O'Reilly of *The O'Reilly Factor* on Fox News interviewed us. O'Reilly's producers told us that Bill was outraged by our firings and he would do whatever he could to help us; we wound up appearing on his show four times, and commenting remotely on two other occasions. O'Reilly did a superb job in reporting the truth and facts about the lab's debacles, as only Bill O'Reilly can do.

Steve and I are convinced that the wieldy, integrity driven investigative reporting of Attkisson and O'Reilly had a significant impact on Energy Secretary Abraham's decision to *lay down the law* on the executives of the University of California and the Los Alamos National Laboratory. Although Steve and I are not socially connected to Sharyl or Bill, we consider both of them dear friends, and we will be forever grateful for their personal stance for truth and justice.

Next up was *NBC Nightly News with Tom Brokaw* in an interview with Joe Johns. A couple of days later, Doran appeared on *At Large with Geraldo Rivera*, although Gregg Jarret was sitting in for Rivera on the broadcast.

The media floodgates were now wide open. The editorial staff of the *Los Alamos Monitor* newspaper, led by Roger Snodgrass, wrote about the newest allegations about Los Alamos cover-ups:

> There may be no more blatant admissions of guilt
> and wrongdoing than firing investigators during an
> investigation. President Richard M. Nixon used the
> same tactics, and he never survived the public out-

rage that followed. The clock is now ticking on how long those responsible at the lab for firing Walp and Doran will survive. The laboratory's apparent cover-up, its relentless attempts to control all information about itself, including its self-shielding processes for handling criminal activity, have become intolerable.

Sue Vorenberg, a reporter for *Scripps-McClatchy Western Service*, noted the inconsistency with which the lab handled personnel matters. "The two accused employees (Bussolini and Alexander)," she wrote, "were given administrative leave while the charges are investigated — a stark contrast to the immediate firings of the investigators." Doran was quoted in the article, saying, "We told DOE IG the truth, and in a few days we were both fired because we supposedly didn't fit. Let your readers come to their own conclusion as to why we were really fired."

POGO's Stockton stood by our side in print. "They're going to rue the day they did this. This ranks as one of the stupidest things I've ever seen an institution do. Lab employees who are suspected of committing fraud are still collecting paychecks. On the other hand, two people who uncovered these, and other problems at the lab, were fired and escorted from the property by armed guards in retaliation for a job done too well."

Steve and I were admittedly gratified by the public exoneration. It was a welcome relief to the relentless pounding we had taken for months from lab higher-ups. Nevertheless, we took every opportunity to drive home our concern for national security, because of the serious problems at Los Alamos. In a December 9 article in the *Los Angeles Times* newspaper, I said, "These guys (Bussolini and Alexander) had keys to everything; there wasn't any nook or cranny in the black area they didn't have access to. All it would take, would be somebody to walk up and say, 'I know what you're doing and either you do this for me or I'm going to the cops.'" The next day, Doran was quoted in the same paper: "If you see the way they handle this money and their property, what would lead you to believe they do any better with national security?"

Bill Hemmer of CNN's *American Morning with Paula Zahn* pressed me hard to make a connection between the theft and mismanagement scandals we were investigating and, most worrying, direct threats to national security. The interview occurred on December 10.

"At no time in the ongoing investigation of misuse of government purchase cards, or the alleged conspiracy to defraud the lab through misuse of the purchase order system, has there been any indication whatsoever of a compromise of national security," Hemmer said. "What about it, Glenn? You say taxpayers have lost hundreds of millions of dollars in this. What about national security? Has any of this been violated?"

"There's a reason for this concern," I responded. "Two individuals, Bussolini and Alexander, had all the keys to the kingdom of that very secure area. They had purchased RF (radio-frequency) detectors, which indicate if a bug is in the area. They had multiple GPS systems and a GPS finder system, meaning that if you bury something, you can find it later. They had lock-picking devices, glasscutters, precision cameras, night vision binoculars; they had what we call spy-type equipment. We brought that to the attention of our superiors and they made Steve take it out of the report. My concern is this: What are these people, who are changing light bulbs, doing with this spy-type equipment within their possession? They've been doing this for over two years. Where was management, where was the control?"

The *Los Alamos Monitor* wrote about the Los Alamos National Laboratory's culture of deception in a Christmas Day editorial. "The lab has a don't-tell culture. It is a culture that seeks to control all the information that leaves the laboratory for public consumption, putting the spotlight on its glorious achievements, while hiding its ailments. Lab officials, through the public affairs spokespeople, have delayed, denied and deceived. Malfeasance or incompetence makes it hard to hold anyone accountable for mistakes, failures, breakdowns or crimes."

For its part, lab officials adamantly denied that Steve and I were dismissed in retaliation for our exposure of the misman- agement, corruption and cover-ups. One lab official even had the audacity to say our firings were not in retaliation for anything, but rather because Steve and I were within our probationary one-year periods. Therefore, he said, we could be fired without cause or proof of poor performance. The lab did not need to give any reason or produce any documentation on why we were fired, he said, say- ing, "We didn't fit" was enough.

The lab spokesman also was quoted as saying that the Department of Energy Inspector General never informed lab officials as to whom they interviewed, or what the content of those interviews may have been. But a few weeks later, University of California officials told Steve, me, and our attorney that the lab was well aware who was being interviewed, and that their original intent was to fire Steve and me before the Department of Energy had a chance to interview us. Doran's visit to Detroit on November 18 evidently foiled those plans — when Madison and Falcon busted into my office in a sweat — so the lab had to wait until November 25 to do its dirty deed.

The media wasn't buying the labs "didn't fit" explanation and reporters turned to Phil Kruger, the lab's human resources deputy director for answers. Kruger tried to reinforce the notion that, because Doran and I were still in our probationary period, the lab wasn't required to come up with any concrete reason. Kruger then proposed another reason: that we had lost the confidence of several lab divisions and an outside organization. "They basically," continued Kruger, "lost the confidence of several organizations and people with whom they had to have effective relationships, including Audits and Assessments, legal counsel (Richard), human resources, the chief operating officer (Shapiro) of the lab, in-line management (Matt M. Falcon), within the security division, and an outside organization as well." Kruger refused to identify who the outside organization was, but Steve and I first heard Kruger was referring to PriceWaterhouseCoopers. Later, UC officials told our attorney that Kruger was actually referring to the FBI and the U.S. Attorney. During a congressional hearing Richard denied he was part of that bold lie, and placed the blame exclusively on Shapiro.

Neither Steve nor I disputed Kruger's in-house list, though. These were the very groups and individuals who were involved in various degrees of attempting to cover-up and/or interfere with our investigations. As Doran said, "Of course these people would say they have no confidence in us. We're the two that are going to burn them."

POGO's Brian chimed in too. In a statement quoted widely by the media, she said, "All signs indicate that leaders at Los Alamos were motivated in the firing by a desire to silence these individuals who were uncovering widespread corruption."

Shapiro denied all accusations of wrongdoing to the media. Our terminations were not in retaliation for speaking to DOE investigators, he said. "I don't know anything about those conversations," Shapiro told reporters. University of California officials later released documents proving Shapiro had knowledge of our scheduled interviews by Department of Energy investigators, and specifically gave an order to fire us before we could speak to the investigators.

By early December, many lab employees began to vocalize their support for Doran and me. One northern New Mexico newspaper printed a letter from Betty Ann Gunther, a lab computer programmer. "In the end, LANL is about making management look good and protecting their high salaries. Doing good work as a fraud investigator obviously doesn't make management look good. As one of my colleagues said, 'They looked into the wrong person's garage.'"

The dominoes that were lining up to topple Doran and me had now dramatically changed direction and momentum. Indeed, many current and former employees were now giving us a great deal more information about improper and illegal activities that had been occurring at the lab:

- A former employee of Johnson Controls of Northern New Mexico said he was aware of millions of dollars in fraud that involved doctored timesheets. He was willing to identify the individuals and records that were involved, and he indicated that his superiors were aware of this fraud. This information was given to the FBI.
- A former employee of the Department of Energy Inspector General said he worked on a timesheet fraud case (not associated with Johnson Controls) in the mid-1990s that involved at least $1 million. He said he completed his investigation and turned it into his superiors, but knows that nothing was ever done to prosecute the individuals involved in the fraud. This person said he was threatened that if he continued with his investigation, that, "chemicals could be placed on the seats of his personal car that would give his family cancer." This information was given to the FBI.
- A current employee of the Los Alamos National Laboratory said he was aware of a recent incident involving misappropriation of federal research funds. Another employee made a similar complaint, but within another lab division. In both cases, the individuals said the misappropriations occurred when federal funds directed for one research program were illegally diverted to other pet research projects that they could patent, and make money from it. In order to divert the money, documents forwarded to the federal government had to be doctored.
- A current employee of the lab indicated he has been fighting a retaliation and harassment case against the lab for years and it had to do with discrimination. This individual subsequently aired his situation on *CBS Nightly News with*

Dan Rather.

• An S-Division employee said he was aware of a security incident where plutonium in Technical Area-18 was left unguarded for a period of time, and officials were attempting to keep this incident from the media and the public. When news media sources attempted to get information on the incident, lab officials denied the incident had occurred. The media continued to pursue the matter and got lab officials to admit the incident had occurred, but they were unable to discover exactly how long the plutonium was unguarded.

The winter holiday season was now approaching and I had long planned to spend time with my family in and around Pennsylvania. When my new attorney, Lynne Bernabei, learned of my plans, she asked me what I planned to do with the reams of notes and other personal items I had collected to support my case. She knew I kept them at my home.

"You know you're taking on some very powerful people, Glenn," she told me. "These people have a lot to lose." I don't want to alarm you, continued Lynne, but you know it's not unusual for some whistleblowers to have their homes burglarized or burned. I know you have a security system, but you should also call the police to have them watch your house or have someone else watch your house, and you should also take all your documents to a secure storage facility for protection, said Bernabei.

I took all of her advice. Not that I hadn't thought of it before. Mullins, Doran, Agent Campbell, and I often discussed how our investigations were placing us in possible harm's way. The three of us agreed we would look out for each other and our families. Still, none of us ever felt completely safe. For example, on the night of September 25, I had just fallen asleep when Mary and I both heard footsteps on our roof. I owned a pueblo-type house with a flat-roof construction. While painting my home earlier that summer, I learned that no matter how gingerly a person may walk on that roof, if you were inside the house it sounded like the person above was about to crash through the ceiling. These footsteps were directly over the master bedroom, heading toward the east side of the house where a kiva ladder providing easy access to and from the roof was located. I quickly jumped out of bed, grabbed my .357 Magnum and a 5-cell flashlight and ran outside. By the time I got there, the person had already fled. I contacted the Santa Fe Sheriff's Department, and two deputies arrived to investigate. I told them who I was, and what I had been involved with at the lab, and I asked them to make sure the incident and my comments were recorded in their official police files. From that moment on, Mary and I were even more cautious and alert than before. As far as we knew, there were no other prowlers.

Doran encountered similar problems. After he was fired, Steve noticed several drive-bys at his Los Alamos home at all hours. He identified some of those in the vehicles as lab employees. Some of the individuals parked their vehicles near Steve's house for hours, Steve presumed, to monitor who was visiting him. Doran contacted a friend at the lab and told him to put out the word that unless the activity stopped, he would take the necessary action to stop it. There were no more drive-bys at the Doran abode after that.

When Steve and I were summonsed to University of California headquarters in California, FBI Agent Jeff Campbell offered to keep an eye on our residences. This is serious stuff you two are involved in, and it is always possible there are some people at the lab that would wish you harm, said Campbell. I will do my personal part to ensure that does not occur, continued Campbell. And Jeff did, keeping a close watch on our residences and our families during our many absences, all on his personal time.

XXV

Beheading the Organization

Responding to intense media pressure and the watchful eye of University of California President Atkinson, Director Otto Harmon revealed, for the first time on November 28 that there were serious problems at Los Alamos. "The laboratory has worked as quickly as possible to address theft and cover-up allegations while making systemic improvements," Harmon said. "The lab has been committed to management improvements since the first indication of a problem."

That same day, Bussolini and Alexander were, suddenly but finally, fired.

The university issued a memorandum to all Los Alamos lab leaders in early December concerning PriceWaterhouseCoopers' three draft review reports (dated September 16, October 8, and November 7, 2002). Presented under the authority of Shapiro and Marquez, but signed by university auditor Patrick Reed, the memo indicated his office would be reviewing the steps the university had taken to resolve management issues as proposed by PriceWater-houseCoopers.

Reed's memorandum clarified that all questionable items would be researched until resolved. A team of six university auditors would be assisted by other UC auditors, as lab management deemed appropriate and would arrive in Los Alamos on December 9 to analyze the reports. It turned out that the lab deemed Marcellaa Zambrea and Brian Richard as the "appropriate" auditing assistants. And so, on December 5, Richard Marquez ordered all employees who were giving documents to the Department of Energy Inspector General to provide copies of a set of those documents to Zambrea's attention.

In response, the Department of Energy Inspector General wrote, "The Office of Inspector General anticipates that audits, inspections, and investigations can be conducted without impediment. We are troubled by any statement that could be interpreted as hindering full and open cooperation with the Office of the Inspector General."

Backtracking, Marquez issued another lab-wide e-mail that said the instructions contained in his previous missive "may not be entirely appropriate." The mandate instructing employees to provide information to Zambrea would be suspended, but, to encourage the free flow of information, a designated laboratory point of contact would deal with documents requested by the Office of the Inspector General.

Some lab employees were skeptical. "Who is the person who will receive the documents now?" asked computer programmer Betty Ann Gunther. "How do we know the person is trustworthy and will not turn the employee in? If they really want to know what's being investigated, they should hear it from the Inspector General." Employees were laughing about Marquez's latest e-mail, Gunther said, because it showed that "management did not...understand what employees were worried about; that there is no guarantee of privacy for the person who supplies the documents."

Project on Government Oversight's Danielle Brian emphasized Gunther's concerns. "This ongoing desire to know who is talking to the Inspector General continues to be inappropriate," she told reporters. "The Inspector General should have unfettered access. Employees need to feel the freedom that management isn't going to do to them what they did to Walp and Doran."

On the day I was terminated, a top-level University of California crew sent by Atkinson arrived at Los Alamos to investigate mismanagement, fraud, and cover-up. The resulting report, presented to Atkinson on December 6 and immediately forwarded to Harmon, was accompanied by a scathing letter that did not cast Los Alamos management in a favorable light. In a word, Atkinson was furious. The report indicated that a total of $3.78 million in procurement card purchases had not been reconciled, $790,000 in questionable costs remained unresolved, more than a quarter of the 790 lab employees who had been issued procurement cards were more than 30 days late in reconciling their statements, some statements had not been reconciled for nearly two years, and Audits and Assessments staffers had frequently closed statements without verifying them.

The report also included this statement, "Where theft is involved, we understand that law enforcement officials are notified." Evidently, whoever spoke to Atkinson's crew willfully misled them on how the process worked when a theft was reported to the Office of Security Inquiries.

After Doran and I were terminated, lab officials soon announced they had updated their whistleblower policy to place it "in sync" with UC's policies. A whistleblower should be protected, University of California spokesman Jeff Garberson said, and LANL's new procedure would make the system more effective. Chris Mechels, the former lab worker who had spoken out against the company's management procedures, told reporters the whistleblower policy "… still remains woefully inadequate. You need some place where you can report a whistleblower complaint without getting your head taken off." The new policy still called for employees to report improprieties to their direct superiors, who may well be part of the problem. "At Los Alamos, there is no provision for protecting your confidentiality," Mechels said. Furthermore, even though the lab had made a point to specifically publicize a new policy, Mechels found that a search for the word whistleblower on the LANL website turned up nothing. "They don't want anybody to blow the whistle," Mechels said. *"At Los Alamos, its blow the whistle, eat the whistle."*

Apparently, lab leadership continued to float down the river called denial. Falcon had met with Office of Security Inquiries staff during the first week of December and told them, according to Mullins, that whenever an OSI inquirer identified a suspect, all information was to be given to Falcon. According to Mullins, Falcon still mandated that the information would then be forwarded to Richard, *who would ultimately decide what to do.* It seemed that despite the empire crumbling beneath the feet of lab leadership, they were attempting to maintain some semblance of control. But in Mullins' opinion, Falcon, and perhaps others above him, probably couldn't help knowing that their days of being a Los Alamos National Laboratory leader were numbered.

Scrambling to respond to Atkinson's increasing wrath, Harmon wrote, "I commit to you that I will hold my senior executive team and myself personally accountable for ensuring that all areas identified for improvement are addressed by our laboratory in a prompt manner." Harmon attached a report titled "LANL Report on Recommendations of the UC Special Review Team" in which he re-stated his late-August directive to Marquez regarding revised procurement-card procedures. "All laboratory managers and staff are expected to give unqualified and prompt cooperation to law enforcement, the Inspector General, and university personnel engaged in investigations or reviews of laboratory activity," stated Harmon in his report. Harmon listed other recommendations, including revising current procedures regarding "unlocated" property, security policies, and media communications. "With respect to the termination of the two employees of the Office of Security Inquiries," Harmon wrote, "the DOE Inspector General is including this matter in his current review. The laboratory is fully cooperating with the Inspector General and will continue to do so."

But it was too little and too late. On December 9, Representative James Greenwood told the media how upset he was with Atkinson that Doran and I had been fired. He also told Atkinson that his committee had decided to conduct a congressional investigation at the lab. The investigators would arrive in Los Alamos within the week.

"These dramatic new developments warrant a congressional investigation," committee spokesman Kenneth Johnson told the media, "and we intend to use every resource at our disposal, including hearings and subpoenas, to determine what's going on at that lab." One could only guess what Los Alamos leadership was thinking when they heard that, especially given my September conversation with Falcon, when I expressed my disgust with the attitudes of lab leaders, especially Richard, and told him the lab's misdeeds were worthy of a congressional review.

Atkinson received the official notice from the House committee on December 10, which expressed the body's frustration that the university and lab had not sufficiently addressed fraud and abuse issues. Congressman Greenwood; Louisiana Republican Billy Tauzin, the committee chairman; Michigan Democrat John Dingell; and Florida Democrat Peter Deutsch signed the letter. The committee issued a sweeping demand for new documents, including whether missing computers contained classified information, all information concerning various theft cases, the Nonproliferation and International Security Division theft case, my March theft report, all documents related to my and Doran's terminations, and Mullins' resignation (James 'Jim" Mullins resigned from lab employment shortly after our terminations — *he had had enough of LANL ways*). The committee also requested that Dennis Nally, the Price-WaterhouseCoopers chairman, send copies of all audit documents related to their review.

"Our investigators are coming to New Mexico on December 16, armed with subpoenas, to get whatever information is necessary to get to the truth," Johnson told reporters.

The latest turn of events compelled a *Santa Fe New Mexican* fiery editorial on December 11, alleging that LANL had enjoyed six decades free of serious questions from a Congress that supported it with American tax dollars, but now:

> Not even the most hawkish among senators and representatives could continue to coddle LANL's impaired management system. Although LANL's scientific knowledge is beyond question, somewhere along the way, some of them began forgetting they were public servants. Consequently, a dictatorship developed among its administrators - and woe to anyone who so much as mentions an indiscretion. We have ways of making you sorry, say the bosses without actually having to say so. In the wake of publicity generated by the Wen Ho Lee case, and the case of the missing computer hard drives, lab management hired Glenn Walp and Steven Doran to investigate theft and other problems. They did their job too well; Walp and Doran uncovered evidence that millions of dollars have been lost or stolen – or were about to be. For their efforts, Walp and Doran were fired because they didn't play well with others, or words to that effect.

Then, on December 12, more trouble surfaced when John Layton released PriceWaterhouseCoopers' final review of the lab's purchase card system. Immediately after reading the report, Harmon sent an e-mail to everyone in the lab finally revealing that some Los Alamos laboratory employees had indeed abused the trust placed in them by their colleagues and by the American public.

Secretary of Energy Spencer Abraham paid a visit to the Los Alamos National Laboratory the next day, expressing his concerns about management. Speaking to reporters, Abraham said that since his department paid the university to operate the lab, "We expect them to do it the right way. We are looking to the University of California to provide leadership. We made it very clear to them that they are responsible."

A senior Department of Energy official accompanying Abraham took it a giant step further. "The University of California runs the lab with our federal money and they have a job to do, so when they find problems, they need to fix them," he said. "If they can't do it, we'll find someone else to do it. We're here to listen, but when they (UC) find problems, they need to fix them."

The lab was even losing support of its closest allies. New Mexico Republican Senator Pete Domenici offered his own stinging criticism. "Clearly," said Domenici, "what I am hearing does not bode well for the management of this laboratory."

POGO's Stockton took that as a small, but positive sign. "The notion the administration would even consider opening up the Los Alamos contract represents progress," he said. "New management might be able to cut out entrenching bureaucrats who are failing to address problems or are causing problems. If a new contractor came in, they would pay attention to the people who cause the current problems and they would take those people out. You simply behead the organization."

Harmon seemed now to be making his last stand. He took his case to the *Albuquerque Journal*'s editorial board in a remarkable, revealing interview. Harmon indicated he wanted to run LANL more like a modern business, and, in order to do that, he needed to take a more personal role in reviewing key weaknesses in the lab's management systems. Harmon went on to say that until recently he had not been provided details on the many problems that led to the investigations by House and Senate Committees, the FBI, and the Department of Energy Inspector General. "What I need to do is really get my hands on certain issues," Harmon said. His meeting with Abraham helped crystallize the urgency; "Abraham's message was very forceful and very direct," he said. "I left that meeting with no doubt in my mind what I had to do. That included making quick changes in management philosophy, holding personnel more accountable, and being as open with the media as possible."

As for Doran and me, Harmon seemed to distance himself from our firings, saying he let his senior managers make the decision. Harmon said he was under the impression that Steve and I were trying to operate within the lab as police officers, although we were "on the right track." Harmon also said he had to improve management and make personnel changes. "I don't think I can wait a year to make changes," he said. "In some cases, we need different kinds of people with different skills, and in other cases, managers simply need more training." He admitted he should have had more knowledge about what was going on.

Yet I felt the interview also revealed that Harmon didn't have his finger on the pulse of the lab. He talked about a 1998 review of the lab's purchase card system that indicated systemic weaknesses including insufficient documentation of purchases, improper recording of assets, and policy that allowed the purchasing system to be susceptible to abuse. "Why does that not rise to my attention?" Harmon asked. "Someone should have been charged with a directive to make...changes. I am struggling to make the lab run like a business."

It is unknown to whom Otto Harmon was referring when he, expressing particular disgust, said, referring to unauthorized purchases by Bussolini and Alexander, "We had a year and no one told us about this — how am I supposed to run this place if no one tells us?" It would make sense that Harmon was probably referring to someone working in S-Division in 2001.

As for the culture of fear of retaliation that prevents employees from coming forward, Harmon said, "Somehow I've got to figure out a way to break that down."

The *Los Alamos Monitor* quickly swooped in with this editorial:

> Los Alamos National Laboratory Director Otto Har-
> mon...saying that nobody told him ... doesn't absolve
> him of accountability. While Harmon is not directly re-
> sponsible for the alleged crimes...the laboratory has
> developed a policy of "don't tell"....The main purpose
> of the lab's Public Affairs office is to prevent the flow
> of possibly damaging information. If this office must
> report something negative, it does so through care-
> fully crafted press releases. And when questioned,
> rarely does any more information come through....
> Questions of substance are not answered candidly,
> and usually not answered at all without invisible (to
> us at least) scurrying and furtive consultation....As
> some Public Affairs employees have admitted in less-
> guarded moments, nobody tells them, either....The
> "don't-tell" culture permeates the laboratory, as Steve
> Doran and Glenn Walp learned when they lost their
> jobs after telling too much. And Harmon wonders why
> nobody told him something was wrong. Somebody
> should have told, instead of thinking that by hiding the
> problems, no one would ever find out....It is a culture
> that has been fostered during at least the past few
> years, a culture that seeks to control all the informa-
> tion that leaves the laboratory for public consump-
> tion, putting the spotlight on its glorious achievements
> while hiding its ailments...lab officials, through their
> Public Affairs spokespeople, have delayed, denied
> and deceived....Not a bad thing, perhaps, when it has
> to do with national security. But it is a very bad thing
> when it means covering up malfeasance or incompe-
> tence, making it hard to hold anyone accountable for
> mistakes, failures, breakdowns or crimes....Nobody

told me, Harmon said. Nobody told us, either, probably for the same reason: fear of retribution.

Commenting on Atkinson's declaration that the lab would enforce a zero-tolerance policy regarding illegal activity at the lab, most media, including the *Albuquerque Journal North,* were skeptical, asking in an editorial, in part, "How much credence does the lab have that whistleblowers will be protected? How much credence should the public give the policy of zero tolerance for any level of illegal activity? How much credence should the public attach to lab assurances that it is doing everything it can to cooperate with federal law enforcement agencies and root out crime?" The editorial concluded by proposing — as Doran, Mullins, and I had claimed all along — that the Los Alamos National Laboratory was more interested in hiding embarrassing information than it was in straightening out its abysmal record keeping.

In short order, at least three congressional committees began looking at the lab's mismanagement problems, and Pete Stockton of Project on Government Oversight raised the question of whether the University of California should continue to be the contractor at Los Alamos. "Congress would be wise to reconsider the issue," Stockton told reporters. Then, Edith Holleman, a House Energy and Commerce Committee staffer, told the media that her group had already requested documents from the lab and had interviewed the lab contractor who sold goods to Bussolini and Alexander. Holleman indicated that committee members had considered sending representatives to Los Alamos to conduct a congressional investigation. Then Holleman telephoned Doran and me to ask if we'd cooperate if they decided to conduct an investigation of the Los Alamos National Laboratory.

"With pleasure," we responded.

XXVI

Doran and Walp Speak, Congress Listens

On December 15, Mary and I welcomed to our home three Committee on Energy and Commerce members: Edith Holleman, Ann T. Washington, and Michael Geffroy. The meeting lasted into the wee hours of the following morning because they had many questions. I had an equal number of answers. Doran hosted them the next two days, even secreting to his home under cover of darkness several lab informants who brought with them damning information to assist with the congressional investigation.

Secretary Abraham, continuing to act forcefully and quickly, sent a Christmas Eve, red-bowed package to University of California President Atkinson, which included a letter chastising him for the Los Alamos fiasco, "Of most immediate concern…are the events surrounding the dismissal of Mr. Walp and Mr. Doran, and their allegations of cover-up concerning matters they were investigating," Abraham wrote. "The inescapable conclusion is that the actions relating to Mr. Walp and Mr. Doran reflect a systemic management failure, one for which the laboratory management must be held accountable. I expect the university to continue its efforts to ensure that these failures are corrected. Taken together, these problems have called into question the University of California's ability to run the Los Alamos National Laboratory. I intend to fully evaluate the university's capacity to operate LANL, notwithstanding the 5-year contract extension."

Abraham ordered this evaluation, along with recommendations on how to move forward, by the middle of the following spring.

But before that, the university took dramatic action. Harmon and Shapiro, the university announced on January 3, 2003, were resigning. All lab Business Operations Division personnel were now reporting directly to Anne Broome, the University of California's Vice President of Financial Management, with LANL's Audits and Assessments personnel now reporting directly to University of California Auditor Patrick Reed. That took Marcellaa Zambrea out of the picture. University officials said she was being reassigned to another, undetermined position at the lab.

Harmon accepted what Doran, Mullins, and I felt was his well-deserved fate amiably by authoring a resignation letter that said in part, "I am fully accountable for the performance of Los Alamos National Laboratory in all matters. Improvements are needed in security, facility operations, business systems, and communications. More operational and administrative changes are needed at LANL, and must occur more quickly than in the past."

Shapiro refused to resign, saying the lab would have to fire him. And so they did, on January 31, 2003.

The changing of the guard was a positive development in the eyes of POGO's Danielle Brian; but she remained wary. "It's a tremendous statement for the two heads of the lab to be forced to resign, but I don't believe that by itself is going to be enough to change the culture of the lab," she said. "As long as the managers of the lab, whoever they may be, believe they have the contract for life, it's impossible for there to be any accountability. Until now, this really has been a contract for life, so why should UC take anything that DOE says seriously?"

Jay Coghlan, a member of the *Nuclear Watch of New Mexico*, said, "I think Harmondid the right thing, but the root problem is a bad manager in the form of the University of California. That management contract ought to be put out to bid."

Naturally, the media were interested in what Doran and I thought. "Everybody says they like Otto Harmon, yet these people are on our side because they say Harmon was a horrible administrator," Doran said. "They continued to cover-up and to conceal the situation at the lab, and finally they've had to pay for what they've done."

I told reporters I was elated, "...but this is just the first chapter. There will be a lot of top-level leaders...walking off that hill."

The *Santa Fe New Mexican* had this to say:

The forced resignations of Los Alamos National Laboratory Director Otto Harmon and his Deputy Director Marion Shapiro, is a first step in correcting the management problems at Los Alamos. As Secretary of Energy Spencer Abraham put it, "The nation needs the same confidence in the business management and security of Los Alamos as it has in the laboratory's weapons design and basic science." That confidence is now gone. The firing of Walp and Doran who uncovered evidence of millions of dollars in theft and losses happened with the acquiescence of lab leaders. This delivered a message to lab employees that those who point out problems are punished, not praised. America can't afford anything but the best management for our national laboratory. It is the key to the security of United States and the entire world.

Harmon was quickly replaced by U.S. Navy Retired Vice Admiral George P. (Pete) Nanos as the lab's acting director. But UC President Atkinson made a sour-grapes comment that the University of California would not compete if the Department of Energy decided to put the contract out for bid. "Such a decision is a vote of no confidence, and the university would step aside," Atkinson said. "The university can survive without the lab, and we gain nothing... in terms of funds."

Some University of California Regents were outraged by those ill-conceived remarks. They quickly chastised Atkinson, telling him his comments were not helpful to UC, and ordered him not to make such public statements in the future. And he, indeed, backtracked.

As for Madison and Falcon, the university announced on January 8 they would be reassigned to non-management positions not yet determined. But neither would take a pay cut; Madison would still make $180,000 a year and Falcon $165,000.

I liked Madison to the very end. Steve, Jim, and I always felt he tried to support us the best he could, to give us the full green light to clean up the mess, because we knew he was an honest man. His shortcoming, we opined, perhaps a weakness to pressure from above.

Falcon's shortcoming was, in our opinions, perchance kowtowing to the whims of higher authority.

What was the root cause of Madison and Falcon's eventual reassignments to non-management positions? Perhaps it was their unwillingness to jeopardize the comfort of their healthy salaries, benefits, and prestigious positions. Perchance it was that they were victims of military habit, executing orders from above unquestioningly. And maybe it was, as proposed by David Broder of *The Washington Post,* concerning some high level officials caught up in these types of situations that they "...wrestle with the conflict between their conscience and their sense of obligation to the administration in which they serve." For sure, in Steve's, Jim's, and my opinions, both

Madison and Falcon were steadfast in obeying the lab's *corporate philosophy/rule* to look out for the Los Alamos National Laboratory corporation.

That Madison and Falcon remained employed and maintained their robust salaries did not please many observers. "Allowing Madison and Falcon to stay employed at LANL is outrageous," Danielle Brian said. "It's a continuing indication of LANL's policy to protect their own. These guys keep their job at the lab while the heroes who uncovered the problems lost their jobs. What's important from the public policy standpoint, however, is that the people who weren't taking security seriously...are no longer in charge of security."

Joe Gutierrez, a lab employee who had previously won a retaliation lawsuit against the Los Alamos laboratory, agreed. "This disparity and treatment between those with the right connections and a base of power and regular workers is likely to create a division between the rank and files and management," he said. "It does not modify behavior; in fact, it reinforces that there are no consequences for letting issues slide or not doing their job."

It was the opinions of Steve, Jim, and me that Los Alamos National Laboratory leadership made it clear, that one of our jobs was to help protect the University of California's contract, and not to root out problems that would make the laboratory look bad. That was the golden thread (protecting the lab) that ran through our experiences at Los Alamos. Law enforcement learned years ago that you need to be straight with the public and the media. You need to be honest. We found that not to be the case at Los Alamos. We see a significant challenge for the Los Alamos National Laboratory is to change their culture of self-protectionism.

In another change, lab officials announced in early January 2003, that all Office of Security Inquiries' investigations concerning criminal issues would now be handled through Audits and Assessments under the supervision of Patrick Reed, the University of California auditor.

I told the media that reporting criminal issues directly to the University of California was an intelligent move. But I still believed that all national laboratory safeguards and security operations, including the protection of national secrets and the investigation into security failures, should not be under the control of a contractor because it has the potential of creating an environment ripe for protectionism and self-preservation, potentially creating serious security problems for our country.

Explaining why Doran and I were fired was raising troublesome questions for the university as it tried to clean up its Los Alamos image. A progress report the university submitted to Abraham on January 10 reported, "One of the university's highest priorities remains establishing an understanding of the facts surrounding the laboratory's dismissal of Glenn A. Walp as office leader of the Office of Security Inquiries and Steve L. Doran as OSI security specialist." The report indicated that university attorneys would be scheduling an interview with us "in order to learn first-hand their concerns about the laboratory practices and management actions regarding their investigations."

Meanwhile, the House Energy and Commerce Committee continued its investigation. Billy Tauzin and James Greenwood asked David M. Walker, the Comptroller General in the U.S. General Accounting Office (GAO), to expand its probe into UC's management practices at two of its other Department of Energy labs: The Lawrence Berkeley and Lawrence Livermore National Laboratories. Tauzin and Greenwood indicated the current allegations of procurement fraud and abuse at Los Alamos piqued their concern that significant procurement problems may not be confined to LANL. The Senate Finance Committee was already waiting for a GAO report concerning these matters.

It was now time for the University of California Regents to meet and discuss the scandal that was engulfing the lab they were purportedly managing. In his news report the day following the January 15 meeting, *San Jose Mercury News* reporter Dan Stober wrote that, historically, neither the university president nor the regents had offered the labs much direction or oversight. Some lab employees, continued Stober, claimed they regarded the labs as free-floating empires charting their own course. According to these employees, Stober wrote, the university issued the paychecks, but for most of the lab's existence, the university's oversight staff consisted of one individual. As a result, this hands-off supervision "has led inevitably to problems, from environmental negligence, security lapses, huge cost overruns and political lobbying."

Nanos, the newly appointed acting director, told the regents that in order for him to correct LANL's problems, he would be "draining the swamp." He would be making immediate personnel and management changes based on findings from a study he had initiated to develop 21st-century business systems throughout the lab. The regents wasted no time in telling Nanos they were aghast that it appeared Doran and I were fired because Los Alamos leadership allegedly was attempting to cover up a host of improprieties. Darling jumped in, claiming the university would be meeting with us within the next two days to hear our stories directly for the first time.

For nearly six hours, Doran and I, with our attorney, Lynne Bernabei, met with University of California officials in Atkinson's conference room at University of California Headquarters in Oakland, California. I provided copies of the personal notes I eventually had given to Schleck and Westfall, the two Department of Energy Inspector General investigators.

Bruce Darling, the university's interim vice president for laboratory management, told us that during his November 25 visit to Los Alamos — the day we were fired — Brian Richard told him one of the reasons for our terminations was because FBI investigators didn't like us and were angry with us. To determine if Richard's statement was true, said Darling, the university sent former U.S. Attorney Charles LaBella to interview members of the FBI and the U.S. Attorney's office. If it turned out to be false, Darling said *severe and immediate action would be taken against Richard for lying*. As

Steve and I already knew, LaBella learned that the FBI and the U.S. Attorney's office had an "extremely positive working relationship with us." In fact, the FBI gave both of us letters of commendation for assisting the FBI in their multiple LANL investigations.

Naturally, we wanted to know what was going to happen to Richard. So did members of the media.

After much prodding, finally, Nanos said, "I do believe that Richard had become too involved in the criminal investigations. I think Richard was inappropriately used. He was being assigned tasks that were not his usual duties. The way he was used was not entirely proper."

Incredibly, Richard remained untouched. Then, Nanos told the media that Richard, LANL's main lawyer, was really employed by the University of California, not the Los Alamos National Laboratory. This gave the impression that it was up to the University of California to take any action against Richard. As far as anyone was told, the University of California never did take any action against Richard, despite Darling's strong statement.

On the same day Steve and I told all to University of California officials, House Energy and Commerce leaders sent a letter to Atkinson telling him that if Doran and I were not put back on the payroll, it would "make it very difficult for the committee to view seriously UC's statements that their intent was to change the culture of secrecy at the Los Alamos National Laboratory. Your failure to take these actions will serve as yet another reminder to the thousands of hard-working personnel that those who try to do what is right will only be punished for it."

As many in the media had noted, the committee leaders wrote it was "both ironic and sad" that the only people now without a job and health benefits are the individuals who tried to correct the fraud problems at LANL, "while those who either permitted or ignored the problems continue to be gainfully employed at their own salaries with full benefits." The committee also asked Atkinson why no UC official attempted to prevent our firings on November 25, even though all were aware of our imminent terminations. The University of California's treatment of us, they wrote, has been "appalling." Almost immediately, Robert Van Ness, a university assistant vice president, in an apparent appeasement mode, told the media that the salaries of Madison, Falcon and Zambrea *would probably be cut* as soon as they were reassigned to actual positions.

Doran and I were about to be offered reparation. During the afternoon session on January 17, Darling asked both of us if we'd agree to be rehired by UC, retroactive to the date we were fired, at our same salaries as before. Our job would be to serve as President Atkinson's personal consultants in helping repair LANL's bankrupt security and management systems.

Doran and I consulted with Bernabei and then agreed to Darling's offer with a firm condition: we would be entirely independent, free to work with any and every investigative body and to communicate openly with the media. "If they continue with the plan and let us clean out the lab," Doran told a reporter, "I'm a happy man."

"Finally, someone at UC is starting to get it," Energy and Commerce spokesman Ken Johnson said. "It was the right thing to do, and it was a critically important thing to do from an investigative standpoint because potential whistleblowers would be reluctant to step forward if they can be fired without cause."

The lab nearly bungled this latest development. While speaking about our rehiring to Adam Rankin, an *Albuquerque Journal North* reporter, Pete Nanos said Doran and I had acted like "Dirty Harrys," treating lab personnel like perpetrators, when what the lab really needed were "Columbos." Bernabei was outraged and immediately complained to John Lundberg of UC's legal staff. Bernabei told Steve and me that Lundberg stated that Nanos was saying a lot of things he shouldn't be saying, and he would take care of it.

Two days later, a letter by Bruce Darling appeared in the *Albuquerque Journal North*. "I take exception to the reported comment made by Interim Director Pete Nanos," Darling wrote. "We found Walp and Doran to be credible, sincere and motivated by the best interest of the laboratory and the nation. We appreciate their cooperation in helping the university identify and end any improper, ineffective business practices, to report all criminal matters to the appropriate authorities, and to restore the nation's focus on the laboratory's pre-eminence in science and technology."

Nanos also wrote a public letter of apology. "I would like to apologize to your readership if remarks made during my recent interview were misconstrued," Nanos wrote. "Some of the remarks could be interpreted as critical of Mr. Walp and Mr. Doran. In fact, those remarks as made were critical of laboratory management for their less-than-adequate performance. Mr. Walp and Mr. Doran performed their tasks with professionalism and expertise, and are to be commended for their outstanding commitment of service to the laboratory and this nation."

Nanos' later comments were extremely complimentary to Doran and me. When we were fired, he said, "The reaction... was one of disbelief. Some of the more senior managers said they couldn't believe we did this. You don't turn away any source of data if it's credible data. The university is finding Walp and Doran credible. They did exactly the right thing in terms of rehiring them and taking advantage of what they know."

Madison was in apparent agreement with Nanos. A few months later while in Washington, D.C. attending a congressional hearing, Madison, who signed our dismissal papers, stated to POGO's Peter Stockton that firing Walp and Doran was the dumbest thing the lab could have done.

Nanos admitted that the lab's management problems were so huge that he could only implement short-term fixes between January and the time the Department of Energy Secretary decided on the contract. Still, he'd begin to lay the groundwork for long-term changes.

Soon after Nanos' comments, University of California officials said on January 17 that they no longer had confidence in the information LANL was giving them. University of California spokesman Michael Reese maintained that a case in point was Director Harmon's report in which he indicated the lab had tracked down most of the questionable transactions and missing property. Reese pointed out that after four months of intense investigating, UC had to throw up its hands and acknowledge it had no idea of the depths of the losses. Gaping holes in LANL's accounting systems could make it all but "impossible" to track down what Doran and I had been claiming; that millions of dollars in goods and property had been improperly purchased or taken by employees. LANL officials originally said they had reconciled all but $120,000 of $3.8 million in questionable purchases and transactions, but LANL and UC auditors later added $500,000 to that figure and said it could still grow. "I'm not even going to begin to defend those numbers," Reese said. "We do not have a good enough fix on these things to defend the report. Consequently, the report had been abandoned. A close examination of Harmon's report and the earlier audits makes it clear the university may have missed many of the improper transactions by lab employees because of weaknesses in the accounting system itself."

At one point, I turned to Doran and said, "Steve, tens of millions of dollars in property fell into a bureaucratic black hole. Theft was all but undetectable."

"They don't even know," Doran responded. "What's more, they may never know."

Suddenly, and unbelievably, Arleen Roybal and Eric Martinez, the two lab employees instrumental in calling attention to weaknesses in the lab's purchase card system, were told by LANL officials they were going to be reassigned. Roybal and Martinez had written critical reviews of the lab's purchase card system in 2001, but their supervisors failed to take any action. They also gave significant information to congressional investigators and Doran, Mullins, and me.

Roybal and Martinez brought their situation to the media. "We were informed that they needed to make some cosmetic changes, so Arleen and I would be reassigned to some other positions," Martinez said. "I had a choice of applying for some positions that might be available. But none of the positions they offered me matched my interest or skills."

Added Roybal: "I found these messes, I reported them, and now I'm gone?"

When a reporter contacted Nanos, he immediately acted to stop the transfers.

There was no doubt in my mind; this was another Los Alamos National Laboratory retaliatory act. Now, however, political and media pressure forced the laboratory officials to fold and reverse their actions.

So for a three-month period – between November 2002 and January 2003 – University of California and Los Alamos National Laboratory officials were reeling from congressional, public, and media blows for the first time since the inception of the Manhattan Project. Every time they attempted to defend, justify, or rationalize their blatant failings, they got slammed for their ineptness, arrogance and incompetence.

XXVII

Media Blasts

Thanks to the national and international media, the truth of the failures and corruption at the Los Alamos National Laboratory was permeated throughout the world. Headlines in international, national, and New Mexico newspapers on January 29, 2003, one day after Department of Energy Inspector General Gregory Friedman released his "Special Inquiry Regarding Operations at Los Alamos National Laboratory," validated the wrongdoing and security risks Doran, Mullins, and I had been exposing.

"Fraud Confirmed at Los Alamos Laboratory"

"Officials say Lab Theft Grossly Underreported and Workers Abused"

"Culture of Cover-Up at Los Alamos"

"Report Shows Workers Advised to Evade Investigator Questions"

"Energy Department Report Calls Whistleblower Firings Incomprehensible"

"Energy Department Blasts Los Alamos Firings"

"Energy Department Decries Los Alamos Firings"

Friedman's report was a culmination of his fact-finding mission. He and his team documented evidence concerning lab management's alleged cover-ups, illegal activities, and, even more, expressed peril for our country, because of dangerous security breaches. Doran and I felt some satisfaction when Friedman vehemently pointed out the incomprehensiveness of the lab's firing of both of us. Friedman added that he expanded his review to determine if our terminations were a result of our vocal criticisms of the lab's procedures.

Friedman's inquiry noted that a November 20 memorandum dated five days before we were fired, which stated that the lab's rationale for our terminations — that we did not get along with lab management, FBI investigators, or DOE inquirers — did not withstand scrutiny.

Friedman concluded that a series of actions constituted "flagrant management failures."

Though Doran and I already were aware of the awful truths now documented for others to read in Friedman's report, to the rest of the world the facts were appalling revelations. Some of the damning findings that had finally become public showed that the Los Alamos National Laboratory:

1. had poor or non-existent property controls, a lack of personal accountability for property, substantial dysfunction in communicating how to handle property loss and theft, and inadequate control over its purchasing systems;

2. had inadequate policies regarding the reporting of illegal activities to law-enforcement agencies;

3. had issued, then immediately rescinded without adequate explanation, a memorandum requiring corrective actions to address "disturbing negative trends regarding laboratory management of government property."

4. had published documents urging loyalty to the lab at the possible expense of disclosing potential problems. This included a memo called "Surviving Inspection and Evaluation Audit," distributed by LANL's chief information officer before the DOE was to conduct a cyber-security review in the last two months of 2002. The document was as close as it could come to explicitly proving management was guilty of cover-up activities, telling employees to "resist the temptation to spill your guts," warning them "handwritten notes can be easily damaging... they are not easily disavowed," and "finger-pointing will just make the program look bad."

Friedman's report made the Los Alamos National Laboratory look worse than bad.

About Doran's and my being fired, Friedman wrote, "These events raise doubt about Los Alamos' commitment to solving noted problems, had the potential to have a chilling effect on employees who may have been willing to speak out on matters of concern, and were inconsistent with laboratory and University of California obligations under its contract with the Department of Energy."

Friedman also skewered the lab's Audits and Assessments Office, indicating that A&A had a Code of Ethical Conduct Statement, based on the Institute of Internal Audits Code of Ethics, but the office didn't pay attention to it because it required its auditors not to use information that could damage the university, the lab, or the Audits and Assessments Office. "The code," Friedman wrote, "gave the appearance of a lack of independence for Los Alamos auditors by inappropriately ordering them to 'exhibit loyalty in all matters.'"

As for my March theft report, I felt the Department of Energy corroborated every single one of my findings. Friedman described shoddy inquiries regarding theft and property loss, inadequate security, no accountability, dysfunctional communication, and an absence of purchasing and property controls.

Most troubling to Friedman was how poorly thefts were

239

tracked. Friedman noted:

1. Even though a BUS report documented a 2001 loss of a security radio, it did not provide information about what frequencies might have been compromised.

2. The quality of lab theft reports were of such poor quality that even though they were being submitted to the Los Alamos Police Department and the FBI, those agencies were not entering them into the National Crime Information Center.

3. Even though one of the lab's counterintelligence officials, Ken Schiffer, indicated that theft of lab property could have national security implications, no questions were ever asked regarding the type of data that may have been on stolen computers, handheld radios, and digital cameras. And yet, the lab's information office released a memo on December 18, 2002, concluding that none of the 319 lost/misplaced computers or forty-four stolen computers reported between 1999 and 2002 contained classified information.

Friedman also observed that my March theft report indicated that lab employees were frequently not held accountable for lost property. Friedman's report commented that the Department of Energy Inspector General found that lab management generally chose to "write off" missing property at the end of an inventory cycle. An accounts receivable official could not recall ever having received restitution from any Los Alamos employee for a lost or stolen item for which he was responsible.

As for the "drop points" where new equipment was delivered, Friedman protested that many were in open spaces with little or no security.

Control over purchase cards was non-existent. The lab failed to reconcile monthly statements, failed to resolve disputed transactions, and failed to properly account for controlled property, the report said. In addition, many restricted items were purchased in violation of lab policy, insufficient documentation existed for purchases, sanctions for non-compliance were inadequate and ineffective, purchase-approvers received insufficient training, audit and review procedures were lacking, and cardholders' spending limits were not properly managed.

Finally, Friedman concluded that the Department of Energy would not be responsible for paying for the inquiries or for any monetary settlements offered to Doran or me. The university would have to foot the bill.

My telephone continually rang that day as reporters sought my reaction.

"The report overwhelmingly confirms everything I have been saying," I said. "The lab is riddled with theft, and lab managers are obsessed with protecting their golden calf; the DOE contract."

Doran chimed in, too. "The report's indication that our firings did not withstand scrutiny and that the timing of the terminations was suspect pretty much says everything we've been saying," he said.

Hearing the evidence, Congress was incensed. James Greenwood, the Pennsylvania congressman, declared, "I am appalled at what we have learned about the thievery that has occurred at the laboratory."

Massachusetts Representative Edward Markey took it even further. "The verification of the allegations of mismanagement, cover-up, and retaliation against the brave individuals who were just trying to keep Los Alamos secure is yet another reason to remove the contract from the University of California. You also have to wonder why DOE isn't taking a look at the university's contract for Livermore as well, in light of this report. Enough is enough."

Or, as POGO's Stockton said, hopefully, "It's a nail in the coffin of the contract."

For their part, university and lab officials appeared contrite. "Guilty as charged," admitted Atkinson.

"We accept the blame; there are no excuses," Darling added.

University of California Regents told Atkinson in so many

words to fix it, and fix it now.

Nanos, the lab's acting director, said he would move as quickly as possible to strengthen the management of the lab. Directing his comments to unnamed lab officials, Nanos said simply, "You guys did some really dumb things."

No one commented on how the mismanagement possibly would, or already had, jeopardized the important work going on at the nuclear lab by not adequately protecting secret discoveries, materials and data.

XXVIII

On the Eve of the Hearings

On the dawn of Groundhog Day, 2003, University of California officials had to be hoping they wouldn't have to weather six more weeks of stormy publicity. But dark clouds shrouded their skies as they continued to be pelted by heavy rain from Department of Energy Inspector General Gregory Friedman's devastating January 28 report. Then on February 3, United States President Bush released his budget proposal, which included a declaration that a blue-ribbon commission would be empanelled to help decide when national laboratory contracts should be open to competitive bidding. The proclamation would long echo in terms of the tempestuous impact it would have on United States' national laboratories.

A week after Bush's announcement, and with lucid understanding that the University of California's contract with Los Alamos was in definite jeopardy, University of California spokesman Michael Reese tried to stop the grind stone by saying the most recent university audit reduced the amount of potentially misspent LANL funds from $4.9 million to $195,246. Reese said UC was "pleased" that the lab was able to document or justify the majority of the transactions questioned in the previous, very damning review. However, just a few weeks earlier, Reese had declared the university no longer had any confidence in LANL reports because of the errors they contained. But now, suddenly, only four percent of questionable purchase card transactions were now in dispute.

Acting Director Pete Nanos led off with a blustery report. "There is good and bad there," he said, "but the transactions still in question are a fairly localized problem."

Politicians now alerted to the storm at Los Alamos were not accepting the balmy local weather report. "This stuff; this is just the tip of the iceberg," Bart Stupak, a House Energy and Commerce Committee member, said. "Lab officials are just picking out a couple of them and saying, 'We're doing something about it,' but they have a long way to go." As Stupak suggested, the report only addressed a minor portion of purchase-card transactions - less than five million dollars of a thirty-five million dollar-a-year purchasing system. The University of California, feeling heavy squalls were coming despite a momentary calm, issued a press release that notwithstanding the months of work that had gone into the new review, the report had a "very limited" scope.

An incredulous Doran pointed out after reading the report that it failed to include the already-verified improper purchase card purchases that amounted to over two million dollars.

University of California officials seemed confused at a press conference when they were questioned about the purchases. Reese didn't answer the issue, but he admitted that University of California auditors found employees who made unauthorized purchases. To mollify those who might not have been paying attention, Bruce Darling said the university would negotiate to repay the Energy Department for any misspent money.

"The audit was a step in the right direction," said House Energy and Commerce Committee spokesman Ken Johnson, "but from our perspective, it's not good enough merely to say, 'Oops, sorry, we'll pay the money back.' We need to determine if fraud and theft were involved as well."

Before he was asked to resign as lab director, Otto Harmon indicated his desire to conduct a wall-to-wall inventory – the lab's first in five years. Nanos followed through on that wish beginning on February 2. More than sixty lab management employees were involved. The inventory was supposed to track down "every" piece of lab equipment worth at least $5,000, or deemed "sensitive/attractive." That meant, however, that an item costing $5,000 in December 2002 but depreciated to $4,999 by the time of this inventory would not be scrutinized.

Rich Gitto said that 96 percent of the lab's 78,984 inventoried items had been tracked down, accounting for about 98 percent of the inventory's total value.

As with the university's claim that only $195,000 in questionable purchases remained unsolved, some skeptical individuals found the numbers less than believable. Jeffrey Allen, a staffer working on the inventory told Doran:

> There are thousands upon thousands of items worth millions and millions of dollars that were not part of the wall-to-wall search. One of the BUS property personnel I was working with told a person who could not find several laptops that he was responsible for, "Don't worry about it, they must have been salvaged, don't you think?" We can complete the form (Report of Lost, Damaged, or Destroyed Property) and take them off the system. And that's what they did – and they did it many times. And I observed it.
>
> It was impossible for the lab to do a wall-to-wall search within the timeframe allotted.
>
> Realistically, it would take years just to get

the paperwork straight to know where to even begin to do a proper inventory. The wall-to-wall inventory was the biggest farce I've ever encountered. We were told that if we could not find anything, accept the word of the responsible person, and don't question it, just close out the books. When spokespeople for the lab came out saying they found nearly all the items, I felt people were scared about losing the contract and their jobs and they would have done anything to save themselves and the contract.

In his annual State of the Laboratory address, Nanos said the university was on track to win the upcoming competition for management of LANL, citing the success of the wall-to-wall inventory. There were those who knew that not all of the lab's property was found. Not even close.

Doran, Mullins, and I had repeatedly discovered a culture in which it was a lot easier at the lab to "fix" things than to do the right thing. We learned another glaring example of that troubled state. Two laboratory informants told Doran that when the laboratory set about to address the deficiencies presented in John Layton's final PriceWaterhouseCoopers report, they were told to just fix it; we don't care how you fix it, just make the numbers match. One of the ways, continued the informants, they did that was to change policy; that's what they did with morale-fund items. For example, said the informants, before the PriceWaterhouseCoopers report it was against lab policy to buy morale items with purchase cards, so they changed the rule to get the books to work. Another method Business Office personnel used was to destroy or delete every document they could when they found items they could not justify, said the informants. And the constant stream of camping gear the lab purchased? They'd just record, alleged the informants, the items under a category that said it was needed for research testing; for example, clothing purchases became uniforms."

246

When they couldn't take it any longer, said the informants, they complained directly to their boss. According to the informants, their boss told them, I don't care what's going on; my fucking job is to protect Otto Hermon.

Calls for a congressional hearing were getting louder and more frequent. On February 19, James Greenwood, the chairman of the Oversight and Investigation Subcommittee of the House Energy and Commerce Committee, announced that the first hearing on Los Alamos would be held in a week. "Our responsibility," he said, "is to find out how it is that the procedures and personnel at Los Alamos enabled employees to steal hundreds of thousands of dollars worth of merchandise from the federal government."

Greenwood indicated the hearings would proceed as a series of steps. "You have the lab, which has the responsibility to supervise its employees. You have the university, whose responsibility is to supervise the lab. You have the Department of Energy, whose job is to oversee the University of California. And you have the White House, whose job it is to oversee its administration."

According to Greenwood, I, Doran, Bruce Darling from the university, a Department of Energy Inspector General representative, and "a secret witness" would be the first ones to testify.

The day before the hearings began Friedman released another Los Alamos audit report. This one caused shudders among those reading and hearing about it. Officials could not accurately account for the loss of potentially dangerous items including more than 1,600 machine guns, pistols, rifles and other weapons – and what was worse, several previous inventory checks had failed to uncover those discrepancies. In response, the University of California released a "Lab Update" the following day that contained this headline: "UC Vows to Fix Problems, Restore Confidence." The University of California was taking full responsibility for the business and administrative problems at the Los Alamos National Laboratory, the story went, and it was aggressively implementing the changes necessary to strengthen financial controls, improve the governance of the lab and restore confidence in the Los Alamos National Laboratory and the University of California's management role.

It was no surprise to us that the public and other authorities, by now, were not convinced.

XXIX

Turbulent Congressional Hearings Begin

As promised by Representative James Greenwood, Congress held three hearings to uncloak the alleged rampant deception and deceit committed by Los Alamos National Laboratory officials. Every significant detail uncovered by our inquiries would be reviewed, and many significant actors in this morality play would turn in significant performances. Greenwood chaired the hearings on February 26, March 12, and May 1, 2003 under the auspices of the Oversight and Investigation Subcommittee of the House Energy and Commerce Committee.

Los Alamos National Laboratory and University of California officials were unmercifully pummeled by the bipartisan committee for their "dereliction of duty," "Keystone Cops performance," and for presiding over "a den of thieves."

Doran and I, along with a secret witness, Jaret McDonald, were selected to be on the first witness panel during the February 26 hearing, "Procurement and Property Mismanagement and

Theft at Los Alamos National Laboratory," which dealt in large part with the thefts committed by Bussolini and Alexander. McDonald was now employed by Kellog-Brown and Root, Inc., who recently acquired LANL's maintenance construction contract, replacing Johnson Controls of Northern New Mexico; he and fellow employee James Stewart made the complaint in the spring of 2002 that alleged the wholesale theft within the Nonproliferation and International Security Division.

Committee members were not shy about letting their strong feelings be known in their first statements. To open the hearing, Greenwood said, "The situation we begin to confront today is not your run-of-the-mill theft and misuse of taxpayer property. We must examine a disturbing breakdown in management controls and oversight at, of all places, an institution that pursues research critical to the nation's security. Simply put, cases of theft, misuse, and loss of government property are not aggressively investigated and usually no one is held accountable when it occurs."

Florida Representative Peter Deutsch referred to "the disgraceful treatment of loyal employees who tried to bring problems to management's attention and get them fixed," and then referred to our terminations. He gave his forceful opinion that "Mr. Shapiro and Mr. Richard had [Walp and Doran] fired based on flimsy justifications, which they knew were false. The real reason was that they were not protecting the laboratory and its contract with DOE. The entire management of Los Alamos National Laboratory needs a complete overhaul. It's not enough to say that there's great science at the lab. Employees have to remember that they are public servants that the public trusts and those individuals who bring fraud, waste, abuse and mismanagement to the lab's attention should be honored, not pursued and ostracized in their community."

Louisiana Representative Billy Tauzin, the chairman of the House Energy and Commerce Committee, zeroed in on "an utter lack of interest by senior laboratory managers to do anything about the theft and fraud that was going on right under their noses. Management turned its back on the good guys trying to make matters right."

Illinois Representative Jan Schakowsky noted, "What troubles me most is the retaliation against Los Alamos personnel who tried to investigate allegations of abuse of taxpayer funds."

At that point, Greenwood introduced McDonald to the committee, calling him the first employee to call attention to fraudulent purchases at the lab.

McDonald testified that he first became suspicious when he saw objects including lock picks, gate openers and two-way radios that were not related to facility maintenance tasks stored in bunkers at TA-35 and TA-33.

When Doran began his testimony, Deutsch asked him about a lab employee's recent misuse of the purchase system. Doran injected a note of levity. He related that when the employee, carrying a number of items, approached the cash register, the young woman behind the counter said, "You'd better purchase everything now, because this program will probably be ending very soon."

"And then they just laughed," Doran said.

Doran testified that Bussolini and Alexander bought items that should have been bar-coded "sensitive" but weren't. The frightening possibilities were obvious to all listening.

When it was my turn, Oregon Representative Greg Walden asked me if I believed the University of California should continue to have the contract. "I think it's time to gut the place," I said. "I think it's time for change. If they're truly serious about changing, then they need to get rid of the people that are there."

I repeated that mantra a bit later when California Representative Anna Eshoo, Democrat-California, asked, "How much do we need to do to cut the cancer out of the organization?"

"You need to get rid of the whole top layer," I said forcefully.

"Do you believe that would cleanse the culture?"

"If you gut it but you bring in the same type of thinking, then it's going to go back to exactly where it was before."

I was more than willing to discuss how, in my opinion, Richard, as the lab's head lawyer, continuously interfered and obstructed my office's investigations and inquiries.

Walden agreed with me, and, then referring to the litany of thefts at the lab, he said, "This is so outrageous it is hard to know where to start."

Naturally, the primary concern was whether the thefts and cover-up were related to possible security breaches. I explained that that had always been my concern. I testified, "Here we had Bussolini and Alexander — people who changed light bulbs — who had the keys to the kingdom of the most secret, blackest areas of Los Alamos. They had items in their possession such as GPS systems, GPS locator systems, high-tech night-vision binoculars, high-tech cameras, radio-frequency detectors, lock picks, and glass-cutting devices."

In her opinion, lab managers, Schakowsky mused, knew about many of the problems, ranging from lack of controls on purchase cards to inadequately investigating theft. "And yet," she said, "the lab did nothing until the matter reached Congress and the media."

"My concern," Michigan Representative Mike Rogers said, "is if you're willing to steal, you're willing to sell information as well."

I vehemently agreed with his assessment, which implied the possible perils for our country in such actions. As I had mentioned in my exchange with Schakowsky, I said, "These people had the highest clearance you can get. One of the factors, when you do backgrounds, is you make sure people are not involved in such things as gambling and prostitution, because they're vulnerable. Here are individuals who are walking away with the farm, and if you had someone from the outside walk up to them and say, 'Look, I know what you're doing, and you either give me what I want or we're going to report you to the police,' then it could place these individuals in an extremely high vulnerability positions. Did anything like that happen? Probably not. Could have? Yes, it could have happened. How can you let that happen in the premier lab in the world, to let that go on without anybody knowing about it?"

"You say it probably didn't happen," Rogers said, "but you don't know for sure if it did or not."

True.

The second witness panel, represented by Gregory Friedman, the Department of Energy Inspector General, first dealt with the retaliatory nature of Doran's and my terminations. His testimony essentially repeated the findings and conclusions of his January 28 report. Again, the discussion reverted to thefts and security issues. "I would not necessarily express a great deal of confidence in the final conclusion that there was no sensitive or classified information compromised in the thefts or property loss," Friedman said. "With 400 computers in three years ... according to the lab's own figures, there can be no guarantees that security was not compromised."

Friedman concluded his testimony with his opinion that the lab contract be put up for bid. "Based on the work that we've done," he said, "is that maximizing competition is in the best interest of the taxpayers."

The university, represented by Bruce Darling, got a chance to state its case on the third witness panel. "I'm not here to offer any excuses whatsoever," he said. "To the contrary, the University of California accepts full responsibility." Among the actions the university has undertaken to correct the many issues were to rehire Walp and Doran, take over direct control of the lab's Audits and Assessment activities, rescind A&A's loyalty oath, and correct the drop-point distribution system.

He said that the university was oblivious to all the wrongdoings because the lab's culture of protecting its own interests was far too ingrained. Darling admitted how troubled he was when he first heard that the lab was "greening the valley" because as "one of the largest economic forces in Northern New Mexico, it made it a very attractive target for thieves, drug trade, or others who might want to prey on the laboratory."

But why, Darling was asked, did the lab allow many of the managers responsible for oversight failures to stay on the payroll with six-digit salaries even after they were removed from management positions? Darling responded that fifteen senior managers had been fired or removed as managers, and provided a list.

That didn't appease Greenwood, for one. "Clearly, some of these people have to go," he said. Why wouldn't Madison and Falcon, for example, "Be out on their ear?"

Because, Darling responded, each had a long and distinguished career with the laboratory.

"Rewarding managers who didn't serve LANL well doesn't fix the problem," Eshoo said.

"Neither did firing those who did serve the lab well," Greenwood stated. "Who made the decision to fire Doran and Walp?"

"I think Madison signed the letter and whether he made the decision or whether Mr. Shapiro made the decision, I think there is some difference of interpretation," Darling said. "I think both might claim responsibility."

Furthermore, Darling admitted there was no evidence that the FBI or U.S. Attorney were displeased with our level of cooperation. "And who was it that said the FBI and the U.S. Attorney's Office were dissatisfied with the gentlemen?" Greenwood asked.

"It was believed to be either Mr. Shapiro or Mr. Richard, or both of them," Darling said. "Shapiro was interviewed and said the FBI thought the laboratory had blown one of the cases, and he attributed the blame to Walp and Doran. Richard however, said that he felt the FBI was saying that it was Shapiro who had blown the case by pushing too hard and preventing the FBI from doing the necessary investigative work that it needed to do."

"What did Mr. Shapiro tell you about his concerns about Walp and Doran obtaining whistleblower status?" Greenwood asked.

"He informed us that the timing of their termination was related to the DOE IG visit, and that he was concerned," Darling said. "He felt that their performance was not adequate, and he was concerned that if they were allowed to meet with the DOE Inspector General on that occasion that would give them, in some technical sense, whistleblower status, and it would make it harder for the laboratory to terminate them for the reasons they felt they should be terminated."

Deutsch said the committee was aware that Richard "was actually working on a daily basis to try to get these two gentlemen fired. Instead of providing legal advice, he also had an operating role." If Richard was responsible for the terminations, then why was he still employed by the university, Deutsch asked. "A meeting will take place early next month with the FBI and the U.S. Attorney that *will allow us to make a decision about Richard*," Darling replied.

Doug Madison, Brian Richard, Marion Shapiro, and Bruce Darling were called to testify at the second round of congressional hearings on March 12. Again, Greenwood presented opening comments about the fact that two weeks before, they had heard very troubling testimony from investigators at the lab.

Then Greenwood noted an appraisal that gave the lab ratings of "excellent" in its procurement and property management areas for Fiscal Year 2000. Yet how could the lab receive those ratings "given the testimony we heard two weeks ago?"

Deutsch brought up the Appendix O commitments the university agreed to in 2000 that were meant to strengthen management procedures in the wake of the lost hard drive and Wen Ho Lee scandals — and which would result in the university's being eligible for $4.7 million in at-risk funds. Even though the university received $3.7 million for its performance rating on October 9, 2002, "have the goals of Appendix O been met?" Deutsch asked.

"The implementation under Appendix O appears to have been incomplete at best," said Deutsch. "The security operations were, and are, in shambles. Mr. Madison proposed strategic staffing with nationwide advertising to find a new OSI Office Leader [so that the lab could meet Appendix O standards]. He wanted someone who could investigate and develop root-cause analysis and solutions. The white hats — consumer service — and the black hats — inquirers — were to be sharply defined and organizationally separated. The hiring of Mr. Walp and Mr. Doran as black hats was a direct result of this effort. Quickly, they were expected to serve Mr. Richard and Mr. Shapiro, the main customers inside the laboratory, rather than to work with law enforcement agencies to root out and fix the problem. Despite Mr. Madison's name of black hats, they just did not fit in. The reasons Glenn Walp and Steve Doran did not fit in was because they uncovered problems and told people about them. They did not put their loyalty to UC above that of the taxpayer."

Walden then began his questioning, starting with a forceful query. He said he was looking forward to hearing the explanation behind our firings. "It is also important to note that the FBI thought very highly of Mr. Walp and Mr. Doran, which is highlighted in Mr. Madison's notes from a conversation he had with an FBI agent."

And Tauzin complained about "what amounts to looting at the lab. Theft of taxpayer dollars and property is bad enough, but this goes beyond that."

New Mexico Representative Thomas Udall went straight to Shapiro and began his questioning. "Several times in your written statement you claim that you had no knowledge that Walp and Doran had claimed whistleblower status," Udall said. Yet in Darling's testimony, when he said he asked Shapiro to explain the firings, he said Shapiro was "afraid that Walp and Doran would achieve whistleblower status and that their new status would prevent LANL from firing them within their probationary period. Darling also told committee staff that you told him that you suspected Walp and Doran had sent the 30-pound box of documents to the *Albuquerque Journal* and you wanted to stop the leaks, so you fired Walp and Doran. Your testimony is inconsistent with Darling's."

Shapiro responded, "I wanted to make sure we did it so that it did not appear to be they were being terminated because of a retaliatory component." He also denied accusing Doran or me of releasing the documents to the *Journal*.

Shapiro further testified that the decisions to terminate were made after the October 24 meeting with the U.S. Attorney and the

FBI, and that he, Richard, Madison, Holt, and Marquez were all at the meetings when the decision was made. The termination letter originated in Shapiro's office, and Harmon knew about it, he added.

"Would it be appropriate to say that the IG request never would have taken place had these stories (*The Energy Daily*, etc.) never been leaked or the anonymous letter sent?" Walden asked Shapiro.

"I would have had no reason."

And what about the lab's relationship with the FBI after Doran and I came in? Walden told Shapiro that Doran had said the FBI and the lab had begun to cooperate better than ever, and cited documents and statements made by FBI Agent Jeff Campbell as proof. Why would the lab say poor relations contributed to our firings? Hadn't Shapiro known about it?

Shapiro responded he had known.

"How then could senior management place the blame on them for blowing the case?" Walden queried.

"I was personally advised by Jeff Campbell that he was very comfortable and felt that Walp and Doran were doing a competent job," said Shapiro, adding that it was a statement made by the U.S. Attorney that the lab had used against us.

"The U.S. Attorney looked at me and said, 'You, the laboratory, blew the case.' I never pursued what was actually meant by that statement."

"My natural reaction would be," Walden retorted, "what do you mean, 'We blew it?' Tell me more. Did anybody ask that of them?"

"No," Shapiro replied.

Representative Eshoo wasn't satisfied. "Can anyone of you give me the short version of why Doran and Walp were fired?" she asked.

"I accept the responsibility for that," Shapiro replied.

"I know you do, but what was the reason for it?"

Although I was hoping for a response, it was really a rhetorical question from Eshoo, and served as a launch pad for the next series of piercing statements. "Your testimony today reminds me of someone from the outside looking in rather than from people that were in charge. During your time, did you oversee and root out this culture that you refer to? What did you do on your watch? In my view, not very much. Otherwise, we wouldn't be here. What did you root out? My observation is you were very adept at knowing who to call outside the institution, but there is a dereliction of duty here. You have more than made reference to what you knew to be wrong, except you didn't do anything about it. I appreciate the fact, Mr. Shapiro that you have come from a law enforcement background, but this sounds like the Keystone Cops to me."

Shapiro replied stammering, "Well, I would address the fact that we did do things and we were proactive and aggressive," he began before Eshoo interjected and snapped, "I don't know what they are, because you are not able to be specific."

Soon, Greenwood introduced a December 11, 2002, e-mail sent to the lab's James Holt with the subject line, "Rationale for Terminations." It said Doran and I had dragged our feet on one case, that we had the case for four days before it was totally taken over by the FBI. "I am not sure how much foot-dragging you do in four days", said Greenwood cryptically. "Do you think Walp and Doran dragged their feet, all four of them, in four days? And, isn't it the case that your office was informed about the NIS theft case in September of the year before?"

Greenwood referred to the admissions of Madison, Richard, and Shapiro that the Office of Security Inquiries knew about the Nonproliferation and International Security Division situation as early as fall 2001, months before Doran and I were hired, but the Office of Security Inquiries took no action.

Madison seemed to blame the FBI based on Marty Farley's memo indicating that he had contacted the FBI, but the FBI in turn failed to do anything. Greenwood pressed, asking for documentation proving the FBI had been contacted, but Madison didn't produce any proof. Greenwood continued his interrogation, wondering out loud what Doran and I had done wrong.

"Can you shed any light on this?"

"I do not subscribe to the notion that there was foot dragging," Shapiro replied.

Walden then went on to talk about specifics. He took time to detail and point out how absurd some of the lab's official purchases actually were.

"I have no knowledge of these," Shapiro said.

Nevertheless, in our opinions, point made.

Walden then turned to Richard, asking whether he discussed with Shapiro the possibility that Doran and I could achieve whistleblower status. Richard said that he did. What role, Walden wanted to know, did Harmon play in the termination decisions?

"He relied upon others and was provided with information before the decision was made."

"Was he actively involved?"

"He was informed before the action took place," said Richard.

"Was the procedure used to terminate Doran and Walp as probationary employees' standard practice?"

"No...," Richard said.

Eshoo picked up where Walden left off. "Is this the very first time on your watch that anyone has raised serious questions where they were caught in some probationary period? Were there others fired that we may not know about?"

Again, her questioning became more rhetorical. "The issues Doran and Walp raised were clearly not appreciated. If I were entitled to characterize this panel, I would say that it is a panel of denial. ... As stewards of a public place and a public contract, I don't know what it would take to get your attention to the things that really mattered."

Shapiro, not surprisingly, attempted to justify the decisions to the committee. At one point, he said the lab brought in an external review team – no doubt, PriceWaterhouseCoopers, to begin looking at the problems of purchasing. "External, internal - Walp and Doran didn't count into this?" Eshoo said, cutting off Shapiro.

"I think you have failed the good people who are part of this place," she continued. "In order to restore confidence both to the policy makers and to the American taxpayer, this place has to be hosed out. I don't think people should be rewarded by contracts. I think that you have failed her [UC] by what you have done and what you have not done. If there is anything that has underscored that today, it is…the denial panel. This is not a management team in my view. I believe this can be fixed, but I don't have confidence in terms of the people.that are still left in charge."

XXX

The Hearing Heats Up

Now Greenwood took his turn again. He wanted to know how evidence was historically safeguarded at the lab. Madison replied, "You put it in the chain of custody and you lock it up in the evidence locker or in a vault." I felt this reply showed his ignorance of what had occurred in the Office of Security Inquiries before my arrival.

The fact is the Office of Security Inquiries never had a professional system of property control until I directed Nguyen to create one.

Greenwood wanted to know from Shapiro and Madison why neither Doran nor I were allowed to defend ourselves after we were fired. "They asked for their resignations and then when they weren't forthcoming, they were terminated two weeks later," Madison said.

And yet, Greenwood said, in one investigation of an employee, it had taken six months to reach a conclusion, and it's now going before a board. "Will that employee have the opportunity to present their side of the story?"

"Yes, they will," Richard said.

Greenwood wanted to know why these were being handled differently from ours.

"Walp and Doran are people looking for perpetrators of crimes," Greenwood retorted. "They are given no opportunity whatsoever to defend themselves. They are told to leave, to resign. They don't resign and they are told that they are fired. They are given a half-hour to get out. An employee in a case the FBI investigated is now going to come before a board. Why would these two matters of dismissal of an employee be handled in such radically different fashions? The answer is because they were on probation?"

"Yes...," Richard replied.

Greenwood continued, "I would assume that is the way you treat all probationary employees: You make allegations about them; they are not afforded an opportunity to respond, and out they go. The allegations against them could be absolutely false but because they are on probationary status, they don't get to offer up their side of the story or defend themselves in any kind of process. Is that the way it is?"

"That is correct...," Richard said.

"That sounds like a terrible policy," Greenwood retorted.

Florida Representative Jim Davis told Darling he was concerned that neither Shapiro nor Richard practiced operational formality or management discipline in their dealings with Doran and me. Both of them, Davis alleged, moved out of their designated roles to try to run criminal investigations instead of leaving that job to us. "Shapiro wanted to direct one FBI investigation on a daily basis," said Davis. "Richard wanted to be in charge of the NIS investigation and control all the communications with the FBI and the U.S. Attorney's office."

Darling's admission was startling. "There were five people who met with me at the laboratory," he said. "All of our views were that Walp and Doran were being held to more an exacting standard than laboratory management was holding other employees, or holding itself."

I felt the reasoning, rationales, excuses, and stories would be flabbergasting to those listening or reading about these hearings. When Darling told Walden he agreed with the Department of Energy Inspector General's comment that our firings were "incomprehensible", this exchange took place:

"If everybody agrees that it is incomprehensible," Walden asked, "then why is it the person who did the firing, and signed the letter, wasn't fired without compensation?"

"Shapiro was terminated without compensation," Darling replied.

"Madison signed the letter, didn't he?"

"Yes, he did."

"And Madison was still being paid his salary," said Waldren. Darling tried to weave his way through an explanation saying that on November 18, when Darling and Co., were at Los Alamos to find out facts, Madison believed he was the one who fired Walp and Doran, but as the day wore on it appeared that Shapiro actually did the firing.

"That is the most bizarre story I've ever heard in employment, and I have been a private employer for 17 years," Walden objected. "I don't understand how somebody thinks they are letting somebody go, and then discovers they really didn't do it."

"That's another instance of troubling issues that left us not only perplexed but troubled," Darling began. Greenwood sharply interjected, "My wife just got me to buy her new drapes and she convinced me it was my idea."

"The problem with the University of California, Mr. Darling," said Representative Markey, "is that they thought they could spray Windex on anything and it would make it okay, like the father in *My Big Fat Greek Wedding.*"

The third panel of the second set of congressional hearings included testimony from Otto Harmon, former Los Alamos Business Office team leader John Hernandez, Los Alamos Associate

Director for Administration Richard A. Marquez, former University of California Vice President for Laboratory Management John P. McTague, Los Alamos Director of Procurement Stan Hettich, and Ralph E. Erickson, the manager of the National Nuclear Security Administration office at Los Alamos.

First, Greenwood focused on the significant numbers of sensitive lost items that were not bar-coded. Desktop computers, pocket PCs, printers, scanners, workstations, network servers, and laptops were not tagged.

"How can anyone sit here with a straight face and say that this property management system is not severely flawed? Who among you had direct responsibility for the purchase card program?" Hettich signaled that he was the man. "How can you justify a self-approval system within the purchase card program?" Greenwood asked.

After much stumbling, Hettich ultimately responded, "I personally disagree with that idea. I agree with you."

"How long have you personally disagreed with that," asked Greenwood?

"I have to admit, I didn't realize that is actually how the structure was," Hettich replied.

Greenwood stared at Marquez and said, "Past procurement card audits dating back to 1998 identified the same systemic issues with the program time and time again."

Like Hettich, Marquez stammered before ultimately agreeing with the system's fallacies. "You have to have sanctions for people that abuse purchase cards," he said.

"As my daughter would say," Greenwood replied, "'Duh.'"

Regarding the Mesa contract, Marquez admitted, "Oversight was clearly not enough. I can't defend why that contract was structured."

Walden paused to reflect. "We have heard today, and before, that there wasn't just cause to fire Walp and Doran. They were the whistleblowers. They identified the problems, and they were fired inappropriately. The people who fired them have been dismissed with a nice severance parachute."

Walden turned to Erickson of the National Nuclear Security Administration, and asked how his Los Alamos office could rate LANL as excellent, despite all the problems that had arisen at that time? Erickson told Walden they did lower it, by one rating grade.

"Just one grade?" said Walden.

"Unfortunately, NNSA didn't take a transactional look at how things really crossed the line between procurement and property and things like that," Erickson said, his voice barely audible. "This year, based on what we found and what we learned, we are changing that process."

The day before the May 1 hearing, Energy Secretary Spencer Abraham announced other entities would be allowed to compete for the rights to manage the lab, which Billy Tauzin called "the equivalent of a political earthquake."

Greenwood began, "Given the length of time UC operated without the threat of competition, it appears that it has been lulled into a state of irresponsible complacency."

Deutsch added, "Laboratory management became arrogant and defiant over the years. When problems were uncovered, they made promises to Congress and others about how they were going to fix them, promises the university took few steps to fulfill....We have found missing hard drives and other classified electronic media for which there are no acceptable explanations. The entire business financial system is in shambles, as is its internal auditing system."

"There is a great deal of blame to spread around," Michigan Representative John Dingell said, "but most of it belongs on the backs of the University of California."

At one point in the final set of hearings, with witness Kyle E. McSlarrow, Deputy Energy Secretary, and Linton Brooks, Acting Administrator for NNSA, Deutsch noted, "It appears that you (Brooks) and Mr. McSlarrow think that most of these problems were of recent origin, even though the DOE Inspector General has been bringing business control problems to DOE's attention for years. The Inspector General said in 2000 and 2001 it could not sign off on the allowability of costs for Los Alamos. Where was DOE and where was NNSA at that point in time?"

"Not where we should have been," Brooks admitted. "The Inspector General has consistently found that the audit function at the lab was ineffective. The university has found that. I cannot explain why we didn't stumble on that fact earlier. In hindsight it's glaringly obvious, and I can't explain why my oversight didn't find that."

Michigan Democrat Bart Stupak threw his own darts. "What is it in big science that prevents us from properly handling computers with classified information? Why would big science prevent us from losing them and not find them?"

"It wouldn't, and it shouldn't, but it has", said Brooks, who obviously felt the sting.

"This OIG report tells me there is a culture there that has to be changed, and I don't see it changed," said Stupak.

"I couldn't agree more, and people have to be held accountable," McSlarrow responded.

"Are you going to hold yourself accountable?"

"Absolutely."

"What are the consequences if it doesn't work?"

"If we fail, we leave," McSlarrow said.

Turning to Brooks, Stupak said, "If the chairman holds a committee hearing next January and things aren't going well, and we still have missing computers, it's my understanding that you guys are going to resign?"

"Actually the way I read the secretary's letter, I may not have to. The secretary (Abraham) has directed me to keep him informed and is tasking back to me, and I didn't read that as bringing him excuses."

The Department of Energy Inspector General Gregory Friedman was the hearing's second witness. Greenwood opened the discussion with the now-well-known but glaring statistics pointing out the weakness of the Local Vendor Agreements that allowed hundreds of thousands of dollars of purchases not tied to legitimate business purposes.

"Do you think the University of California could pull itself up by its business-operation boot straps and start running those portions of the lab effectively and efficiently?" Greenwood asked Friedman.

"I think the jury is out...and remains to be seen," Friedman responded.

Deutsch and Friedman proceeded to engage in an animated give-and-take on the lab's lack of financial controls. It ended by Deutsch asking, "How does Los Alamos compare financial controls in place by other contractors?" He went on asking a penetrating question. "Is it the worst you've ever seen?"

The answer was even sharper. "As far as we're concerned, it's the worst."

Then Deutsch proceeded to the important issue of the high marks the lab received from the Department of Energy for its protection of classified material. "You state that you found such weaknesses in the lab's control of computers used for processing classified data that you do not believe that Los Alamos can provide adequate assurance that classified, sensitive and propriety information is appropriately protected. How do you reconcile these high marks with your failing grade?"

"Well, I can't reconcile the position," Friedman admitted. "We just completed a review of laptop computers and we found that a number of unlocated laptop computers were simply written off the inventory records at the end of the year, and that seems to be a not uncommon methodology for handling unlocated sensitive property and nonsensitive property."

It was and, in Steve's, Jim's, and my opinions, still *is a perilous situation for America.*

XXXI

Red Flags of Cover-Up

Red flags of cover-up flew high over the Los Alamos National Laboratory several years before Steve, Jim and I arrived there.

Chuck Montano, a highly educated and skilled auditor with more than 30 years of auditing/accounting experience, had joined the University of California's auditing unit in 1989. Three years later, the Department of Energy decided to transfer all Los Alamos auditing functions and all of the auditors from California to Los Alamos. It was a decision they deeply regretted when Steve, Jim, and I unraveled the corruption in the Los Alamos Audits and Assessments Unit in 2002.

Even before the ink was dry on the transfer papers, the University of California auditors screamed "foul" since they had been taken out from under the umbrella of independent auditing, and now owed their jobs and futures to Los Alamos management - *the very people they were to audit.*

It didn't take long for their fears to be realized when Los

269

Alamos management almost immediately got rid of the University of California auditing supervisors who were transferred from California and brought in their *own people*. These included Marcellaa Zambrea, the same person the university reassigned in the wake of the 2002 Audits and Assessments debacles that Steve and I had documented in congressional testimony.

Shortly after Chuck's arrival at Los Alamos in 1992, he and other auditors received this cryptic message from management: "We want to re-engineer our activity so that we become a *greater service to management*."

What it meant to Montano and some of the other auditors was, that from here on out, they were to write only audit reports that reflected well on management — "A don't tell" mentality. Additionally, after all of LANL's own specially chosen audit leaders had replaced the old ones, all of the auditors were forced to sign a *loyalty pledge* to the University of California and the Los Alamos National Laboratory, a move unheard of in the world of auditing.

In spite of the lab's efforts to brainwash this new onsite auditing team, Montano, an expert in automated systems and data-center control, was relentless in upholding professional accounting standards after he was assigned to conduct an audit on the lab's *classified data controls*.

During this 1990s audit, Montano said, he raised concerns about the security of research information being downloaded on workstation computers and about classified information that was vulnerable to security failures. Still, Montano alleged, after his report was eventually submitted to the Department of Energy, amid great consternation from his bosses, no one took his concerns seriously. If they had, Montano proposed, most likely the Wen Ho Lee and lost hard drive incidents would never have occurred because he had recommended revised security controls on these very issues.

Interestingly, those two incidents caused the Department of Energy to place strict standards on Los Alamos security functions, including the mandatory hiring of a professional, qualified person to supervise the Office of Security Inquires. Hence, the reason I was hired in 2002.

On another occasion, Montano said he conducted a cost-incurred audit of Johnson Control of Northern New Mexico and found blatant misstatements. Johnson Control officials ultimately confessed to me, said Montano, that they were mandated by lab fiscal personnel to under-accrue various accounts, including workmen's compensation; the reason was so that the lab could balance its fiscal budget, which was, said Montano, a clear violation of Cost Accounting Standards (CAS). My bosses, postulated Montano, true to form, once again attempted to bury the report, but I persisted and eventually forced the higher-ups to send the report to the Department of Energy.

In another audit, said Montano, I determined that lab officials were not properly accumulating costs, which meant that lab-funding sources were being inappropriately charged, and this was another violation of CAS standards. My superiors ignored the report until a lab employee brought this improper practice to light in a public hearing a year later, Montano continued, and the report was then released grudgingly to the Department of Energy.

As the battle ensued within the Audits and Assessments Unit, a frustrated Montano sent countless e-mails to audit officials at the University of California, including the person in charge of all UC audits, Patrick Reed. His missives expounded on the cover-ups, but to no avail. No one responded to my pleas for help, emphasized Montano.

A fellow auditor ran into the same problems. Tommy Hook testified in a 1997 deposition mandated because of an employee's complaint of abuse, that Zambrea "didn't want to aggressively report findings; ...Didn't want to see certain things put in reports," including "unallowable costs;" and other information "...that might be an embarrassment to the university." He continued that Zambrea "threatened" him if he did not comply with the way she wanted to handle audit findings, to the degree that if the "findings cost the university money it could be his job, his staff's jobs, his raises, and his future."

Auditor Michael Aires also received Zambrea's wrath, Hook testified. Aires had gone directly to the Department of Energy with major findings of waste, fraud, and abuse, but was afraid to take it to Zambrea because he felt she would bury or modify the findings, said Hook. Continuing, Hook said that Zambrea told him that after she found out Aires went straight to the Department of Energy, she said, "I'd like to rip his fucking face off."

A year after the thefts, fraud, waste, abuse, corruption, and cover-ups were unraveled in 2002, lab officials were forced to come up with an auditing process that would prove to Congress and the Department of Energy that all was well at Los Alamos; an important façade, since the University of California was now forced to compete to bid for the Los Alamos Laboratory contract. Hook and Montano got the nod to ramrod the audit.

What they found was contrary to the declarations of University of California and Los Alamos National Laboratory officials that all was well at Los Alamos. In fact, they concluded, in part:

- Seventy percent of the transactions reviewed failed to comply with price check verification (reasonableness of cost and compliance with purchase contracts).
- There were improper purchases of personal items and other prohibited items.
- Thirty-five percent of lab employees were not following purchasing rules.
- It was questionable whether DOE should have reimbursed UC for $1.4 million in shipping costs and $800,000 in overpayments to lab vendors.

Montano and Hook submitted their findings to their superiors, who, the two claimed, changed their findings. They said the report ultimately sent to the Department of Energy was totally different from what they found and reported to their bosses.

Montano became infuriated with his superiors' actions and

reported the matter directly to the Department of Energy, who then proceeded to investigate his allegations.

The Department of Energy results were released in its 2005 Annual Cost Report. The Department of Energy report confirmed what Montano and Hook had claimed — that their original findings were never forwarded to the Department of Energy, but rather, they were cut off at the pass by a Los Alamos hired gun.

The Department of Energy's report also questioned $1 million in meals, travel expenses, payroll overpayments, and subcontractor expenses.

After Montano and Hook challenged lab officials (their bosses) for multiple reasons in 2003, lab officials, in their robotic method of handling such matters, retaliated, said Montano.

"Can you enlarge upon the whistleblower issue and how people in the organization will have confidence that, when they make an observation and they act on it, that there won't be punitive action taken against them?" Congresswoman Anna Eshoo asked during the 2002 Los Alamos congressional hearings.

"I agree that terminating a whistleblower sends a chilling message," UC's Bruce Darling responded. "It creates a climate in an organization that is ultimately very destructive to the organization itself."

No more punitive action for telling the truth?

Montano was stripped of *all* his duties in December 2003 and sentenced to an isolated cubicle in one of the lab's dingy basements, with no work assignments. Each day he came to work passing time surfing the Web and reading newspapers. It was "Chinese water torture" said Montano to a *Los Angeles Times* reporter. Chuck also sent daily e-mails to lab managers and Director Nanos begging for an assignment that would justify his $85,000 salary.

But banishment to a LANL *penal colony* was not an uncommon practice at Los Alamos.

Deesh Narang, a specialist in nuclear regulatory compliance, said he has been "unassigned" for nearly a decade after suing the lab for passing him over for a promotion. Narang was awarded

more than $500,000 in that case, and later won a retaliation griev-
ance that accused the lab of wasting taxpayer money for paying his
$100,000 annual salary but giving him nothing to do.

Some lab leaders executed harassment tactics against those
that would dare to bring organizational improprieties to the fore. These
tactics could include being buried in an office with nothing to do, being the recipient of an unwanted lateral transfer, and discrediting an
employee by questioning their mental health or competence.

Montano not only made it known to University of California,
Los Alamos National Laboratory, and Department of Energy officials that the lab's auditing procedures violated professional standards of auditing conduct, but that it also affected national security.
"This defiance of oversight and accountability places our national
interests at risk," he said to DOE officials. "If the employees closest
to the internal workings of our national labs can't feel secure in exer-
cising their constitutional rights, professional standards of conduct,
and legal responsibility to reveal fraud, waste, and abuse, what then
is the likelihood they will dare report laxness and failures in security
programs at our national labs?"

Steve and I often talked about how the lab would probably
ostracize us. We figured we would come to work one day and have
someone tell us we were reassigned to count pine trees in the Los
Alamos Acid Canyon, or some other *critical* function. As we found
out later, Shapiro and Madison saved us from that type of ordeal by
putting a hubristic bullet between our eyes on November 25, 2002.

Hook eventually retired from lab employment. As for Montano, after many legal battles with Los Alamos, he was finally able
to lobby for a meaningful job outside the laboratory. In March 2007,
he was placed on a Change-of-Station assignment with the New
Mexico Office of the State Auditor. In this job, Chuck is helping this
state agency to establish capabilities in investigating fraud. As far as
Chuck knows, U.S. taxpayers are paying his salary and benefits.

XXXII

No Gain? Not Exactly

When Doran, Bernabei, and I met with University of California officials on January 17, Bruce Darling told us the University of California was concerned and annoyed with the problems uncovered at Los Alamos. Darling said he told Atkinson he was so frustrated that he wasn't sure if he'd even recommend to the University of California Regents that they continue the Department of Energy contract when it expired in 2005. The university has never made money off the contract, Darling observed. From the very beginning, he insisted, UC has managed Los Alamos for the sake of America as a public service.

"We have not wanted to receive any additional money beyond our costs, and we have not wanted to spend any university money beyond what it costs to run these programs," Darling had told California Representative George Radanovich during the first set of Congressional hearings. "The university, from 1943 until today, has done this as a no-gain, no-loss".

I found Bruce Darling to be a true professional and a man

of integrity, but was Darling's comments completely accurate? Although the University of California may use the multi-billion dollar annual federal funding to conduct research and cover costs for that research, there is a caveat.

During the second set of hearings Oregon Representative Greg Walden broached the same issue when he said, "I guess the entrepreneurial spirit is alive and well at the lab." Walden was referring to a situation in which a Los Alamos Laboratory employee admitted that, for a number of years, he had been selling Los Alamos computer source codes and then using the proceeds to purchase new computers for his division, all the while routing the money through his personal bank account.

"What are the safeguards? How do you know that somebody else isn't doing this that hasn't come forward or hasn't been caught?" Walden asked.

Perhaps taken off guard, Darling's response was a bit convoluted. The result was a product of the Patent and Trademark Law Amendments Act of 1980, better known as the Bayh-Dole Act, said Darling. "The idea was to take ideas ... and put them to work in the marketplace, and drive the creation of new companies; jobs for people," Darling said.

The University of California, he explained, is the largest licenser of technology of any university in the United States, with revenues approaching eighty million dollars from licensing their technologies. "You are obliged as an employee when you go to work at the university, or one of our labs to ... turn over all patentable inventions to the University of California. We then have a process that provides an incentive back to the scientists so that they will receive some of the money in return."

The law was the result of the idea that the federal government was not doing enough to promote the adoption of new technologies. Consequently, Congress determined that the public would benefit if universities and small businesses were to receive federal funding to invent new technologies and to become directly involved in the commercialization process. The law permits exclusive licensing when an invention goes to the marketplace for the public good. Indeed, the act did stimulate the U.S. economy through the licensing of new inventions from universities to businesses that, in turn, manufactured the resulting products in United States.

Before the law, there was considerable debate over whether Americans should be paying for research and inventions that would result in university profit. Legislators concluded the public would benefit because new technologies would help all Americans in a variety of ways, such as in job creation and health-care advancement.

A major stipulation was that universities had to share a portion of any revenue they received from licensing the inventions with the university-employed inventor. Any remaining revenues, after expenses, must be used to support scientific research or education, the law provided.

Seventeen years later, the University of California adopted a patent policy that mirrored Bayh-Dole. Like the 1980 law, it was not without its detractors. In essence, some claim the new law enabled "profiteering" by universities more interested in inventing things for public consumption and profit rather than for "big science" creativity.

For one thing, the detractors proposed, professors who are inventors often have large investments in the companies to which they sell patents, and they receive large cash bonuses as a result. They also proposed that inventors are not required to disclose their financial interest in their research, which opens the door to the possible skewing of research results at the expense of objective experimentation. There was also a fear that basic science, the building blocks of applied science, may be abandoned in favor of applied science alone. Lack of basic science could result in a dearth of out-of-the-box thinking which is the foundation of all innovation, the detractors suggested. The law could make it difficult for professors and universities to collaborate or volunteer without receiving a warning from university licensing departments.

After Doran and I were terminated, multiple lab employees

offered the opinion that one of the reasons Los Alamos managers misappropriated federal funding was to invent a product that could be patented, thereby giving extra funding to the inventor. Of course, the department that the invention represented, the lab, and the university would also benefit.

In an article for *Small Times*, senior writer Tom Henderson interviewed William Hoskins, the director of the office of technology licensing at the University of California, Berkeley. Hoskins said that at his campus, after all legal expenses are paid; inventors receive 35 percent of licensing revenues, with 15 percent going to a research fund in the inventor's department. Of the remaining 50 percent, 16 percent goes to a university-wide fund and 34 percent goes to the chancellor, to be used, as the law specifies, to "support education or research."

So, University of California officials may have been waving the American flag when they said they managed Department of Energy contracts on a no-gain basis, but the university most certainly did make a substantial profit from taxpayers. That profit amounts to approximately $80 million a year. A significant part of these millions can then be used by university officials to help support their educational or research programs, whatever university officials determined that to be. This funding is extremely beneficial to the University of California in particular, and to California taxpayers in general. Additionally, the more money that is funneled into research theoretically means more inventions, and more inventions means more licensing money for all involved.

In addition to the patent profits, in February 2005 the Department of Energy Inspector General reported that over a five-year period the Department of Energy overpaid the University of California by thirty million dollars. This money, said Inspector General Friedman, was used by the University of California to pay for such things as student recruitment, capitol expenses, and *faculty home loans*. There was no requirement that the university had to pay the money back to the U.S. taxpayer, and apparently, UC. officials *didn't catch* that they were being overpaid.

Consequently, the statement that the University of California administers the Department of Energy contract at no gain is not exactly accurate.

XXXIII

Fallout, Aftermath

Although we'd been commended by Congress, back at the Los Alamos National Laboratory, Doran and I weren't exactly heroes among those who defended the status quo. Art Husson, a close friend of Steve, Jim, and me, who still worked in S-Division, called me on March 10, 2003. He related that he and some of the remaining OSI staff had met with Scott Gibbs (who replaced Madison), Victoria Snelling, and Barbara Stine (who replaced Shapiro), for the purpose of discussing Steve and me. Your congressional testimony upset them, Art confided. Some OSI inquirers felt they were being portrayed as fools, and lab employees were looking at them as if they were idiots, and the lab was not supporting them, Husson continued.

Husson related that Stine said the hearings were part of the process for the lab to keep the Department of Energy contract, and that comment really upset the other inquirers. The reason was, he continued, to them it substantiated what Steve and you had been saying all along; everyone is concerned with keeping the contract to the detriment of everything else, to include lab employees, namely them.

Art continued that after that meeting came another one with Director Pete Nanos to discuss the assertion that the lab didn't support the Office of Security Inquiries. Nanos told us, continued Husson, that he was only dealing with issues that occurred while he was there, and that he really didn't want to hear negative things about you or Doran, and that Doran and you should not have been terminated. But he also said, said Husson, that the February hearing was your day in the sun, and after that, things would begin to settle down. Nanos also told us that because of the things the University of California were doing to correct their deficiencies, they would probably be able to keep the contract, concluded Husson.

When that meeting ended, Husson said, Holt called for still another one, this time with OSI supervisor Glenn Teghmeyer, Scott Gibbs, and the same Office of Security Inquiries staffers. According to Husson, at this meeting, Holt said he wasn't aware of everything that happened in the Office of Security Inquiries because he had always depended upon Madison and Falcon to take care of things. Holt told us, said Husson, he figured Madison and Falcon, whom he said he trusted would go directly to Shapiro and Richard and keep him out of the loop. Husson continued, stating that Holt alleged it was Shapiro who ordered the firings of Steve and me against Holt's advice. Holt said he had advised there would be repercussions, but Shapiro, Holt alleged, told him he really didn't care, Husson said.

About a week later, Art continued, the university sent Terry Owens to interview Office of Security Inquiries staffers, ostensibly to check on morale and get a grasp on the group's operations. Three OSI inquirers tried to castigate Steve and you, Husson said, but Owens cut them off. Owens told them he didn't think Doran or you should have been fired and, in fact, that you and Steve had set OSI operations in the right direction, said Husson. Interestingly, Husson continued, Owens also said he was Madison's friend, and that Madison had always agreed in principle with us, but Owens said whatever Richard and Shapiro told him to do Madison did because he wanted to be a good soldier.

Husson stated he then had a private meeting with Owens. Owens apparently came out of the meeting with the sense that the Office of Security Inquiries was fragmented and full of conflict, said Art, believing that many of the older OSI employees didn't really seem to want to do the job, whereas many younger employees did. On a larger scale, said Husson, Owens appeared to feel that certain Los Alamos managers were not being truthful with the University of California on a variety of matters.

It was around that time that Madison resigned from the lab. A couple of months after he resigned, he created a stir at the lab when he reappeared on site. That news was leaked to the media, and reporters pounced on lab officials, wanting to know why Madison was back.

The official word was that Madison was working as a consultant for MOG Technology, a federal contractor based in Miami. As if his appearance wasn't perplexing enough, the explanation of his employment was even more curious. Madison was allegedly consulting for Los Alamos' D-Division (Decision Applications Division), but D-Division didn't have a standing contract with MOG; however, S-Division did. A lab spokesperson said Madison would be doing most of his work at a Nuclear Regulatory Commission site in Tennessee, and would be at the Los Alamos National Laboratory only briefly, to attend a few meetings.

Reporters asked me my opinion on Madison's return. I told them, "If Madison has been contracted to work for S-Division, or LANL in general, it could be the last nail in UC's coffin."

POGO's Peter Stockton agreed. "It really is extraordinary," he said. "He was the responsible person for firing the two whistleblowers, and it's absurd that they would bring him back — for any reason."

The Los Alamos National Laboratory began the restructuring of all remaining Office of Security Inquiries' operations in March

2003. Earlier that year, all criminal-type inquiries had been assigned to the lab's Audits and Assessments office, which was now under the direct control and management of the University of California. All other security responsibilities were scattered throughout other S-Division groups, *bringing to an end the Office of Security Inquiries*. In a memorandum, S-Division's acting deputy division leader explained the reasons for the reorganization:

1. The failure of OSI to professionally carry out their functions has culminated in nearly defunct OSI operations.
2. Given the current reputation of OSI, it is questionable whether qualified candidates could be recruited to fill vacant OSI positions.
3. The name-recognition associated with OSI is viewed as detrimental to the ability of the office to carry out its activities.
4. Critical OSI functions are stagnating, leaving the laboratory vulnerable to further damage from the failure to carry out these activities.
5. Prompt action is required to correct the dysfunction of OSI.

PriceWaterhouseCoopers' John Layton released his second financial review in April 2003, in which he found purchasing weaknesses, lax procurement policies, and inadequate controls within the Local Vendor Agreements and Just in Time contracts. The report stated that the LVA and JIT systems allowed "any" lab employee issued a lab badge to use it as a blank check to buy merchandise without prior approval. This conclusion supported what Gitto had claimed months before, and Agent Campbell had verified in his investigations.

Furthermore, "another $1.76 million in questionable purchases, which may or may not have been allowable under the Department of Energy contract, were lacking documentation, or required further explanations," Layton wrote.

This time University of California reaction was swift.

Bruce Darling stated, "The audit team's criticism of lax procurement policies, lack of timely and reliable data, and inadequate management are being addressed by an overhaul of the lab's business system. We believe that these actions...will give the American taxpayers greater assurance that their tax dollars will be better managed at the Los Alamos National Laboratory."

Pete Nanos said, "Problems are being rapidly addressed by a complete re-engineering of the laboratory's business practices. We are committed to ensuring that business processes meet the level of accountability expected by the American public. We will accept nothing less."

Rich Marquez responded, "Much of the weaknesses in the report were expected, but I was a little surprised at the extent in some areas. I was optimistic that we were in better stead than we are with the Just in Time contract."

Jay Johnson, LANL's Acting Comptroller replied, "A new system is being implemented that requires employees to justify their purchases. The system we are putting in place is going to help immensely."

Anne Broome, UC Vice President for Finance Management said, "We are disappointed that we do have so many control weaknesses."

But, in my opinion, the report represented only a cursory review of the lab's multi-billion-dollar purchasing systems. I told reporters, "A deeper, comprehensive investigative audit would, without a doubt, reveal staggering amounts of unauthorized purchases."

My call for an *investigative audit* was in line with my recommendations to the University of California's President Atkinson as part of my new consultant duties. In my second report to the university president, submitted through UC Deputy General Counsel John F. Lundberg, I wrote:

"In the past few months, I have heard about audits that UC has done and plans to do concerning

285

issues related to purchase cards, purchase orders, the LVA and JIT systems, vouchers, and whatever other systems of purchase have been used at LANL. Although these types of audits may be of some profit, they fall significantly short of accuracy because they are not "investigatory" audits. There is a quantum leap between a normal audit and an investigatory audit. LANL is good at manipulating the systems to make it appear that all is well in their auditing, when in fact it is filled with flaws. Consequently, any audit process of any of the purchase systems must be effectuated by investigating purchase by purchase (that is, every purchase), purchaser-by-purchaser. This involves going back to the agency it was purchased from to determine what in fact was purchased, when, how, where it was delivered, when it was delivered, etc. Then checking LANL records to ensure they coincide; then tracking down the item and viewing it with your eyes; or if classified as lost, salvaged, missing, retired or the like, reviewing the visible paper trail to ensure it meshes with all other investigatory facts. This activity must be pursued with the caveat that the dismantled, salvaged, retired, and so forth classifications may have been used to bury the truth; the fresh-ink phenomenon. Anything short of that process is a waste of time and paper. You will find many cases where LANL employees have retired/resigned and took all their government computers and other equipment with them, and nothing was done. When you check the dismantled, salvaged, etc. records, you will, I suggest, find many cadavers. Yet the normal audit will record these transgressions as clean, but the fact is they're not. We left in Steve's office a stack of questionable purchases by a Lab employee. Although my plan was to fully investigate all purchasers' transactions, I never had the chance. Hence, these transactions were never followed up from an investigatory perspective. It will take considerable time and significant effort to track down these purchases to determine if in fact they were valid. Be careful of the words, 'We have taken a situation to the point of diminishing returns.' What that normally means is we don't want to pursue this any further because it is taking a lot of time, and it is not really worth it. I strongly state that it is worth it, because the American public has the right to know. It is their money, contrary to what others at LANL propose. As an example of what needs to be done from an investigatory approach, Steve picked one purchase and called the vendor. When someone answered the phone, it was a travel agency. In fairness to the Lab purchaser, the number could have been changed since the purchase. But you will never know that unless you do an investigatory audit. It may mean traveling to certain locations to determine the facts, but that is an investigatory audit as compared to a normal audit. UC should ensure investigatory audits are conducted on ALL LANL purchase processes and voucher transactions for at least the last decade. Any other type of audit is fluff.

A most important area of investigatory audit need is the LVA and JIT systems. The investigator must go back, vendor by vendor, purchase by purchase, purchaser by purchaser, to determine who purchased what, when, where it was delivered, and the like, and then compare the vendor's records with the LANL records. I think you will find this to be the most egregious area of theft of all. Understand, in the NIS case, the FBI thus far has only dealt with the purchase order system, but a NIS suspect has already confessed to his major theft in the LVA and JIT systems."

In still another scathing report of inadequate oversight of business operations at the Los Alamos National Laboratory, Department of Energy Inspector General Friedman indicated that the lab misused another $14.6 million in taxpayer funds between 1999 and 2002. Further, Friedman's report stated the auditors found memorandums written by Audits and Assessments Unit supervisors that warned lab auditors against *throwing grenades*, but rather, encouraged them to *work with management*. "Such admonishments could have encouraged a reluctance to report audit findings to the department," Friedman wrote.

The report also noted that Friedman's investigators encountered *reluctance* on the part of Los Alamos Audits and Assessments Unit personnel to share documents with their auditors, and that although the Los Alamos National Laboratory had planned to conduct thirty-two internal audits between 2000 and 2002, only eleven were completed.

"Based on the record we developed, in our judgment, business operations at the laboratory have not been given adequate emphasis," Friedman wrote. "As a result, the caliber of business operations is simply inadequate given the nature and size of operations at Los Alamos and the requirements of the university's contract with the Department of Energy."

As the university made its attempts to understand the depth of the problems at the lab, it commissioned Ernst and Young to conduct a top-to-bottom evaluation of the lab's business practices. In its report released on April 22, 2003, the company recommended ninety ways the University of California should change how it did business at Los Alamos.

Four days later, Deputy Secretary Kyle McSlarrow and Linton Brooks, the acting chief of NNSA, recommended to the Department of Energy's Abraham that the University of California's contract should be put out for bid. At the same time, they admitted the Department of Energy and the National Nuclear Security Administration shared the blame for the lab's failures by allowing systemic management problems at the lab to go unchecked. That, they said, allowed the negative culture to flourish, which propagated a disconnect between science and business.

"For years, there has been a general acknowledgement of a 'Los Alamos way' that was unique and that devalued business practices," Brooks said. "Evaluations of Los Alamos in recent years always showed it slightly inferior in overall performance to the other two weapons laboratories, but never by enough to cause strong concern. It's hard to argue for any other course (than to open the contract to bid)."

New Mexico Senator Pete Domenici agreed the contract should be opened up for competitive bidding after Department of Energy Inspector General Friedman released another rebuke on Los Alamos laboratory operations on April 29. It was the sixth of its kind in four months. The report prompted Ken Johnson, the spokesman for the House Energy and Commerce Committee, to say, "It's another black eye for Los Alamos. If this were a fight, UC would be losing the punch count by a wide margin."

Underlying Friedman's latest report criticizing LANL's security, management, and accountability processes in reference to computers dedicated to classified processing, were the *inherent dangers this posed for our country*. The report strongly echoed my March 2002 theft report, especially as it related to lost and stolen computers.

In brief, Friedman observed that the lab didn't place strict and necessary control on its thirty-five thousand computers, including laptops that contained classified and proprietary information. He found five laptop computers that processed classified information were not even recorded on the lab's Office of Cyber Security list as single-user, stand-alone computer; two computers listed as classified were not approved to process classified information; four computers used for classified information were never entered into the lab's property database tracking system; and missing computers were written off the lab's property inventory without a formal inquiry.

And perhaps most sinister of all, some laptops that were downloading secret information had not been "accredited" — meaning they had not been cleared by managers to make sure they met technical requirements to protect the vital information about our country's top secrets.

With the release of Friedman's report, Secretary Abraham sent a letter to McSlarrow and Brooks that agreed with their recommendations. "I intend to open the management of the Los Alamos National Laboratory to full competition when the current contract expires," he wrote. "The management of the nuclear-weapons complex is my most important responsibility as Secretary of Energy, and it is important that business services be as good as the science. It is my intention to make it clear that, in dealing with nuclear weapons and materials, only the highest standards of performance are acceptable."

Finally, on April 30, Abraham announced what had been unthinkable for nearly sixty years. "The Los Alamos culture exalted science and devalued business practice," Abraham wrote. "Changing this culture will be the most difficult long-term challenge facing the laboratory, no matter who manages it. The university bears responsibility for the systemic failures that came to light in 2002. Given that responsibility and the widespread nature of the problems uncovered at Los Alamos, I plan to open the management of Los Alamos to full competition when the current contract expires (September 2005)."

Although most observers expected the announcement, University of California officials, as well as many Americans, were still stunned when his decision was officially released. After all, the university had held on to lab management through six decades of noncompetitive contract extensions.

"The idea that UC is entitled to the contract by some divine birthright is absurd," Congressman Greenwood said. "Given the length of time UC operated without the threat of competition, it appears that it had been lulled into a state of irresponsible complacency."

I found sweet vindication in the announcement. I told reporters, "I knew we were taking on a giant, and we won. The irony is that UC may lose the very thing our supervisors were trying to protect."

But, in my opinion, what this announcement was really about was justice for the American taxpayer, and security and safety for an imperiled national security.

Financial failures at the Los Alamos National Laboratory uncovered by Jim, Steve and me in 2002, amounted to millions of taxpayer dollars being lost to theft and greed. If this egregious mismanagement resulted in the waste of millions of federal dollars at just one federally run program, one can only imagine the total amount of squandered money when considering all federal operations. In 2010, America is experiencing unprecedented financial issues with no solid solutions in sight. Perhaps an appropriate place to begin to bring United States' budget into logical balance is to ensure professional oversight and management of all federally run programs. Federal officials certainly did not do their oversight job at the Los Alamos National Laboratory, and in my opinion, they still don't.

The two rogue nations of Iran and North Korea, and maybe others, apparently have come into possession of some highly sophisticated nuclear weapons information. Was this classified nuclear weapons information extracted from the hidden chambers of the Los Alamos National Laboratory? As Michigan Representative Mike Rogers implied during the February 2003 congressional hearing, and I agree, "Who really knows?" Buttressing this possibility, was the sworn statement of Gregory Friedman, the United States Department of Energy Inspector General, who proposed during the same hearing, that there can be no guarantees that *classified information* was not contained on the over 400 computers lost or stolen between 1999 and 2001 at the Los Alamos National Laboratory.

Unbelievably and alarmingly, the Los Alamos National Laboratory has had security failures nearly every year between 1999 and 2009. Based on these proven security failures concerning classified information, including lost/stolen computers, files, flashcards, disks, thumb-drives, and hard drives, in Jim's, Steve's, mine, and apparently Representative Rodgers' and Inspector General Friedman's opinions, *nuclear weapons secrets that may now be in the hands of Iran, North Korea, terroristic entities, and perhaps others, could possibly have been stolen from the Los Alamos National Laboratory*. I ask anyone to prove to the American citizen, with absolute certainty to the converse. These facts and possibilities should cause every American to demand that their government officials take immediate action to ensure these incomprehensible and unforgivable failings never occur again at the Los Alamos National Laboratory or any other national laboratory.

When referring to nuclear weapons secrets, it is not just the secrets of the 1940s-1990s that we need to protect. But rather, there are the perpetual new and current secrets created or in progress as America attempts to keep a step ahead of the enemy. In September, 2009 a uranium enrichment plant was identified buried inside a mountain near the city of Qum, Iran. U.S. defense experts propose there may be hundreds, perhaps thousands of tunnels in Iran that could hide nuclear research facilities and weapons. As a result, the Pentagon is racing to develop a new tunnel busting weapon called the Massive Ordnance Penetrator, which could be used as a weapon against these deeply buried mountain bunkers. It is axiomatic that America must keep these types of secrets out of the grip of the enemy - without falter.

XXXIV

Missing Plutonium – Missing Keys – Missing Security

Earlier, University of California President Richard Atkinson had taken the stoic position that the university would not compete for the contract. But now, after extensive pressure and chastisement from University of California Regents, Atkinson did an about-face. "My instinct continues to be to compete, and to compete hard," he announced. "We believe, with every fiber of our institutional being, that continued UC management is in the absolute best interest of the nation's security."

Not everybody at the university supported him. The scientists generally supported Atkinson, while those in the liberal arts were not so sure. "It's extremely important that we have the outstanding scientists who are working on trying to preserve the security of our country," said Chris McKee, chairman of UC-Berkeley's physics department. "The University of California has demonstrated that it can create and maintain an atmosphere which fosters outstanding science."

But Robert Bellah, professor emeritus of sociology, disagreed. "Who needs that kind of prestige?" he said. "Our prestige comes from the quality of the faculty above all. I don't think it [keeping the lab contract] has much to do with the quality of the faculty."

Shocking revelations were to come. At about the time of Spencer Abraham's announcement, the Department of Energy announced that the Los Alamos National Laboratory had experienced two major plutonium contamination violations in 2002. The first incident occurred in March and involved seven employees "receiving uptakes" of radioactive plutonium at Technical Area-55, the only facility in the nation authorized to handle all phases of plutonium processing. "Significant plutonium contamination was spread throughout the room," NNSA official Linton Brooks said. The second violation occurred in September, when two lab workers were exposed to potentially hazardous levels of radiation.

Doran's and my growing fears about how all the mismanagement and corruption could lead to peril for America came to fruition when, on June 12, 2003, Los Alamos officials admitted they had lost two vials of plutonium oxide. It is a highly carcinogenic substance that can be used to make "dirty bombs." The plutonium was "most likely" discarded in a waste drum on site, lab managers said, but they couldn't confirm this theory. The official position was stupefying, "The lab plans to establish a system to keep better track of such material," a lab spokesman said.

The problem was that even a small amount of plutonium oxide is highly carcinogenic and could pose a public health or safety threat if criminals, or worse still terrorists, got hold of the substance. "Plutonium oxide is every bit as dangerous as weapons-grade if you wanted to disperse it in a dirty bomb or just get it airborne," POGO's Peter Stockton said. "But the real concern is security. We have hundreds of tons of plutonium and rich uranium in the system. This raises questions about the reliability of that system if you can't find an unidentifiable quantity of plutonium."

Two other University of California managed labs – Lawrence

Livermore National Laboratory and Lawrence Berkeley National Laboratory – also began to receive their share of public attention as a result of security issues.

On May 15 2003, University of California officials stated that a set of Lawrence Livermore National Laboratory security keys had been missing for a month. Susan Houghton, a spokeswoman for the Lawrence Livermore laboratory, said she wasn't sure how many locks the missing keys would unlock, but hundreds of locks would have to be changed. A later Department of Energy Inspector General report indicated approximately seven million dollars in American taxpayer money was spent to replace these locks because of lost keys, an amount Lawrence Livermore officials stated was exaggerated.

"First there were missing computers at Los Alamos, now there are missing keys at Livermore," an angry Ken Johnson, the House Energy and Commerce Committee spokesman said. He went on, "It all adds up to a management team that has been missing for too long now."

Less than a month later, more risks of national jeopardy surfaced. Media scrutiny intensified when reporters revealed that in April 2003 a Lawrence Livermore laboratory security officer had lost an electronic badge that provided access to 3,000 offices, some of them containing classified nuclear information. The loss wasn't reported to senior managers until May 29. This episode launched an investigation of all security issues by a Washington-based National Nuclear Security Administration team.

The Department of Energy Inspector General released another report in mid-June that identified several more problems at both Livermore and Berkeley laboratories, including the revelation that neither maintained strong controls of sensitive/attractive property. In fact, to locate all the sensitive/attractive equipment, the report stated, it took a level of effort that "exceeded normal expectations", as long as ten days. In addition, neither laboratory updated its records when employees with high-level security clearance had left employment. The report went on, of 150 recently terminated employees, seventeen of them had a total of forty-one sensitive/attractive items still assigned to them, and the laboratories also have problems tagging computers built on-site, leaving them susceptible to theft. And — shades of the danger for national security at Los Alamos — the report stated the equipment delivered to the Lawrence Livermore Laboratory could be delivered to a drop point without a signature.

XXXV

Our Settlements

To mollify us for our wrongful terminations, the University of California offered Doran and me a variety of full-time positions, both in California and in New Mexico, after we had been hired as consultants to UC President Richard Atkinson in January 2003. Partly because I had acquired a pretty decent retirement nest egg, I declined the offers. In addition, I had already heard the stories of lab employees who had spoken out against the Los Alamos National Laboratory and what happened to them. Yes, I was being welcomed back with verbal open arms, but in my opinion lab officials were not about to change the way they did business, despite their congressional beatings and pleadings to reform. It was my position, that if I accepted any offers, I would be banished, buried, and shunned. That was not what I wanted to do for the remainder of my career. Doran, younger and needing a steady income, took a position as the Director of Public Safety and System Security at University of California Headquarters, in Oakland, California, in April 2003. That job was short-lived, Doran quickly deciding to move on after dealing with more, said Doran, UC driven manipulations.

But there was still the issue of winning a real settlement from the lab, which we believed had wrongly terminated us when we were exposing not only the faulty management of Los Alamos but, even more importantly, the risks to which such practices exposed our country. I added another lawyer to assist Lynne Bernabei. Consequently, Gary Gwilliam of the Gwilliam, Ivary, Chiosso, Cavalli and Brewer law firm in Oakland, California, and Bernabei formed a formidable tag team in bringing negotiations to a successful conclusion.

The university, represented by John Lundberg, Jeffrey Blair, and Joseph Mullinix, started out with a $400,000 settlement offer, but I demanded something closer to one million dollars. I told my attorneys I wouldn't meet with the university until I received an offer closer to that amount. As summer 2003 rolled around, we finally met in Oakland to begin our talks.

The attorneys took over. After four hours, Gwilliam and Bernabei came to me and said the best Lundberg would do was "about" $700,000, and he would not budge from that figure. Well, I wouldn't budge from mine, and I told my lawyers, look, you told me UC was going to make a serious offer, and they already knew that I would not think about settling out of court unless the figure was in the one million dollar range. I came here today because I thought they were serious.

I told Gwilliam and Bernabei to return to the negotiating room and tell the university's attorneys that unless they make a serious offer, I would initiate court action.

My reasoning was simple and straight-forward. I accepted the position at Los Alamos because I believed in the job. I worked for the University of California, the lab, and most of all, the American people. All I wanted to do was fulfill my responsibilities. Nevertheless, I felt their actions indicated the lab and university just wanted me to sit in a chair, collect a check like many other lab employees, help them meet Appendix O requirements, and keep my mouth shut. I value my reputation and, in my opinion, they damaged it by not letting me expose corruption, cover-ups, and retaliation. And it was clear to me lab officials would have interred me if they could have. Thus, fighting for a just settlement through the courts was the only process I had for proper retribution. I told my attorneys if the opposition wouldn't negotiate in earnest, then I wanted them to file the lawsuit immediately.

Forty-five minutes after returning to the negotiating table, Gwilliam and Bernabei walked back to where I waited. We told them Glenn is pretty passionate about this, he will absolutely take you to court and bring you to your knees, said Gwilliam. You're not going to believe this, Glenn, Gwilliam continued, but they are willing to give you $900,000, plus three months salary.

And so, we agreed to settle out of court, as did Doran, whose settlement was equally satisfactory. The university agreed to give me $900,000 in an outright payment, plus 3-1/2 month's salary (approximately $30,000).

Having suffered the consequences of wrongful termination, we were anxious to reveal our vindication for the truthful revelations we had made about Los Alamos to the media, and hoped for a strong public reaction. One of the first news stories came from Wired News. Noah Shachtman's lead paragraph was "Los Alamos National Lab: 0, Whistleblowers: $1 million. That's the score after the University of California agreed Wednesday to pay former lab investigator Glenn Walp nearly one million dollars for being wrongfully fired last year."

In interviews with reporters, Bernabei said, "Walp's settlement should send a clear message to managers in the nuclear-weapons complex that retaliation is a risky and expensive business. The courage of Walp and Doran in pursuing these issues has finally brought some measure of accountability to the national labs."

Added Gwilliam: "There is a culture of retaliation at these laboratories against anyone who stands up against management. There is a barricade mentality: 'We're the best and the brightest, leave us the hell alone.'"

I issued a statement. "It represents a solid victory for all Americans whose hard-earned monies were egregiously wasted and misused by leaders and managers at the Los Alamos lab. Hopefully, this settlement will initiate the dawn of a new approach wherein all national lab contractors conscientiously strive to be wise stewards of tax dollars, and aggressively and appropriately address the issues of corruption and crime that, regrettably, appears to permeate these environments. May this settlement send a searing message to all national lab leaders, that they need to concentrate their efforts on the security of all Americans and not personal or corporate gain."

I stressed that the settlement with Doran and me wouldn't resolve the lab's problems. "What I encountered, mismanagement and corruption, is so ingrained within the laboratory's philosophy that the only thing that will correct it will be a new contractor," I said.

From my perspective, the lab's ongoing problems emanated from the arrogance of staff members who had worked there for many years and were unwilling to change their antiquated approach to management. I told reporters I was definitely pleased with my settlement, but "I don't believe justice took a big enough swath or cut deep enough. At this very moment people who were just as involved in wrongdoing as other LANL employees who have now resigned or were removed, are still receiving a salary, still in leadership positions, and still making leadership decisions. If you are truly going to cleanse the swamp, then you need to drain it. The only way to change the culture — whose most salient feature is arrogance — is to change the contractor and root the place out. I'm encouraged to believe that the trailing effects of my settlement will make all national laboratory managers around the country re-evaluate their operations to ensure prudent stewardship of tax dollars."

Regrettably, tax dollars paid for my settlement, even though Inspector General Friedman had noted in his January 2003 report that taxpayers shouldn't have to pay for UC's failures. Darling, too, testified before Congress that UC would not seek reimbursement from the federal government for any settlement agreements. But University of California officials told the media that my settlement was paid from the university's Management Fee, which averages about fourteen million to seventeen million dollars a year. That money comes from the Department of Energy to help the University of California cover the lab's administrative costs. The university may not have asked the Department of Energy for any additional funding, but the fact is, all settlement costs came from United States taxpayers.

Massachusetts Representative Ed Markey pointed out that, in a five-year period, the Department of Energy paid out $331 million in settlements. "When a contractor for the DOE gets sued, 95 percent of the time its legal fees and settlement costs get reimbursed by the federal government," Markey said. "Underwriting the cost of defending against lawsuits provides little incentive for Energy Department contractors to act within the law."

Markey drove home a case-in-point. After the University of California fired Dee Kotla, for alleged personal use of a lab telephone that amounted to $4.60, a jury awarded Kotla a $2.1 million settlement in 2007. The jurors indicated they felt she was retaliated against for blowing the whistle on the University of California. The fight to defend the $4.60 call cost American taxpayers over $8 million. That ridiculous UC driven action could have paid for a lot of medical bills for millions of Americans in dire need of crucial health care.

Charles Tiefer, a professor of government contracting at the University of Baltimore Law School, called for the government to revise its requirements on reimbursing company legal costs. "While you'd expect all corporate management to spend lavishly on their legal self-defense, only a few have the privilege of using a key to the Treasury — namely, generous, 100-percent cost-reimbursement contracts — to make the taxpayer foot the bill."

Soon after our settlements were announced, Markey nominated Doran and me for the Paul H. Douglas Ethics in Government Award. "These modern-day Paul Reveres embody the spirit of the

Ethics in Government Award. They did their duty to the highest ethical standards, but sadly, paid a high price for doing so."

Doran and I also received letters of commendations from the FBI. Signed by David M. Varner, acting senior supervisor resident agent in Santa Fe, it said in part:

> I am expressing my appreciation for the cooperation extended to the Santa Fe Resident Agency of the Federal Bureau of Investigation during your tenure at LANL. Although I have not had the pleasure of personally meeting you, I am cognizant of the outstanding efforts you extended to staff in Santa Fe. Special Agent Jeffrey W. Campbell has conveyed to me the efforts you put forth which resulted in the successful development of several investigations. I am therefore, taking this opportunity to convey my sincere appreciation for your assistance to the FBI.

Despite our sweeping vindications, Doran and I still remain tainted by being labeled whistleblowers. We never perceived ourselves as whistleblowers; we feel we were just doing the job we were hired to do. But the label stigmatizes those who are so titled. Regardless of an applicant's credentials, many employers shy away from hiring a whistleblower. I applied for more than 30 police executive positions, but did not receive a nod until late 2005. On many occasions, various grapevines have revealed information to me that I had been rejected for this or that job because of the whistleblower tag. In 2008, I landed a consulting/teaching position with Penn State University. My first project was to build a program from scratch entitled, "Management-Driven Ethics", for presentation to national and international police executives. My experiences at Los Alamos are, obviously, a significant part of that presentation.

Like me, Steve had problems finding satisfying permanent employment. After leaving University of California employment, he ricocheted for a while from one policing job to another, attempting to find the health and stability he enjoyed before accepting employment at Los Alamos. In 2005, he accepted a consultant/investigator position for a private corporation, and in 2009, he became the host of the internationally-broadcasted Shilohtv.com program *Trail Boss.*

The word whistleblower had its origin from the practice of English bobbies who would blow their whistle when they observed the commission of a crime. I suppose, in a way, all police officers who do their jobs are whistleblowers.

On the day Steve and I were fired, Pete Stockton had said, Glenn, you need to know, if Steve and you fight the lab it can bring unbelievable pressures into your lives. Many whistleblowers have had their lives permanently disrupted, their finances depleted, their marriages/relationships destroyed, and some have even committed suicide. I will gladly help you fight this battle, continued Pete, but for the sake of you and your loved ones, you really need to think this through.

Pete was right. History reveals that once whistleblowers go public, their lives are *forever changed.* Stress, anxiety, frustration, and apprehension are words totally inadequate to describe what really happens. *Permanent chaotic disruption* gets closer to illustrating what actually occurs. Clearly, doing what is right, at times, has a *high* price tag.

I was asked by the media: "Based on the reprisals you are enduring for telling the truth, would you do it again?" My answer was quick and certain, and still is, "Without hesitation, because it is the right thing to do."

Yes, Steve and I, now, more than ever, fervently believe that exposing the wrongdoings at the Los Alamos National Laboratory was, for the sake of humankind, the right thing to do; the only thing to do. We have also learned that to truly enjoy and understand the peace, beauty, and contentment of life's mountaintops, one must first walk through the valleys of uncertainty and pain. Consequently, from the moment Steve and I were told "we didn't fit", we have found unending strength in the words of the greatest man to ever walk the Earth, who stated:

> "If the world hates you, know that it hated me first...if you did the things of the world they would love you...but you are not of the world, therefore they will hate you."

Steve and I know that in the next world beyond this physical world, "*we will fit;*" and that's what is important.

XXXVI

Past Failures

During the fall and early winter of 2002, Doran, Mullins, and I faced continual resistance from our superiors. Notwithstanding, we mutually agreed it was game on, and we would be relentless in our pursuit to do the right thing. It was clear to us that the opposition was equally inspired to stop us in our tracks. The battle was on.

Although we were hell-bent on addressing the lab's theft and corruption issues, this was not our main concern. It was our positions that those who cast a jaundiced eye towards theft and corruption had also failed, and failed miserably, in ensuring *ironclad* security of the lab's nuclear weapons secrets.

We brought our concerns to lab leaders but that didn't work, so when the opportunity finally arose, we told members of Congress and federal investigators.

But we were not the first to express these concerns. The Los Alamos National Laboratory has a long and continuous record of bankrupt security, economic flaws, and environmental failures.

305

The following represents a few of those shortcomings:

- A month before the Trinity test, Klaus Fuchs, a Los Alamos scientist, passed nuclear secrets to the Soviets.

- In 1979, Los Alamos National Laboratory thermonuclear weapons data was erroneously declassified and given to a public library.

- In 1980, the Department of Energy pleaded with the FBI to help them improve Los Alamos security. Victor Rezendes, the Director of the General Accounting Office's Energy, Resources, and Science Issues Division, testified in front of a 1999 House Committee that the FBI withdrew its staff from Los Alamos after attempting to help out, "because of resistance to security measures" by Los Alamos leaders.

- Since 1996, Los Alamos has been attempting to produce plutonium pits (used to trigger a nuclear bomb explosion). The new pits are required to replace old ones pulled from the active nuclear weapons stockpile for testing, to see if any have become defective with age. Los Alamos leaders said they would be able to produce twenty to fifty per year by 2003, with a cost of $310 million. As of 2006, no pits had been produced. The revised estimated date of completion was 2007, with a cost of $1.7 billion.

- In 1996, the Department of Energy had announced they would fund the building of a massive laser machine to be built by the University of California's Lawrence Livermore National Laboratory, a "critical tool" for maintaining U.S. nuclear weapons. The initial cost was estimated at $1.7 billion, to be completed by 2002. It didn't happen. University of California management then projected the completion date to be 2009, with a cost of $6.7 billion.

- In 1988, Los Alamos proposed building machines, at a cost of $30 million dollars, to make three-dimensional X-rays of exploding nuclear weapons parts; a process they called "essential" to their research. As of 2006, the machines have cost taxpayers $300 million and still did not work.

- In 1999, Los Alamos Laboratory officials admitted that seventy-eight percent of their security personnel failed required skills tests.

- Between 2002 and 2004, thirty-two percent of all nuclear-safety complaints filed concerned the Los Alamos National Laboratory. In fact, the fines levied against Los Alamos were four times the total assessed against all other National Nuclear Security Administration facilities.

- In the first six months of 2004, top-secret data at the Los Alamos National Laboratory was improperly transmitted via e-mail eighteen times, more than three other major national labs combined.

- In February 2004, the New Mexico Environmental Department fined the Los Alamos National Laboratory $854,000 for environmental violations under the state's Hazardous Waste Act, just one month after it had levied a $282,000 fine for similar infractions. In 2005, the lab was fined another $63,000. The lab was cited for failure to perform adequate hazardous waste determinations on chemicals discarded in the lab's Technical Area-35, failure to adequately track mixed waste in eight hazardous waste drums, failure to protect waste piles at Technical Area-39, storing hazardous waste in open containers, failing to properly label hazardous waste, and failure to maintain adequate hazardous waste operating records.

- In 2008, a waterline break at Technical Area-21 released nearly 4 million gallons of potable water. As a result of the break, along with several storms, New Mexico officials reported that elevated levels of plutonium-238, americium-241, strontium-90, and plutonium-239/240 were found in the Rio Grande watershed. The officials also reported contaminates did not reach the Rio Grande River, and that the situation did not pose an *immediate* threat. Of concern however, is how far this concentration of contamination is from the river; the Rio Grande River is slated to become the future drinking water supply for the City of Santa Fe.

According to some security experts, history has shown that the Los Alamos National Laboratory Protective and Security Forces are not adequately prepared to keep U.S. secret weapons codes from the eyes of spies, nor is it capable of totally protecting the facility against terrorist intrusion.

Security experts propose that a terrorist attack on the Los Alamos National Laboratory would not only be a surprise, but extraordinarily violent, considering the conventional weaponry and explosives available to terrorists today. Some experts question whether the protective force has the training or experience, or would continue to fight under these circumstances. These experts propose, and so do Steve, Jim, and I, that it is not a question of the personal courage or dedication of the protective force, but the daunting circumstances under which they are placed by the system.

The federal government tests the lab's security capabilities by conducting mock force-on-force exercises.

Experts point out that there are virtually no surprises in a force-on-force test. Once the lab's Protective Force personnel are outfitted with laser simulation equipment, they know the attack will take place within an hour or two at the most. The controllers and the observers always tip off the specific location of the attack during a safety walk down. A safety walk down is performed across the whole area where a battle will be simulated, to ensure that no obstacles or other land variations can injure the protective forces during the exercise. Obviously, this does not create a realistic scenario.

In 1997, a special unit of the U.S. Army Special Forces played the role of adversary during a force-on-force exercise at the Los Alamos National Laboratory. The normal scenario is to "steal" enough Special Nuclear Material to build a crude nuclear weapon that could fit in rucksacks. The Special Forces attacked Technical

Area-18, loaded a garden cart they had bought from Home Depot with nuclear materials, and snuck out of the facility. The invaders achieved the simulated objective of the game; stealing enough Special Nuclear Material to make an atom bomb. According to the official report on the exercise, attackers mainly did it by using hidden snipers in the hills to kill the first lab guards who arrived. Because those killed were the commanders, the rest of the force was thrown in disarray. Other guards were killed as they arrived in small groups down a narrow road leading to Technical Area-18. This invasion succeeded despite months of Los Alamos security training on dozens of computerized battle simulations, showing that the Los Alamos security force, the defenders, would win.

As a result of the poor force-on-force evaluations, in 1998 the Department of Energy's Albuquerque operations office classified security at TA-18, and other critical Los Alamos sites, as totally unsatisfactory.

Consequently, in 1999, Secretary of Energy Bill Richardson's security team recommended that TA-18 be shut down, and immediately de-inventoried because, based on tests and evaluations, they claimed it could not be defended. In essence, it was a monumental disaster waiting to happen. Secretary Richardson realized how dangerous the situation was and ordered that all weapons-grade material be removed from Los Alamos and placed at a Nevada test site by 2003. It took Los Alamos officials until November 2005, to remove the weapons-grade material.

The force-on-force failures continued:

- In one 2000 force-on-force exercise, a Los Alamos convoy of lab security personnel, responding to an attack, hit a minefield placed there by the adversaries. Amazingly, the other vehicles behind the initial convoy continued through the minefield. Los Alamos management's response; they didn't have time to stop.
- Again in 2000, a team of Department of Energy inspectors found a TA-18 burst reactor with large loads of highly en-

riched uranium fuel sitting in the middle of an open area, fuel that should have been contained in a secure vault.

- In still another force-on-force exercise, adversaries gained access to the TA-18 reactor fuel. This intrusion had the potential of morphing the denotation of an improvised nuclear device that could have taken out a major chunk of Northern New Mexico and caused a nuclear winter downwind. All the intruders needed to do was place one highly enriched plate on the floor, get on a stepladder and drop another like plate on the floor plate; the intruders having access to both plates. If this activity occurred, it would have caused a nuclear explosion equal to Hiroshima.

- In one of the force-on-force attacks, the attackers captured the targeted cache, weapons-grade nuclear material. Los Alamos officials complained that the enemy didn't play fairly, because the tactics used by them were not on the Department of Energy's approved list of weapons for war games.

- During one security test at Los Alamos, the Department of Energy Inspector General found that thirty percent of the lab's security personnel were pressured by management to change their assessments of the lab's security in order to make the lab's Security Operations Division "look good" rather than report actual security conditions.

Testifying in June 2003, before the House Government Reform Subcommittee on "National Security, Emerging Threats and International Relations," POGO's Danielle Brian stated concerning these force-on-force exercises:

> The nation's nuclear-weapons labs house nearly 1,000 tons of weapons-grade plutonium and highly-enriched uranium. In mock terrorist's attacks, these facilities regularly failed to protect the material. I have spoken to Homeland Security officials about

this issue and they said, "You realize we are more concerned about the lack of security at DOE facilities than you are."

Although most force-on-force scenarios are based on the terrorists getting into the facility and back out with the material, of concern now is that the terrorists simply gain access to the weapons facilities, which could result in a sizeable nuclear detonation at the facility itself. Thus, a terrorist group, to be effective, does not have to steal nuclear material, create a nuclear device, transport it to the United States, and detonate it in a major city. They can simply gain access to the material at a U.S. nuclear facility – some of which are near large metropolitan areas – and accomplish the same outcome. Such a detonation can be created by using conventional explosives brought into the facility in a backpack and combined with particular kinds of Special Nuclear Materials stored at these sites. In a mock attack test on TA-18 at Los Alamos, an area that contains tons of Special Nuclear Material, the mock terrorists successfully entered the facility and the guard force could not get them out. The mock terrorists had enough time to have been able to create a sizeable nuclear detonation.

One of the ways to harden up security is to place the nuclear materials in a more secure location. Case in point, once again, is TA-18 at Los Alamos. In 2000, then-Energy Secretary Bill Richardson directed that this site, which is at the bottom of a canyon and very difficult to be protected, be de-inventoried of its Special Nuclear Material by 2003 and transported to a hardened underground facility at the Nevada test site. As of June 2003, not one gram has moved in that direction. Although Otto

Harmon was told to expedite the de-inventorying in 2003, excuses kept emanating from Los Alamos. Now, Los Alamos officials are saying it will take until 2006 for that task to be accomplished. I believe they are betting on turnover at DOE headquarters, and the inattention of the Congress.

To add to the problems, currently the tests are seriously dumb-downed – often to the point of absurdity. In a recent mock-theft scenario, terrorists were not allowed to go out the same hole in the fence they came in, requiring them to run all the way around the fence line to leave the facility. If they had been allowed to use the hole, they would have been able to leave the facility without even having engaged any of the protective forces. In another recent example, the mock terrorists were required to stay on the road in order to leave the facility. DOE should use training adversary forces – for example, the Special Forces unit out of Fort Bragg, or the Navy SEALs – to perform these tests. These teams are trained to think and act like terrorists. Instead, typically, protective forces from other sites are used as mock terrorists – yet they lack this very specialized training. In addition, advanced warning is given to the sites – often months in advance – that a test is scheduled, and the tests follow scripts of what the terrorists can and can't do. The three advantages a real terrorist has are surprise, speed, and violence of action – elements that are not factors in these dumb-downed tests – yet the mock terrorists still accomplish their mission all too often.

A way to improve security is to move security oversight out of the Department of Energy. Perhaps, it could be moved to the Department of Defense under the nuclear command and control staff.

Before I left lab employment, the lab's PTLA used contracted security personnel from other national laboratories as the attacking entity in force-on-force scenarios, rather than using highly skilled military personnel. Using highly skilled military personnel, such as recommended by Danielle Brian, would make the scenario more akin to a realistic attack. I highly recommended to federal authorities that force or force activities at all national laboratories, starting with Los Alamos, use trained military force personnel to test the lab's true capabilities of defense.

In October 2003, Richard Lavernier, a twenty-two year veteran of the Department of Energy who had long been a critic of lax security at the Los Alamos National Laboratory, wrote an article for *Vanity Fair*.

Lavernier spent six years running war games for the United States government at the nine nuclear weapons laboratories in United States. "In more than 50 percent of our tests at the Los Alamos facility, we got in, captured the plutonium, got out again, and in some cases didn't fire a shot, because we didn't encounter any guards," he wrote. Not only that, but LANL's security force knew the exact dates of the drills months in advance, Lavernier maintained.

Following the *Vanity Fair* piece, Ed Bradley of *60 Minutes* on CBS interviewed Lavernier on February 15, 2004. Lavernier told Bradley, and an international audience, that poor security at national labs, including Los Alamos, jeopardizes America more severely than the after effects of the World Trade Center attacks. Bradley cited several Department of Energy reports that indicated many labs leave security gates wide open, fail to repeatedly respond to alarms in top-secret areas, and are caught sleeping on the job. Lavernier supported that with this anecdote: He had made an unannounced visit to a national lab in Colorado one January Sunday, only to find the vast majority of the patrols in a building watching the Super Bowl. For those hours at least, the lab was wide open to attack.

Bradley also interviewed Chris Steele, a Department of Energy employee responsible for protecting United States citizens against nuclear accidents at Los Alamos. Steele said he'd give Los Alamos a failing grade because of its systemic nuclear safety violations. In 2003, Steele said he gave Los Alamos an unprecedented forty-five major nuclear safety infractions, but lab officials cavalierly regarded these violations as mere "glitches" — never mind that in Steele's opinion, these violations were eagerly inviting disaster.

Shortly after Lavernier's *Vanity Fair* piece came out, a National Nuclear Security Administration official denied the article's sweeping claims and announced that the nation's nuclear-weapons facilities were "not vulnerable to any type of attack." In response to the *60 Minutes* broadcast, Los Alamos laboratory officials' basic statement was, "That's old news."

Not according to Noah Shachtman, a reporter for *Wired News*, an online news service. In his investigation of alleged lax security at Los Alamos, Shachtman wrote, "To sneak into the Los Alamos National Laboratory, the world's most important nuclear research facility, all you do is step over a few strands of rusted, calf-high barbed fence. I should know. On Saturday morning, I slipped in and out of a top-secret area of the lab while guards sat, unaware, less than one-hundred yards away."

Other examples of security perils were equally troubling.

In September 2002, two classified flashcards belonging to the Nonproliferation and International Security Division, which had been entered into the classified removable electronic media (CREM) database in September 2001, could not be located. An Office of Security Inquiries inquirer said in his findings that the missing materials did not contain any classified data. "Thus," he wrote, "the event is *not considered a security incident*; rather, it is recognized as a failure of the CREM database."

I challenged the inquirer. How do you know the CREM didn't contain classified data? The reply, I really don't know that as a fact, it's just that that's what they told me.

"Who's 'they'?" I asked.

"People in NIS."

314

I felt if that was the only information he had, how could he conclude there weren't risks to the national security of our country?

Madison and Falcon said that if that is what NIS personnel said, then that is what I must conclude in my report, said the inquirer, and so I did, but if you're asking me if I know that as a fact, or can I prove that as a fact, I can't; I have no idea what was on the flashcards.

I was speechless.

I revealed that incident and several others to congressional investigators. I included information on a missing classified hard drive, and as a result, these things became public knowledge. Nanos confessed to University of California Regents on January 16, 2003 that a hard drive, the one I was referring to, containing classified information, might be missing. "I am deeply troubled that the Los Alamos National Laboratory is unable to account for computer equipment and other materials as part of the lab's management inventory control and audit program," Nanos said.

The most disturbing thing about these incidents was lab officials' nonchalant reaction. Of the missing hard drive, a lab spokesman said, "If it existed," it didn't contain nuclear-weapons information and it "most likely" contained old security plans. And the missing flashcards? A lab official stated that the missing flashcards "probably" did not contain classified information, but they could not prove it.

Energy Secretary Abraham was not impressed. "This is yet more examples of poor management of business practices that the University of California and the new laboratory management must resolve, and resolve quickly," he said.

POGO's Peter Stockton also weighed in. "Nobody knows what's going on as far as I can tell. My trust level of LANL is next to zero," he said.

It would get worse. Ten classified disks disappeared in November 2003 from, once again, the Nonproliferation and International Security Division. The lab's position again was that none of the disks held information that jeopardized national security. Nanos' response: "This situation is totally unacceptable."

Nanos took unprecedented action in December 2003, by placing several employees, including managers, on paid investigative leave.

National Nuclear Security Administration's Linton Brooks added, "We are disturbed that after all of the revelations and reviews about security and document control over the past few years, lab employees still have not learned to manage their classified media."

Failures continued to pile up against the Los Alamos National Laboratory and the University of California. I suggest one of the major reasons is, as was expressed in 2004 by Robert Foley, who replaced Bruce Darling as Vice President of the University of California's Laboratory Management, "At Los Alamos there has been a lack of accountability, virtually a sense of entitlement that developed over the years in the culture at LANL....When they did something wrong, it was 'musical chairs.' They could move from one job to another. People didn't get fired...and that's intolerable.'"

XXXVII

Will LANL Ever Be Secure and Safe?

Doran and I had been proposing to Congress and the Department of Energy that the protective forces at national laboratories be placed under the control of a specially trained federal security force, such as a U.S. Special Forces Unit. In May, 2004 Energy Secretary Abraham may have been following up on our recommendation when he announced plans to create an elite federal guard force to protect the nation's supply of plutonium and weapons-usable uranium from terrorists. Abraham was alternately praised for the concept, yet warned by some that contractors — most notably the University of California — had a long history of stonewalling security reforms. Regrettably, Abraham's plans never materialized. Six months after his announcement, he told President Bush he would be leaving his cabinet position. Bush replaced Abraham with Samuel W. Bodman, a former Deputy Secretary of Commerce and Deputy Secretary of the Treasury.

Bodman faced a daunting task because security and safety

issues continued to plague the Los Alamos National Laboratory. On July 7, 2004, two computer Zip disks containing classified data were reported missing from the lab's highly sensitive DX Division. Upon hearing the news, UC officials ordered Nanos to halt all classified work at the lab. University of California Regent Ward Connerly was so infuriated with Los Alamos' latest security debacle that he told reporters, "This is the third incident in about eight months. Part of me wants to say, 'Get rid of the damn labs.'"

Nanos apparently heard approaching hoof beats. He quickly placed twenty-three employees on investigative leave. Long-held suspicions that Nanos' real priority was to save the Department of Energy contract were renewed. Nanos told lab employees, "This is no longer an issue of competition. It's an issue of survival." Nanos' original task of attempting to save the Department of Energy contract had now evolved into saving Los Alamos as an institution. Because the DX- Division performed critical nuclear weapons research, reporters asked Nanos if espionage could be involved. Nanos, contrary to previous lab leaders, plainly responded, "Nothing could be excluded."

New Mexico Senator Pete Domenici responded with an open letter to lab employees, stating, in part, "Today, in Washington, Los Alamos' reputation as a crown jewel of science is being eclipsed by a reputation as being both dysfunctional and untouchable." Colorado Senator Wayne Allard took bolder action by introducing federal legislation that not only would ban the University of California from bidding on the new contract, but would immediately terminate the university's contract and replace them with an interim manager.

Not only were university officials and Nanos rocked by the latest security failure, but the Department of Energy's top brass was also incensed, promptly asking the FBI to conduct an investigation into the missing disks. The Project on Government Oversight group demanded the firing of Brooks, the NNSA chief. "Brooks has failed in his role as chief overseer of (LANL's) security," a POGO statement said. Not that Brooks had his head in the sand; he had once acknowledged the lab's failings when he said, "I believe there is something about the Los Alamos culture that we have not yet beaten into submission."

As if the loss of the two disks containing national nuclear weapons secrets was not enough, a few days later a lab student intern suffered a retinal lesion from a laser accident in the lab's Advanced Chemical Diagnostic and Instrumentation Group. Secretary Abraham said that these egregious security and safety breaches proved that failure to follow appropriate security and safety procedures was rampant throughout Los Alamos operations.

Nanos quickly fired four employees and disciplined nine others, while another employee resigned, most of them scientists. He called those responsible for the loss of the disks and the laser mishap "cowboys" and "buttheads." Finally recognizing the gloomy depth of the situation, and validating my long-held opinions, Nanos admitted that the lab's diseased culture needed to change. "I misread the signals," he told reporters. "I thought the security lapses stemmed from an antiquated infrastructure, but I was wrong. I now find it had to do with the attitudes of the employees."

In 2005, because of the combined factors of the alleged security mishap and safety failure, the lackadaisical attitudes of some employees, and mounting political pressures from all fronts, Nanos took the boldest director action since the beginning of the Manhattan Project, mandating the total shutdown of all Los Alamos operations. "All lab functions will remain silent until assessments and corrections can be made to all lab security and safety operations," he said. "This willful flouting of the rules must stop, and I don't care how many people I have to fire to make it stop."

But cultures die hard, as Nanos discovered when he found an underground lab bumper sticker that called the lab a "Work-Free Safety Zone." Indeed, some lab employees struck back, calling Nanos a dictator and accusing him of being a leader out of control.

Although it may have been Nanos' only remaining option, the shutdown, according to the Department of Energy, cost Americans $367 million in unrecoverable taxpayer funds. Meanwhile, with University of California officials reeling, the university's vice president of lab management, Robert Foley, made a bold political statement, suggesting that some of the employees' attitudes could be attributed to Domenici, the New Mexico senator who had earned the nickname "St. Pete" for bringing federal funds home to Los Alamos. Because Domenici had always supported the financing of LANL, Foley contended, Los Alamos employees were provided a comfort level that had made them complacent in terms of security and safety measures. Domenici sternly denied Foley's allegation.

Citing the lab's loss of the disks, Secretary Abraham ordered a nationwide shutdown of all Department of Energy work where computer data storage devices containing classified information were used. The shutdown would stay in effect, Abraham said, until all national labs were able to account for all Classified Removable Electronic Media (CREM).

The media launched into full attack mode. An *Albuquerque Journal* editorial stated that Nanos' firing of lab employees wouldn't come close to bringing back public trust of UC management. One article in *The Santa Fe New Mexican* newspaper stated, "At Los Alamos National Laboratory, our nation's nuclear bomb factory, someone is still treating security as a joke."

In early August 2004, another possible area of threat was pointed out. The Department of Energy Inspector General followed up its 2003 report concerning the lab's failure to properly manage its classified computers, identifying continuing problems at the lab that prevented classified computers from being properly "managed and safeguarded from loss or theft." The report cited classified laptop computers that didn't match with lab paperwork, and classified desktop and laptop computers that didn't match actual classified equipment. The report also highly criticized the lab's safety record, stating that unless Los Alamos placed a higher priority on stabilizing its radioactive materials, it could negatively affect the safety and health of the lab workers. "We would be hard pressed to claim that the lab's safety record is best in class," Lee McAtee, the Health, Safety and Radiation-protection Division Leader at Los Alamos, admitted to *The Santa Fe New Mexican*.

In December 2004, shortly after Secretary Abraham announced his plans to resign, the Department of Energy released another report addressing the alarming problem of security at all national labs. "The department must ensure that its most sensitive materials, facilities, and information are secure and protected from hostile groups and countries," the report said. But it went on to note that Department of Energy investigators had found weaknesses in the Los Alamos lab's ability "to assure that laptop, desktop, and related equipment are appropriately controlled and adequately safeguarded from loss or theft, and that classified computer use did not meet security standards."

Meanwhile, the mystery of the missing DX- Division Zip disks was apparently solved. In January 2005, the FBI and the Department of Energy released a report that suggested the disks never existed. Although lab records indicated twelve disks were prepared, someone had apparently prepared bar codes for two disks before they were actually made – so only ten disks ever existed. However, the report contained a footnote that was not so assuring: "The forensic evidence does not prove that no other disks were created, only that they need not have been." Thus, despite the report, the question still lingered. In 2005, Los Alamos' new director, Robert Kuckuck, confirmed the nebulous conclusion, stating that the "disks, *probably* never existed." Were there disks, and if so, were they stolen, placed behind a copy machine, or sold to one of our country's enemies? No one apparently really knows with surety – at least, no one who should know.

Bill Desmond, acting associate administrator for Defense Nuclear Security stated that the National Nuclear Security Administration was unaware of the extent to which Los Alamos employees disregarded security procedures. "An inventory," said Desmond, "showed that large amounts of top-secret material, besides the questionable pair of Zip disks – were not being properly tracked."

With the enigma of the missing DX disks allegedly solved, Nanos was about to tell his DX-Division personnel to resume their normal duties. But the lab had a few more alarming calamities to deal with.

On February 9, 2005, a few hours after President Bush announced he wanted to fund Los Alamos with an extra four million dollars to study new weapons that could destroy hardened, deeply buried targets, the lab experienced its own "bunker buster" denotation.

Don Brown, a lab contractor responsible for evaluating quality control over Department of Energy nuclear facilities, told "CBS Evening News" that he had uncovered several safety violations at the lab's Technical Area- 18, where sub-critical nuclear experiments were being performed. Brown said the types of problems he discovered would put a halt to work at any other nuclear facility. For example, he found more than 1,000 faulty welds, which made the facility susceptible to nuclear accidents many times worse than in Chernobyl. Brown tried to explain. "I attempted to resolve the problems with UC and LANL officials, but they ignored me," he said. "Instead, they sent me a letter telling me they were taking those assignments away from me."

In response to Brown's charges, I feel lab spokesperson Kevin Roark gave few details of what exact actions were being taken. "There is a very aggressive program in place to rectify the very issues," he said.

A weary Nanos resigned as director in May 2005, being the shortest serving director in the lab's history, and was replaced by Robert Kuckuck. Kuckuck didn't have long to wait until feeling the sting of LANL ways. In July 2005, a long-time lab employee failed to follow procedures when opening a package containing radioactive americium-241. This safety violation resulted in the americium-241 contaminating houses and another lab in four states. Terry Wallace, the lab's associate director for strategic research, called the contamination "low level, but serious." More grim news came soon. On

August 3, 2005, Kuckuck was told that nearly three weeks earlier, two lab employees had inhaled nitric and hydrochloric acid fumes, sending one of the employees to the hospital for nearly a week. Contrary to policy, the employees did not report the mishap to occupational medicine that day, and no one told the new director until August 3. Three employees were placed on paid leave pending investigations of both potentially serious safety violations.

A few years ago, this situation may have been handled differently at the Los Alamos National Laboratory. In the 1980s, lab employee Ben Ortiz became violently ill, believing his illness was caused by his toxic exposure at the lab. His superiors made an appointment with him with the lab's paid physician. Although Ortiz had been soldering silver and cadmium and working bare handed, nearly elbow-deep in vats of chemical solvent for years, the doctor had a unique diagnosis. Ben, I think this is being caused by your age (he was 50 at the time), or maybe it is just your imagination. Then the stinger, "Ben, do you know what, *En boca cerrada no entran muscas* means?" "Yes", said Ben. "It means keep your mouth shut."

Regrettably, to the disadvantage of all Americans, Steve, Jim, and I propose the Spanish words *En boca cerrada no entran muscas* was a common Los Alamos concept, and we postulate it still is.

All of us should ask our representatives and ourselves what risks, frightening lapses, and hazards will the laboratory pose for our country in the wake of ever widening terrorist threats? Will LANL ever be secure and safe? Another security breach at the Los Alamos National Laboratory in 2006, emphatically proclaimed – "Probably not!"

XXXVIII

Meth Lab Connection

By October 2006, Los Alamos officials believed that all was finally well at the lab. This idea slipped away when, on October 17, 2006, Los Alamos County police officers responded to a domestic violence call. What they encountered instead was local illegal drug user Justin Stone and lab employee Jessica Quintana hunkered down in her house trailer. Search of the residence disclosed methamphetamine, Los Alamos National Laboratory USB thumb-drives, and classified documents.

The FBI responded and determined that the thumb-drives and the 400-plus pages contained classified nuclear research data, ranging from national security intelligence information to secret data about nuclear weapons.

Quintana was a contract employee who held a Sigma 15 Q-cleared classification that allowed her to read classified documents that could contain information on how to bypass "permissive action" links, which ensures only authorized use of nuclear weapons information. She had been laid off in September 2006 from the lab's Hydrodynamics Experiments Division (HX). The HX- Division was formerly a part of the now-infamous DX- Division, created when the new contractor took over lab management in June 2006. Stone was incarcerated for a probation violation and possession of drug paraphernalia; Stone claimed to officials that the classified "stuff" was not his. Stone was eventually sentenced to two years in prison.

In December 2007, U.S. Magistrate Lorenzo Garcia sentenced Quintana to two years probation. As the sentence was handed down the judge told Quintana how her actions harmed, among others, her former employer, which had lost its contract with the lab. Quintana, who had pleaded guilty to one misdemeanor for mishandling classified matter, said, "*I knew there was lax security, and I took advantage of it.*" Her attorney, Stephen Aarons, argued that Quintana should not have to pay proposed restitution of nearly $400,000 because scores of other governmental officials had mishandled classified matter and received little more than a slap on the wrist.

I am curious as to exactly what Aarons was alleging.

As POGO's Danielle Brian had said years before, "What does it take for UC to suffer the consequences of screwing up?"

What was both clear and alarming was that this 22-year-old contract employee readily removed classified nuclear weapons research information from the Los Alamos National Laboratory by concealing it on her body in a backpack. It was that easy seven years ago when Steve, Jim, and I worked there, and it is obviously that easy now.

In response to the Quintana security failure, Department of Energy spokesperson Craig Stevens said, "We want to know how this could happen."

For me, the answer is disconcerting but simple: The lab's security program is severely lacking. Checks of vehicles, briefcases, people, and other property are next to nil. A lab employee who has worked in various classified lab areas since the 1980s told me he had been checked three times in the last 21 years – the latest about seven years ago. X-ray machines, personal searches, metal detectors, and the discarding of personal effects are a way of life at our airports. A breach of security in the airport environment could endanger the lives of hundreds, perhaps thousands. A breach of security at our national labs could endanger the lives of millions, perhaps the entire world population. Yet, a rank-and-file employee with association to a person involved in illegal drugs can easily walk out of the lab's front door, taking with her mounds of classified information – untouched.

It appears Los Alamos leadership still doesn't get it, or is so embedded in unadulterated arrogance that they thumb their noses at rules, laws, and promises.

The warning siren is wailing across America but it appears we are deaf to its pleadings. On October 16, 2006, Secretary of Homeland Security Michael Chertoff sent a sobering message to international law enforcement officials at the International Association of Chiefs of Police Conference in Boston. "Let me start by talking a little bit about what we are most concerned about at the Department of Homeland Security in terms of the emerging picture of threats to the homeland from terrorism," he said. "The first…is the possibility of a weapon of mass destruction being introduced into one of our cities or towns here in United States. We're talking about a radiological weapon, chemical weapon, a biological weapon, even a nuclear weapon…And, obviously, the consequences of such an attack are so great, we have to do everything in our power to prevent this from happening". In January 2009, incoming Homeland Security Secretary Janet Napolitano echoed the thoughts of Chertoff to a reporter for the *Arizona Republic* newspaper, stating, "We would be wrong to tell American people there would never be an attack on American soil again. What keeps me up at night: There are a lot of what-ifs in this job."

The "we" and the "our" about whom Chertoff speaks are the leaders of these United States and our national labs, and what causes Secretary Napolitano to lose sleep *are indeed the "what ifs."*

May these leaders enact measures post haste to protect our national labs against the "what ifs" with *impregnable* safeguards and security, before it is too late. For the future of humankind, I propose, it must be America's charge.

XXXIX

Clear and Present Dangers 2009

After the failures and debacles at the Los Alamos National Laboratory were exposed in 2002, the federal government, the University of California, and the Los Alamos National Laboratory attempted to initiate steps to finally bring professionalism and expertise to the management of the Los Alamos National Laboratory; regrettably, it was business as usual:

- In 2009, the Los Alamos National Laboratory had to contact nearly 2000 current and former employees and visitors because of potential exposure to beryllium. Beryllium, a toxic metal used in the casings surrounding plutonium pits, can cause lung disease. Los Alamos officials stated that the chances of someone falling ill from the beryllium are remote. New Mexico Senator Tom Udall apparently disagreed, stating the situation was of "great concern", and requested the lab conduct a full investigation.

- The National Nuclear Security Administration released a report in February 2009, stating that Los Alamos had *another* 69 computers either lost or stolen, with 13 of them vanishing in 2008. LANL officials did not even know they were lost or stolen until January 2009, when three lab computers *were stolen from a scientist's home* in Santa Fe. This prompted lab leaders to do an inventory, which revealed the lost or stolen computers. In addition, lab management admitted that a lab Blackberry was lost "in a *sensitive* country." So much for wall-to-wall inventories and Department of Energy mandated audits. A lab spokesman presented their now tattered statement, "None of the computers contained classified information". But an NNSA memo outlining the loss of the computers stated the "magnitude of exposure and risk to the laboratory is at best unclear as little data on these losses have been collected and pursued," since LANL treated these missing computers as "*property management issues.*"

- Chris Mechels stated regarding this security failure, "...they handle...equipment, in the easiest manner, not the correct manner. The solution; put a few of them in prison where they belong."

- In February 2009, National Nuclear Security Administration officials released more alarming news. The officials sent a letter to Los Alamos Director Michael Anastasio, chastising the Los Alamos laboratory for failure "to conclusively determine control of special nuclear material as there is no reconciliation of the physical inventory that includes calculation and evaluation of the ID (inventory difference)." The officials stated that this failure "exceeded alarm limits," and the items of the inventory included huge stocks of plutonium and highly enriched uranium – enough for the making of hundreds of nuclear weapons. The failures identified by the NNSA officials at the lab's Technical Area-55 included:
    - compliant Nuclear Material Control & Accountability (MC&A) program.
    - lack of qualified and experienced personnel in critical positions.
    - inattention to performance indicators.
    - lack of procedures for key processes.
    - conduct of operations deficiencies.
    - inadequate quality assurance practices.

The officials said in their letter that these weaknesses had the potential of diminishing "...the ability of the facility to continue operations."

Interestingly, although the Department of Energy was aware of these inadequacies as early as June 2008, they still granted the Los Alamos National Laboratory a $1.43 million performance award fee, even though one of the areas of performance evaluation was "*material control and accountability.*"

A report released by the Project on Government Oversight organization in February 2009, concerning the February 2009 NNSA letter referenced a cover-up type tactic. That is, the report stated, "DOE appears focused on preventing this latest LANL bad news from becoming publicized and sent out messages to staff *warning them not to release critical information to the public.* If the information was sensitive enough to pose a security concern, there is a process in place at DOE to classify the information. However, the letter is stamped 'Official Use Only,' which is not a classification marking but is generally used to prevent internal documents *from seeing the light of day.*'"

Is it any wonder that in 2009, Steve, Jim, and I still opine, that security at the Los Alamos National Laboratory remains just a word, a word without sufficient meaning.

Yes, based on a bevy of personal knowledge and unbiased investigatory disclosures, Steve, Jim, and I maintain that security at the Los Alamos National Laboratory is still sorely inadequate.

There are encouraging signs that federal hierarchy may agree with us. In April 2009, a report released by Washington D.C. officials, concerned Transforming the U.S. Strategic Posture and Weapons Complex for Transition to a Nuclear-Free World. The report came at a time that United States and Russia were, once again, negotiating reducing their nuclear arsenals. Dr. Robert Civiak, the lead author of the report, a physicist and former White House Office of Management Budget examiner, recommended that United States' weapons-grade and weapons-quantity nuclear material be consolidated into fewer sites in order to enhance nuclear weapons security. Supporters of the report concurred with the consolidation view, stating that sites housing nuclear weapons remains major *homeland security vulnerability.*

In April 2009, while emphasizing his concern for the security of 21st century nuclear weapons, United States President Barack Obama told world leaders "...the *theft of nuclear material* could lead to the extermination of any city on the planet." An Obama senior administrative official added, "The United States... needs to...turn their attention to *the threat of nuclear terrorism*...to focus on the growing and urgent danger of *loose nukes.*"

In these days of bona fide and ever-increasing fear of nuclear terrorism, there are genuine concerns regarding the solid protection of United States' nuclear secrets. According to security experts, three major concerns exist at the Los Alamos National Laboratory:

1. **Theft of nuclear weapons codes**

   Some security experts suggest that threats from the inside are of the greatest concern. In 1999, former Senator Warren Rudman (R-NH), the Chair of the President's Foreign Intelligence Advisory Board, was asked to review security at all Department of Energy weapons laboratories. The board's report stated the major threat to our nuclear secrets is the insider - *the trusted employee.* "Virtually," the report indicated, "all of our known spies have been insiders with the higher security clearances...the insider is a priority problem."

   Indeed, it was Klaus Fuchs, the Los Alamos laboratory physicist who passed nuclear secrets to the Soviets in 1945. It was *somebody* from inside the Los Alamos National Laboratory in 2000, who had the two missing hard drives for three weeks. Los Alamos officials *believe* the missing 2004 Zip disks most likely did not exist, but they *can't prove it.* In addition, it was Wen Ho Lee, the Los Alamos laboratory scientist, who admitted he illegally downloaded classified information.

Neither allegations nor evidence indicates that Bus-solini or Alexander, who both held high U.S. security clear-ances, were in the spy business. Evidence pointed to the fact that they were just thieves. Yet these individuals – trust-ed employees - who were in charge of changing light bulbs and cutting weeds, had access for years to the keys to the locks, and the lock picks that could be used on the locks to one of the lab's most secret areas of nuclear weapons re-search.

How easy would it be to get classified information out of the lab? A device the size of a GameBoy can down-load the equivalent of 1,100 floppy disks off a computer in three minutes and fourteen seconds. Another device called a memory stick, the size of a stick of gum, can hold the equivalent of forty-four floppy disks. The tiny, easily hidden USB thumb-drives used in the Quintana incident normally have the capacity to hold 128GB. These are just three of several devices that can be used to quickly and proficiently download classified documents and easily be hidden upon the person.

2. **Exploding an Improvised Nuclear Device (IND)**

An IND can be created at the Los Alamos National Labo-ratory on site because of the presence of Special Nuclear Materials in bomb grade quality and quantity. How such a crude weapon can be created is highly classified. However, experts point out that any self-respecting college physics student already has the knowledge. Explicit instructions on how to build a nuclear weapon are on the Internet. With the proper material and knowledge, little time is required to make an IND, and an IND explosion could cause a chain reaction on par with the devastation of Hiroshima and Na-gasaki. Thus, a terrorist would not have to steal nuclear material, then create a nuclear device and transport it to the United States, but rather they would just need to gain access to the material at the Los Alamos National Laboratory, and within minutes create the IND on site, and then detonate it on site.

3. **Radiation sabotage**

   Blow up nuclear material with conventional explosives, and dispersing radiation into the surrounding areas. An insider in the Los Alamos National Laboratory, an outside terrorist getting inside, or a truck bomb could achieve this.

What would happen if terrorists entered the halls of the Los Alamos National Laboratory and exploded a dirty radiation bomb? A good portion of New Mexico would be enshrouded in a radiation nightmare. What would happen if terrorists breached the lab's innermost chambers and exploded an Improvised Nuclear Device? It would mean the end of Northern New Mexico, and depending on wind direction, other parts of New Mexico, and perhaps some surrounding states, as we know them. What would happen if an insider stole codes to the laboratory's most secret nuclear weapons research and passed them to rogue nations like Iran and North Korea? If we don't heed the warnings to protect our national secrets, we may be forced to a frightening observation, to paraphrase J. Robert Oppenheimer who gave a dire warning on a hot 1945 summer morning as he watched the explosion of the first atomic bomb; we will become death – our world will be destroyed.

XL

A Nation at Risk

On multiple occasions, Doran, Mullins, and I were told that we were to make the lab feel like a college campus, not a military installation.

We were also told that lab leadership used the words inquiry and inquirer as opposed to the common terminologies of investigation and investigator. The reason, because lab leadership felt the words investigation and investigator were too harsh for the type of people who worked at the lab, but the words inquiry and inquirer were much softer, and consequently, more acceptable to the campus environment atmosphere they wanted.

When Steve and I were summoned to University of California Headquarters in Oakland, California in January 2003, we were asked to tell the university's top officials all we knew about the lab's mismanagement, theft, cover-ups, corruption, and failed security. We told them that our superior directed us multiple times, to ensure that the lab maintained a college campus environment, and not have a military feel, because it would offend the lab's employees –

especially the scientists. We explained how that perspective, in our opinion, had a negative impact on lab security and protecting our nation's top secrets.

As we looked across the table at the University of California elite, no one flinched at those comments. We expected shock, but we both saw and felt none. In the police world where Steve and I came from, failure to deny the allegation is an indication of guilt. From their facial expressions, we judged that our comments were not a revelation.

Perhaps, as we were told at the Los Alamos National Laboratory, the order for a campus environment came directly from university headquarters in downtown Oakland.

In Steve's, Jim's, and my opinion, the Los Alamos National Laboratory remains unsafe and unsecured, and it will remain that way until the Department of Energy and lab management make our country's top secrets and security a major priority. We must get rid of the campus environment mentality and realize we live in times of extreme terrorism threats where real dangers to our national nuclear facilities and data secrets increase daily.

Are Steve, Jim, and I overreacting? Are we crying wolf? We think not.

In the early 1990s, I attended FBI National Executive Institute training at the FBI Academy in Quantico, Virginia. During that training my fellow classmates and I were told by terrorism security experts, that United States law enforcement needed to get prepared for terrorism on American soil. They theorized the attacks would occur around the turn of the century. Regrettably, they were right on target. These same like experts are now telling us that terroristic events as great as, and perhaps beyond the tragedy of 9-11 could be coming to these United States again. Hopefully they are wrong, but I don't think so.

In March 2008, Chi Mak was sentenced to nearly 25 years in a federal prison for secretly copying U.S. secrets on Navy ships and submarines, and then having the data transferred to Chinese authorities by courier. Mak admitted he had been placed in America more than 20-years-earlier in order to burrow into America's defense-industrial establishments to steal secrets. According to U.S. Intelligence and Justice Department officials, the Mak case represents a *small facet* of the spy intelligence gathering operations that are *continually growing* in size and sophistication in America.

In June 2009, Walter Kendall Myers and his wife Gwendolyn Steingraber Myers were arrested by the FBI for alleged spying for Cuba for 30 years. Joseph Persichini, the FBI's assistant director in charge of the investigation stated that even as U.S. relations with foreign countries change, the clandestine hunt for secrets continues. "When it comes to the intent of other nations pursuing our classified material, our research and development, the Cold War is not over, this activity does continue," Persichini said.

In October 2009, the FBI arrested United States scientist Stewart David Nozette for alleged attempted espionage. Nozette worked at the University of California's Lawrence Livermore National Laboratory from approximately 1990 to 1999, where he designed highly advanced technology, and held a federal clearance that gave him access to information relating to atomic or nuclear-related materials. The criminal complaint alleges that Nozette offered to reveal classified information to an undercover FBI agent posing as a foreign entity. The information Nozette allegedly offered included nuclear weaponry and other major United States weapons systems.

In December 2004, the Department of Energy released the preliminary criteria to potential bidders who wanted to take over Los Alamos National Laboratory management when the University of California's contract expired in September 2005. Several entities expressed initial interest, including the University of California, Northrop Grumman Technical Services, Lockheed Martin, the University of Texas, and The Texas A&M University. In the end, two bidders came to the forefront of competition - the University of California, who partnered with Bechtel National, calling themselves the Los Alamos National Security (LANS) LLC team; and Lockheed

Martin, who partnered with the University of Texas, calling themselves the Los Alamos Alliance LLC team. LANS received the nod and took over management of the lab in June 2006.

For the first time in the Los Alamos National Laboratory's more than sixty-year history, it is now co-operated by an industrial partner. No longer will a purely nonprofit academic institution run the Los Alamos National Laboratory.

As part of the contract, National Nuclear Security Administration officials agreed to conduct evaluations of LANS performance, offering additional fees for high grades of performance. The 2007 LANS Performance Report gave LANS 5 "F's" causing LANS to lose nearly 15 million dollars. The report stated LANS failures included poor leadership, management, environmental protections, and safety. LANS was severely admonished for allowing leaks of classified information. "The length of time it has taken the laboratory to resolve cyber security...and developing integrated corrective actions...did not reflect...urgency or focus", the report said. *Can anyone get it right?*

The Department of Energy gave LANS an overall FY2009 performance rating of *"Good."* Certainly, LANS has improved their overall performance over FY2008, and for that they are to be commended. However, DOE ratings are given within Poor, Good, Very Good, and Outstanding classifications. Thus, although LANS deserves kudos for their improved performance, coming in "Good" as opposed to "Outstanding," is not something to be proud of as an organization, nor does it bring warm and fuzzy feelings to those of us who would hope and expect our premiere national laboratory to be outstanding - not just good. Apparently, some Los Alamos National Laboratory employees are not that enamored with LANS leadership. That is, an employee survey taken in 2009, revealed, that of those who responded to the survey, 71.31% indicated they did not "have confidence in the leadership of the laboratory," and 82.70% believed that no "action would be taken on the results of the survey."

Steve, Jim, and I strongly hoped that Department of Energy

officials would not renew their contract with the University of California. It was nothing personal, but we believed the responsibilities of Los Alamos management needed to be in the hands of an entity that would take national security and stewardship of federal funds as a sworn oath of service, not only for the present generation, but also for our children and our children's children. For us, the facts were undeniable, that certain leaders of the University of California and the Los Alamos National Laboratory severely failed every American on all counts. Yes, the leadership of the University of California and the Los Alamos National Laboratory, as well as the thousands of hardworking and dedicated Los Alamos employees, who have unselfishly labored for America through the decades, should be praised for their dedication, commitment, and expertise that have resulted in noteworthy and *unbelievable scientific advancements*.

However, I postulate, the Los Alamos National Laboratory's inexcusable security debacles and ever-increasing security failures — yea even through the first decade of the 21st Century — necessitates that the laboratory be placed in expert security hands – as *General Leslie R. Groves* would have done. Masterful hands that will ensure, without use of irrational, patronizing excuses, and corporate protectionism philosophies, *fail-safe security* of our nation's secrets. I respectfully suggest that it is time for America to get it right before it is too late.

The headlines of the first eight-plus years of the 21st Century have been replete with corporate corruption. For example, the Enron, Tyco, Martha Stewart/ImClone, WorldCom, Halliburton, Qwest, and Madoff Ponzi scheme scandals have illustrated how far some corporate leaders have plunged into the abyss of corruption while using deceptive business practices to attempt to cover-up their misdeeds. However, it is one thing to steal from stockholders and the public at large, and quite another to be involved in a type of corruption that jeopardizes America's security and national nuclear weapons secrets.

Osama bin Laden, Mahmoud Ahmadinejad and Muqtada al-

Sadr and their minions — including America's homegrown variety — represent entities that pose *real threats to all Americans*. These individuals would not hesitate to steal or destroy our national secrets, and kill every American they can in the process. For leaders of any American institution to be part of a system that places our nation at risk is, to me, unforgivable. And yet, there have been proven acts of egregious deceit, deception, corruption, mismanagement, and/or cover-up by certain employees of the Los Alamos National Laboratory. Regrettably, some of the people appointed as stewards of the defense of our beloved United States have not been of the caliber so desperately needed in these chaotic and peril-filled times.

When Steve, Jim, and I accepted employment at the Los Alamos National Laboratory, our intent was to continue to serve our country, not as police officers as we had done for most of our lives, but as security specialists helping to protect America's national secrets in a period of great potential risk and danger from terrorist threats.

We propose that we encountered some administrators so concerned about maintaining their jobs and associated lucrative salaries and benefits, that they lost sight of what it meant to be wise stewards of America's tax dollars and, even more important, America's security.

I wrote this book in the hope that my findings and revelations will stimulate the public to demand of their governmental officials that they initiate and maintain the necessary actions to ensure that these unconscionable leadership failures and security dangers never occur again. Further, I hope there will be a fresh focus on professionalism, scientific advancement, integrity and security throughout all of America's national laboratories. Let us pray so, for I believe the safety, security, and permanence of these United States of America hang in the balance.

ACRONYMS

A&A – LANL's Audits and Assessments Office

Appendix O – Performance initiatives placed on UC/LANL by the DOE

BUS – LANL's Business Operations Division

BUS 1, 2 and So Forth – Units of Operations within BUS

CI – Confidential Informant

CREM – Classified Removable Electronic Media (such as computer hard drives and Zip disks)

D-DIVISION – LANL's Decision Application Division

DEA – Drug Enforcement Administration

DOD – Department of Defense

DOE – Department of Energy

DOE IG – Department of Energy Inspector General

DX-Division – LANL's Dynamic Experimentation Division

ESA – LANL's Engineering Sciences and Applications Division

FBI – Federal Bureau of Investigation

FMU – LANL's Facility Management Unit

GAO – United States General Accounting Office

HEU – Highly Enriched Uranium

HR – LANL's Human Resources Division or Office

HX-Division – LANL's Hydrodynamics Experiments Division

IG – Inspector General

IND – Improvised Nuclear Device

ISEC – LANL's Internal Security Office

JCNNM – Johnson Controls of Northern New Mexico – LANL contractor responsible for overall maintenance of the Lab

JIT – Just In Time (A LANL purchasing system)

LANL – Los Alamos National Laboratory

LAPD – Los Alamos Police Department

LLC – Los Alamos National Security LLC. The new contractor for LANL in June 2006.

LLNL – Lawrence Livermore National Laboratory

LVA – Local Vendor Agreement (A LANL purchasing system)

NCIC – National Crime Information Center

NIS – LANL's Nonproliferation and International Security Division

NNSA – National Nuclear Security Administration

OSI – LANL's Office of Security Inquiries

POGO – Project on Government Oversight, a Washington D.C. based non-partisan, non-profit government watchdog group whose mission is to investigate, expose and remedy abuses of power, mismanagement, and subservience to powerful special interests by the federal government

PTLA – Protection Technologies of Los Alamos – LANL's security force

PU – Plutonium

PWC – PriceWaterhouseCoopers auditing firm

Q-Cleared – DOE Security Clearance equivalent to DOD Top-Secret Clearance

RICO – Racketeering Influenced Crime Organization

RLDD – Report on Lost, Damaged and Destroyed Property (A

LANL In-House Report)

S-Division – LANL's Security and Safeguards Division

SNM – Special Nuclear Material

TA – Technical Area

UC – University of California

UCR – Uniform Crime Reporting

X-Division – LANL's Applied Physics Division

Zip Disk – Advanced version of the floppy disk

ABOUT THE AUTHOR

Glenn A. Walp was a member of the Pennsylvania State Police for nearly 29 years, retiring from the agency as commissioner, holding the rank of colonel and a member of the governor's cabinet. After retiring from the state police, he accepted positions as Chief of Police in the City of Bullhead City, Arizona and the Arizona Capitol Police. He then accepted an offer by the University of California to be the Office Leader of the Office of Security Inquiries at the Los Alamos National Laboratory, Los Alamos, New Mexico. Because of his skilled investigative efforts at Los Alamos, he was assigned as a personal consultant to the President of the University of California.

Walp has an Associate of Science in police administration from York College, York, Pennsylvania; a Bachelor of Science in criminology/police administration from Indiana University, Indiana, Pennsylvania; Master of Arts in criminal psychology from Prescott College, Prescott, Arizona; and a Ph.D. in Human Services, with a specialization in criminal justice from Walden University, Minneapolis, Minnesota. He is a graduate of the Federal Bureau of Investigation's National Police Academy and National Executive Institute; the Southwest Command College; the Governor's Senior Management Development School at Penn State University; the Secret Service Dignitary Protection School; and the Glynco, Georgia Federal Law Enforcement Training Center. He was a certified police officer in the States of Pennsylvania and Arizona, a certified police instructor for the Commonwealth of Pennsylvania, and held a United States Top-secret Clearance.

Walp graduated magna cum laude from Indiana University of Pennsylvania and was the recipient of the University's 1994 Distinguished Alumni Award. The Pennsylvania Human Relations Commission and the National Organization of Black Law Enforcement Executives recognized him for his strong stance for human rights. He received the Optimist Club Law Enforcement Officer of the Year Award, and the national J. Stannard Baker Award for Outstanding Achievement in Highway Safety. Glenn was assistant task force commander of the Pennsylvania Johnstown Flood of 1977, and the task force commander of the Pennsylvania Camp Hill Prison Riot of 1989. As Chairman of the Pennsylvania Crime Commission, he spearheaded a corruption investigation that resulted in the incarceration of the state attorney general. Because of his criminal investigative efforts at Los Alamos, he received a Letter of Commendation from the FBI, and was nominated for the national Paul H. Douglas Ethics in Government Award. He has appeared multiple times as a guest on national television programs such as *The O'Reilly Factor,CBS Nightly News, NBC Nightly News, and CNN's American Morning with Paula Zahn.*

Dr. Walp is employed part-time as an adjunct professor and consultant for Penn State University in their Justice and Safety Institute, teaching police executives nationally and internationally, and has been consulted by Penn State staff concerning security matters related to the United Arab Emirates. He has served on an Executive Search Team program for the International Association of Chiefs of Police, is the owner operator of Criminal Justice Consulting, and is Operations Manager of Justice Publishing, LLC. Walp's academic works include, *"The Missing Link between Pornography and Rape: Convicted Rapists Respond with Validated Truth"*, *"The Causes of Crime: A Search for Truth"*, and is co-author of *"Criminal Investigation Assessments"*, as published in the FBI Law Enforcement Bulletin.

Glenn, who resides in Gold Canyon, Arizona, has three children, Yvette, Faith and Aaron; a stepson Garett; and seven grandchildren, Adam, Michael, Chandler, Marah, Marissa, Austin and Mason.

ACKNOWLEDGEMENTS

Deepest thanks are extended to the following individuals and, where relevant, their associated agencies, for their dedication and commitment to professionalism and truth. In multiple instances, their journalistic and/or personal efforts have contributed extensively to helping expose/illustrate the crime, corruption, mismanagement and cover-up at America's most prominent national nuclear weapons facility. You deserve the gratitude of all Americans.

Attkisson, Sharyl – Washington, D.C. based Correspondent for *CBS News*

Benke, Richard – Reporter, *Associated Press*

Bopp, Charles – Senior Investigator, U.S. Senate Finance Committee

Brian, Danielle – Executive Director, Project On Government Oversight (POGO)

Broder, David – Reporter, *The Washington Post*

Brown, David – Senior Producer, *The O'Reilly Factor*

Clark, Bob – Commentator, KRSN Radio, Los Alamos, New Mexico

Clark, Louis; Danielle Brian and Jeff Ruch – From their book, *The Act of Anonymous Activism: Serving the Public While Surviving Public Service*

Coile, Zachary – Reporter, *San Francisco Chronicle* newspaper,

Washington D.C. Bureau

Cutler, Kim-Mai – Reporter, *The Daily Californian* newspaper

Daley, Beth – Director of Communication and Development, POGO

Davidson, Keay – Reporter, *San Francisco Chronicle* newspaper

Fredman, Nate – Associate Producer, *The O'Reilly Factor*

Freedhoff, Michal – Senior Policy Associate, Office of Congressman Edward J. Markey (D-Massachusetts)

Friedman, Lisa – Staff Writer, *Oakland, California Tribune* newspaper, Washington D.C. Bureau

Gehrke, Robert – Reporter, *Associated Press*

Gilbert, Thomas – Associated Press employee

Hargrove, Thomas – Reporter, *Albuquerque Tribune* newspaper

Hemmer, Bill – Anchor, CNN, *American Morning with Paula Zahn*

Hoffman, Ian – Staff Writer, *Oakland, California Tribune* newspaper

Hoffman, Leslie – Reporter, As*sociated Press*

Holstege, Sean – Reporter, *The Arizona Republic* newspaper

Jennings, John – LANL NIS employee

Johns, Joe – Washington, D.C. based Correspondent for *NBC News*

Johnson, Carrie – Reporter, *Washington Post*

Kabat, Alan – Attorney and Public Information Officer for Bernabei and Katz, a Washington D.C. based law firm

KOB TV Channel 4 – *NBC News* affiliate, Albuquerque, New Mexico

KOAT Action 7 – *ABC News* affiliate, Albuquerque, New Mexico

KRQE TV Channel 13 – *CBS News* affiliate, Albuquerque, New Mexico

Lobsenz, George – Reporter, *The Energy Daily*, a Washington D.C. based news publication

Lutts, Matthew – Associated Press employee

Monaco, Rob – Producer, *Fox Wire News*

Montano, Chuck – LANL Audits and Assessments Specialist

Multiple LANL employees who requested anonymity at the time they provided information to the author or others

Murphy, Charles – Investigator, Office of U.S. Senator Charles

Grassley (R-Iowa)

O'Reilly, Bill – Anchor, Fox News, *The O'Reilly Factor*

Oswald, Mark – Editor, *Albuquerque Journal Northern Bureau* newspaper

Rankin, Adam – Reporter, *Albuquerque Journal Northern Bureau* newspaper

Richards, Jonathan (Jon) – Cartoonist, *Albuquerque Northern Bureau* newspaper

Rocky Mountain News newspaper, Denver Colorado

Shachtman, Noah – Correspondent for *Wired News*

***Shooter* –** An Antoine Fuqua Film – 2007 Paramount Pictures

Silverstein, Stuart – Reporter, *Los Angeles Times* newspaper

Snodgrass, Roger – Assistant Editor for *The Los Alamos, New Mexico Monitor* newspaper

Sterngold, Jim – Reporter, *San Francisco Chronicle* newspaper

Stober, Dan – Reporter, *San Jose Mercury News*, a Bay Area newspaper

Stockton, Peter – Senior Investigator, POGO

Taylor, Allison – Washington, D.C. based Producer for *CBS News*

Tollefson, Jeff – Reporter, *The Santa Fe New Mexican* newspaper, Santa Fe, New Mexico

Trever, John – Editorial Cartoonist, *Albuquerque Journal* newspaper

Trounson, Rebecca – Reporter, *Los Angeles Times* newspaper

Vorenberg, Sue – Reporter, *Albuquerque Tribune* newspaper and the *Scripps-McClatchy Western Service*

Ward, Jerry – www.wildcoyotephoto.com

Warrick, Joby – Reporter, *Washington Post*

Wong, Raam – Reporter, *Albuquerque Journal North* newspaper

A small portion of information in this book was gathered from Dan Stober and Ian Hoffman's book, *A Convenient Spy – Wen Ho Lee and the Politics of Nuclear Espionage*, published by Simon and Schuster.

Some of the historical information in this book concerning the Los Alamos National Laboratory came from files contained on the LANL website.

Some of the material in this book came from reports authored by the Project on Government Oversight (POGO), *U.S. Nuclear Weapons Complex: Homeland Security Opportunities*, dated May 2005, and *U.S. Nuclear Weapons Complex: Security at Risk*, dated October 2001.

SPECIAL GRATITUDE

Special gratitude to Miss Mary V. Walp, owner/operator of "Sun-Glow Word Processing", Camp Hill, Pennsylvania, who provided the executive stenographical skills necessary for this book's seven-year effort, and Mr. Jon Rochmis of San Francisco, California, the executive book editor. Their unending dedication and commitment to this project, and their superior expertise contributed extensively to the success of this book.

ASSOCIATED FEDERAL AND STATE LAWS

FEDERAL LAW

A. The Inspector General Act of 1978 was created, in part, to initiate an auditing and investigative resource to more effectively combat fraud, abuse, waste and mismanagement in the programs and operations of certain executive departments and agencies. By this Act, the Department of Energy Inspector General (DOE IG) has legislative authority to audit and investigate all issues related to federal funds endowed to federal contractors. Both the Department of Energy (DOE) and the DOE IG have the authority and responsibility to create orders in effectuating all requirements and associated requisites of the Act.

Under the authority of this Act, on March 22, 2001, the DOE, as initiated by the DOE IG, created DOE Orders 221.1 and 221.2. Under Order 221.1, the DOE IG established the policies and procedures for reporting fraud, waste, abuse, misuse, corruption, criminal acts or mismanagement to the DOE and DOE IG. The Order is applicable to all DOE contractors and their employees. This Order directs employees of DOE and its contractors who have information about actual or suspected violations of law, regulations, or policy, including fraud, waste, abuse, misuse, corruption, criminal acts, or mismanagement related to DOE programs, operations, facilities, contracts or information technology systems, to immediately notify the appropriate authorities. The Order directs that employees should, when appropriate, report directly to the Office of the Inspector General, any information concerning alleged wrongdoing by DOE, its contractors, subcontractors, grantees or other recipients of DOE financial assistance; or their employees. Order 221.2 directs that all DOE contractor employees must cooperate fully and promptly with requests from the DOE IG for information and data related to DOE programs and operations.

B. Executive Order 12731 of October 17, 1990, in essence, directs that all executive employees (to include DOE and DOE contractors and their employees who receive federal funding through DOE) are to (a) protect and conserve federal property, and shall not use federal property for other than authorized activities, (b) disclose waste, fraud, abuse, and corruption to appropriate authorities, and (c) avoid any actions creating the appearance that they are violating the law or ethical standards promulgated pursuant to the Executive Order, in order to ensure that every citizen can have complete confidence in the integrity of the federal government. Therefore, each federal employee shall respect and adhere to the fundamental principles of ethical service as implemented in regulations promulgated under the Executive Order.

C. Title 10, Code of Federal Regulations, Chapter X, Part 1010, in essence, directs that all employees of the DOE are subject to the standards of ethical conduct for employees of the executive branch concerning the reporting to DOE IG, or other appropriate authority, about fraud, waste, abuse, and corruption in DOE programs, including on the part of DOE employees, contractors, subcontractors, grantees or other recipients of DOE financial assistance.

D. Title 48, Code of Federal Regulations, Chapter I, Subpart 45.5, in essence, directs DOE contractors to maintain accountability of all government property in their possession. The contractor is directed to effectuate a system to control, protect, preserve, and maintain all government property under their control.

E. Title 18, Section 1516 states "whoever....endeavors to...obstruct, or impede a Federal auditor in the performance of official duties relating to a person receiving in excess of $1000,000.00 directly or indirectly, from the United States in any one period...shall be fined under this Title, or imprisoned not more than five years, or both."

F. Title 18, Section 4944 states "whoever falsely makes, alters, forges...any...contract... public record...or other writing for the purpose of defrauding the United States...shall be fined under this Title or imprisoned not more than ten years or both."

G. Title 18, Section 2232 states that "whoever, before, during, or after any search for or seizure of property by any person authorized to make such search or seizure, knowingly destroys, damages... disposes of, transfers, or otherwise takes any action...for the purpose of preventing or impairing the government's lawful authority to take such property into its custody or control...shall be fined under this Title or imprisoned not more than five years, or both."

H. Title 18, Section 372 states "if two or more persons in any state...conspire to prevent, by force, intimidation, or threat, any person from accepting or holding any...place of confidence under the United States, or from discharging any duties thereof...shall be fined not more than $5000.00 or imprisoned not more than six years, or both."

I. Title 18, Chapter 31, Section 641 states "whoever embezzles, steals, purloins, or knowingly converts to his use or the use of another, or without authority, sells, conveys, disposes of any record, voucher, money or thing of value of the United States or of any department or agency thereof, or any property made or being made under contract for the United States or any department or agency thereof...shall be fined under this Title or imprisoned not more than ten years, or both."

J. Title 18, Chapter I, Section 4 "whoever having knowledge of the actual commission of a felony...conceals and does not as soon as possible make known the same to some judge or to other person in civil or military authority under the United States, shall be fined under this Title or imprisoned not more than three years, or both."

K. Title 18, Chapter 11, Section 218 states "...the President or... the head of any department...may declare void and rescind any contract...authority...in relation to which there has been final conviction of any violation of the Chapter, and the United States shall be entitled to recover in addition to any penalty prescribed by law or in a contract the amount expended or the thing transferred or delivered on its behalf, or the reasonable value thereof."

NEW MEXICO STATE LAW

A. Chapter 30, Section 30-16-1 covers all larceny (theft) that occurs within the state.

B. Chapter 30, Section 30-22-1 states "whoever knowingly obstructs, resists or opposes any officer of this state or any other dually authorized person serving or attempting to serve or execute any process or any rule or order of any of the courts of this state or an other judicial writ or process...commits resisting, evading or obstructing an officer."

C. Chapter 30, Section 30-16-11 states "whoever receives stolen property...knowing that it has been stolen or believing it has been stolen is guilty of the mandates of this statute."

INDEX

A

A&A 69, 89, 239, 253,341

Abraham, Spencer 207, 220, 221, 225, 226, 227, 230, 265, 266, 289, 290, 294, 315, 317, 319, 320, 321

Albuquerque Journal 180, 181, 221, 256, 320, 351

Albuquerque Journal North 162, 178, 179, 224, 233, 351

Alexander, Scott 67, 68, 70, 76, 77, 79, 80, 81, 82, 83, 89, 140, 141, 142, 144, 147, 148, 151, 152, 153, 154,155, 165, 190, 200, 208, 209, 215, 222, 224, 250, 251, 252, 333

Allen, Jeffrey 245

Annual Lost and Stolen Report 40, 46, 62

Appendix F 131, 132

Appendix 0 18, 19, 129, 130, 131, 132, 165, 255, 298, 341

Ares, Michael 64, 68

At Large with Geraldo Rivera 207

Atkinson, Richard 162, 164, 165, 215, 217, 218, 219, 224, 225, 228, 231, 232, 233, 241, 275, 285, 293, 297

Attkisson, Sharyl 206, 207, 349

Audits and Assessments 88, 89, 91, 140, 143, 150, 156, 210, 217, 226, 229, 239, 269, 270, 271, 284, 288, 341, 350

B

Bar-code(d) 46, 162, 165, 251, 264

Bellstrum, George 97, 98, 102

Bernabei, Lynne 205, 213, 231, 233, 275, 298, 299, 350

Berkeley 230, 278, 293, 295

Blair, Jeffrey 298

Blow the whistle 118, 134, 218

Bodman, Samuel 317

Bradley, Ed 313

Brian, Danielle 204, 211, 216, 226, 229, 310, 313, 326, 349

Brokaw, Tom 207

Brooks, Linton 265, 266, 288, 289, 290, 294, 316, 318

Brooks, Marla 41

Broome, Anne 226, 285

Brown, Meredith 59

Brown, Don 322

Bunkers 77, 79, 93, 109, 141, 251, 292

BUS 40, 42, 44, 45, 60, 61, 62, 63, 76, 87, 240, 245, 341

Bush, George (President) 243, 317, 322

Business Operations Division 2, 40, 56, 86, 131, 226, 341

Bussolini, Peter (Pete) 7, 68, 69, 70, 71, 76, 77, 79, 80, 81, 82,83, 89, 137, 138, 140, 141, 142, 143, 144, 147, 148, 149, 150, 151, 152, 153, 154, 155, 165, 190, 200, 208, 209, 215, 222, 224, 250, 251, 252, 333

C

Calles, Gregory 98

Cantu, Michelle 69, 72

Casey, Robert 38, 175

CBS Nightly News with Dan Rather 205, 212, 346

Chertoff, Michael 327

Christmas 41, 154, 201, 209, 225

Classified removable electronic media 314, 320, 341

CNN American Morning 209, 346, 350

Code of Ethics 239

Coghlan, Jay 227

Corporate philosophy 122, 123, 139, 142, 156, 160

Corporate rules 123

CREM 314, 320, 341

Curry, Brandon 103

D

Daley II, Peter, J. 38

Darling, Bruce 165, 231, 232, 233, 241, 244, 247, 253, 254, 255, 256, 262, 263, 273, 275, 276, 285, 300, 316

Davis, Jim 262

D-Division 283, 341

Dingle, John 191

Department of Energy 4, 13, 18, 29, 31, 47, 56, 59, 60, 64, 82, 88, 99, 102, 103, 104, 119, 122, 125, 126, 130, 131, 137, 142, 144, 145, 158, 160, 163, 164, 169, 170, 187, 188, 204, 210, 211, 212, 216, 221, 218, 228, 230, 231, 234, 237, 239, 240, 241, 243,247, 253, 263, 266, 267, 269, 270, 271, 272, 273, 274, 275, 278, 279, 281, 284, 288, 289, 291, 294, 295, 301, 306, 309, 310, 312, 313, 317, 318, 319, 320, 321, 322, 326, 330, 331, 332, 336, 337, 338, 339, 341, 353

Desmond, Bill 321

Deutsch, Peter 219, 250, 251, 255, 265, 267

Didn't fit 197, 208, 210, 303

Dirty bomb(s) 294

Disks 292, 315, 316, 318, 319, 320, 321, 322, 332, 333, 341

DOE 4, 18, 72, 81, 104, 105, 107, 118, 121, 122, 123, 125, 137, 157, 158, 188, 191, 192, 208, 211, 214, 218, 227, 238, 239, 241, 250, 254, 266, 272, 274, 301, 311, 312, 331, 338, 341, 342, 353, 354

DOE IG 82, 88, 105, 122, 208, 254, 301, 341, 353, 354

DOE Inspector General 118, 218, 254, 266

Domenici, Peter (Pete) 221, 289, 318, 320

Drop point(s) 45, 46, 115, 240, 253, 296

DX Division 318, 321, 322, 326, 341

Dy, Jeff 141, 188

E

Eckrote, Ron 42, 43, 46

Energy Daily 157, 158, 160, 204, 257, 350

Engineering Sciences and Application Division 3

Erickson, Ralph 192, 264, 265

Ernst and Young 288

ESA 3, 4, 45, 341

Eshoo, Anna 251, 254, 257, 258, 259, 260, 273

Espionage 2, 53, 58, 135, 318, 337, 351

Estes, Carol 18

F

Facility Management Unit 68, 69, 79, 341

Falcon, Matt (Mack) 14, 15, 16, 17, 19, 20, 21, 25, 31, 32, 33, 34, 35, 41, 43, 46, 56, 57, 58, 59, 60, 61, 62, 64, 65, 70, 71, 72, 73, 78, 80, 81, 86,87, 88, 89, 91, 97, 98, 99, 100, 101, 102, 104, 105, 107, 109, 110, 111, 112, 116, 117, 118, 119, 120, 121, 122, 123, 124, 126, 131, 132, 136, 137, 138, 139, 140, 141, 142, 143, 144, 145, 158, 159, 160,165, 188, 190, 191, 196, 198, 203, 204, 210, 218, 219, 228, 229, 233, 254, 282, 315, 335

Fall guy(s) 107, 111, 112, 113, 190

Farber, Katie 116, 117, 120

Farley, Marty 1, 2, 45, 69, 71, 72, 75, 188, 258

FBI 14, 15, 19, 23, 40, 41, 46, 56, 57, 58, 67, 69, 70,71, 72, 73, 75, 76, 78, 79, 81, 82, 83, 85, 86, 87, 88, 89, 90, 91, 92, 93, 95, 96, 97, 98, 99, 103, 105, 107, 108, 109, 110, 113, 115, 118, 121, 122, 129, 133, 134, 135, 136, 137, 138, 140, 141, 142, 143, 144,147, 148, 150, 152, 153, 154, 155, 156, 160, 176, 187, 190, 191, 206, 207, 211, 212, 214, 221,231, 232, 238, 240, 254, 255, 256, 257, 258, 262, 287, 302, 306, 318, 321, 325, 336, 337, 341, 346

FBI Regional Office 23

Flashcards 292, 314, 315

Flynn Barbara 88, 89, 90, 91, 92, 96, 97, 110, 112

FMU 68, 70, 79, 143, 341

Foley, Robert 316, 320
Force-on-force 308, 309, 310, 311, 313
Forgery 115, 116, 125, 135, 142, 187
Friedman, Gregory 163, 237, 238, 239, 240, 241, 243, 247, 253, 266, 267, 278, 288, 289, 290, 291, 292, 300

G

Gallegos, Adrian 103, 104, 105, 125, 126, 140, 142, 144, 158, 159
Garberson, Jeff, 161, 217
Geffroy, Michael 225
General Accounting Office (GAO) 230, 306, 341
Gibbs, Scott, 281, 282
Gitto, Rich 2, 3, 4, 62, 63, 64, 75, 76, 77, 78, 80, 86, 87, 88, 89, 91, 92, 93, 108, 109, 112, 113, 114, 161, 162, 245, 284
Government Accountability Project 124
Grassley, Charles 160, 351
GPS 209, 252
Greening the valley 253
Greenwood, James 162, 219, 230, 241, 247, 249, 250, 251, 254, 255, 258, 261, 262, 263, 264, 265, 266, 267,291
Gunther, Betty Ann 211, 216, 217
Gutierrez, Joe 229
Gwilliam, Gary 298, 299

H

Hard drive(s) 57, 71, 96, 107, 130, 159, 164, 220, 255, 265, 270, 292, 315, 332, 341
Harmon, Otto 138, 163, 164, 165, 215, 217, 218, 220, 221, 222,223, 226, 227, 228, 235, 245, 247, 257, 259, 263, 312
Hemmer, Bill 209, 350
Holleman, Edith 224, 225
Holt, James 191, 196, 257, 258, 282
Homeland Security 31, 39, 150, 156, 189, 310, 327, 332, 352
Hook, Tommy 271, 272, 273, 274

Howe, Philip 45, 46
House Energy and Commerce Committee 162, 224, 230, 244, 247, 249, 250, 289, 295
HR 341
Human Resources 18, 68, 69, 98, 115, 118, 119, 150, 156, 210, 341
Husson, Art 281, 282, 283

I
Impact Measurement Indexes (IMI) 27
Improvised Nuclear Device (IND) 320, 333, 334, 342
Informant(s) 67, 81, 83, 138, 142, 147, 149, 150, 152, 155, 176, 225, 246, 247, 341
Inspector General 82, 88, 99, 100, 102, 103, 104, 118, 119, 125, 137, 142, 144, 145, 159, 163, 187, 188, 210, 212, 216, 217, 218, 219, 221, 231, 237, 240, 243, 247, 253, 254, 263, 266, 278, 288, 289, 291, 292, 295, 300, 310, 320, 341, 342, 353, 354

J
JCNNM 43, 342
Jennings, John 83, 138, 142, 147, 148, 149, 150, 151, 152, 153, 154, 155, 156, 176, 350
JIT 77, 284, 286, 287, 288, 342
Johns, Joe 207, 350
Johnson Controls of Northern New Mexico 43, 68, 212, 250, 342
Johnson, Kenneth (Ken) 219, 220, 233, 244, 289, 295
Just In Time 77, 284, 285, 342

K
Kotla, Dee 301
Kruger, Phillip (Phil) 210, 211
Kuckuck, Robert 321, 322, 323

L

Labella, Charles 231,

LANS 338

LAPD 15, 41, 122, 342

Lavernier, Richard 313, 314

Lawrence Berkeley National Laboratory 295

Lawrence Livermore National Laboratory 47, 130, 295, 306, 337, 342

Layton, John 102, 220, 246, 284

Leivo, Kenneth (Ken) 115, 116

Ling, Tony 116, 117, 120

LLNL 47, 342

Local Vendor Agreement 267, 284, 342

Los Alamos Monitor 207, 209, 222

Lowe, Mike 23, 71

Lundberg, John 233, 285, 298

M

Madison, Douglas (Doug) 10, 17, 18, 19, 20, 21, 34, 46, 47, 49, 50, 56, 61, 62, 70, 71, 72,73, 75, 76, 78, 80, 85, 89, 91, 92, 100, 101, 107, 108, 109, 110, 111, 112, 113, 122, 131, 132, 133, 134, 135, 136, 137, 140, 158, 159, 160, 188, 189, 190, 191, 192, 193, 195, 196, 197, 198, 199, 203, 210, 228, 229, 233, 234, 254, 255, 256, 257, 258, 261, 263, 274, 281, 282, 283, 315

Matthews, Jason 3, 4

Marquez, Richard (Rich) 60, 61, 64, 76, 89, 191, 192, 193, 215 216, 218, 247, 257, 264, 285

Markey, Edward (Ed) 241, 263, 301, 350

Martinez, Eric 86, 235, 236

McDonald, Jaret 67, 68, 69, 70, 71, 72, 76, 77, 83, 147, 148, 172, 249, 250, 251

McSlarrow, Kyle 265, 266, 288, 290

McTague, John 164, 165, 264

Mechels, Chris 163, 217, 218, 330

Mesa Equipment and Supply 68, 77, 140, 149, 151, 264

Montano Charles (Chuck) 177, 269, 270, 271, 272, 273, 274, 50

Mullins, James (Jim) 16, 46, 50, 90, 91, 96, 98, 99, 100, 101, 103, 104, 114, 115, 116, 117, 118, 119, 120, 123, 125, 126, 135, 136, 137,140, 141, 142, 144, 145, 158, 159, 160,188, 190, 191, 200, 203, 213, 218, 219, 224, 226, 235, 237, 246, 305, 335

N

Nanos, Peter (Pete) 228, 231, 232, 233, 234, 236, 242, 244, 245, 246, 273, 282, 285, 315, 316, 318, 319, 320, 322

Napolitano, Janet 327

Narang, Deesh 273

Naranjo, Richard 40, 189, 190,

National Nuclear Security Administration 132, 192, 264, 265, 289, 295, 307, 314, 316, 321, 329, 338, 342

NBC 350

NBC Nightly News (with Tom Brokaw) 207, 346

Nguyen, Thanh 95, 96, 97, 98, 99,100, 101, 261

NIS 67, 70, 71, 72, 75, 76, 78, 79, 81, 82, 85, 89, 90, 91, 92 93, 96, 116, 134, 135, 136, 137, 138, 141, 143, 149, 150, 151, 152, 153, 154, 258, 262, 282, 283, 287, 288, 314, 315, 342, 350

NNSA 132, 265, 266, 288, 294, 318, 330, 331, 342

Nonproliferation and International Security Division 67, 68, 71, 72, 73, 75, 77, 78, 80, 81, 85, 89, 90, 92, 118, 134, 137, 138, 141, 155, 187, 219, 250, 258, 314, 315, 342

Nuclear Watch of New Mexico I, 227

O

O'Reilly, Bill 207, 346, 349, 350, 351

Obstruction of justice 87, 89, 97, 102, 158

Office of Security Inquiries 1, 7, 10, 11, 14, 15, 17, 18, 19, 20, 21, 22, 26, 27, 28, 29, 31, 32, 33, 34, 35, 41, 42, 44, 45, 49, 59, 60, 62, 63, 67, 68, 69, 71, 73,75, 79, 80, 86, 87, 88, 91, 92, 95, 96, 98, 99, 100, 101, 102, 116, 118, 119, 131, 133, 135, 137, 140, 141, 144,

145, 161, 164, 188, 191, 198, 217, 218, 229, 230, 258, 261, 282, 283, 284, 314, 342, 345

OIG 266

Ortiz, Ben 323

OSI 1,2, 3, 10, 11, 14, 16, 18, 19, 21, 22, 23, 27, 28, 29, 32, 33, 34, 35, 40, 41, 43, 44, 45, 46, 50, 53, 57, 60, 62, 63, 67, 69, 71, 73, 76, 87, 88, 89, 91, 92, 95, 97, 98, 99, 100, 101, 102, 105, 107, 108, 109, 112, 113, 114, 119, 121, 122, 132, 134, 135, 140, 141, 144, 164, 188, 190, 195, 198, 199, 218, 230, 255, 281, 282, 283, 284, 342

OSI Inquiry 22, 23, 27, 29, 89

Oversight and Investigation Subcommittee of the House Energy and Commerce Committee 162, 247, 249

Owens, Terry 47, 282, 283

Oxide 294

P

Padilla, Leroy 40, 41, 42, 46, 61, 62, 161

Palmieri, Thomas 56, 64, 131, 132

Parks, Anna 68, 69, 72

Paul H. Douglas Ethics in Government Award 301, 302, 346

Peterson, Rosemarie 103, 104

Plutonium 213, 293, 294, 306, 307, 310, 313, 317, 329, 330, 342

POGO 165, 192, 203, 204, 205, 208, 211, 221, 226, 234, 241, 283, 294, 310, 315, 318, 326, 342, 349, 350, 351, 352

PriceWaterhouseCoopers 88, 96, 99, 100, 102, 107, 211, 215 216, 220, 246, 259, 284, 342

Procurement card purchase(s) 217

Project on Government Oversight 165, 191, 203, 205, 216, 224, 318, 331, 342, 349, 352

Protective Technology Force of Los Alamos 32, 35

PTLA 32, 34, 188, 199, 313, 342

Purchase card(s) 46, 209, 240, 246, 252, 264, 286

Purchase order(s) 140, 209, 286

Q

Q-cleared 13, 14, 20, 342

Quintana, Jessica 325, 326, 333

R

Radanovich, George 275

Rankin, Adam 162, 233, 351

Rather, Dan 205, 206, 213

Reed, Patrick 215, 216, 226, 229, 271

Reese, Michael 234, 235, 243, 244

Regents 228, 230, 231, 241, 275, 293, 315

Report of Lost, Damaged, or Destroyed Property 42, 43, 245

Richard, Brian 72, 73, 78, 86, 87, 88, 89, 90, 91, 92, 93, 96, 97, 98, 99, 101, 102, 104, 105, 107, 108, 109, 110, 111, 112, 113, 117, 118, 119, 120, 121, 122, 123, 126, 133, 134, 135, 136, 137, 141, 158, 159, 164, 191, 192, 193, 196, 197, 211, 216, 218, 219, 231, 232, 250, 252, 254, 255, 256, 257, 258, 259, 262, 282, 283

Richardson, Bill 204, 309, 311

RICO 56, 342

Ridge, Tom 31, 32, 39

Rivera, Geraldo 207

RLDD 42, 43, 342

Roark, Kevin 322

Rogers, Mike 252, 253, 291

Rollins, Gayle 85, 86, 87, 126

Roybal, Arlene 86, 87, 97, 98, 103, 235, 236

Roybal, Joe 60, 61, 62, 161, 162

S

Santa Fe New Mexican 220, 227, 320, 321, 351

Schakowsky, Jan 251, 252

Schiffer, Ken 14, 15, 16, 17, 20, 21, 23, 40, 56, 57, 59, 65, 71, 72, 240

Schleck, Peter 187, 188, 189, 190, 231

SCIF 80

Scripps-McClatchy Western Service 218, 351

Secret Compartmentalized Information Clearances 80

Secretary of Energy 204, 220, 227, 290, 309

Security and Safeguards Division 10, 13, 17, 18, 145, 164, 343

Sensitive/attractive 162, 165, 245, 295, 296

Shachtman, Noah 299, 314, 351

Shapiro, Marion (Moe) 72, 78, 88, 89, 90, 92, 93, 100, 101, 102, 104, 109, 110, 112, 113, 133, 135, 136, 137, 159, 191, 192, 196, 204, 210, 211, 215, 219, 224, 226, 227, 250, 254, 255, 256, 257, 258, 259, 260, 261, 262, 263, 274, 281, 282, 283

Smith, Marci 56

Snelling, Victoria 18, 49, 50, 75, 159, 203, 281

SNM 343

Special Nuclear Material 308, 309, 311, 380, 383,384

Spying, spy 78, 80, 81, 137, 206, 209, 333, 337, 351

Stockton, Peter (Pete) 165, 191, 204, 205, 208, 221, 224, 234, 241, 283, 294, 303, 315, 351

Stone, Justin 325, 326

Stupak, Bart 244, 266

T

TA   68, 69, 93, 109, 251, 252, 309, 310, 311

Tauzin, Billy 219, 230, 250, 256, 265,

Terminated, termination(s) 32, 171, 184, 196, 197, 199, 200, 205, 207, 211, 217, 218, 219, 231, 232, 238, 241, 250, 253, 254, 255, 256, 257, 258, 259, 261, 263, 277,282, 295, 297, 298, 299,

Terrorism 45, 137, 143, 327, 332, 336

The O'Reilly Factor 207, 346, 349, 350, 351

Theft report(s) 27, 44, 46, 49, 56, 59, 60, 62, 131, 162, 219, 239, 240, 289

Top-secret(s) 68, 80, 130,137, 157, 307, 313, 314, 321, 342

Tringe, Heidi 160

Trulock, Notra 160

U

Udall, Thomas 256, 329

Uniform Crime Reporting 15, 40, 41, 343

University of California 4, 19, 29, 33, 39, 47, 60, 87, 102, 121, 130, 131, 158, 160, 161, 162, 164, 207, 210, 211, 214, 215, 217, 221, 224, 225, 226, 227, 228, 229, 230, 231, 232, 234, 236, 239, 241, 243, 244, 247, 248, 249, 251, 253, 263, 264, 265, 267, 269, 270, 271, 272, 274, 275, 276, 277, 278, 279, 282, 283, 284, 285, 288, 289,   290, 293, 294, 295, 297, 298, 299, 301, 302, 306, 315, 316, 17, 318, 320, 329,335, 336, 337, 339, 343, 345

U.S. Attorney 61, 98, 102, 107, 108, 110, 113, 133, 136, 211, 231, 254, 255, 256, 257, 262

V

Van Ness, Robert 233

Vanity Fair 313, 314

Vorenberg, Sue 208, 351

W

Wagner, Gene 43, 44, 46

Walden, Greg 251, 252, 256, 257, 259, 263, 264, 265, 276, 345

Wallace, Allen 60, 61, 162

Washington, Ann T. 225

Wen Ho Lee 57, 71, 102, 107, 129, 130, 159, 163, 164, 206, 220, 255, 270, 332, 351

Westfall, Garrett, 188, 189, 190, 231

Whistleblower(s) 83, 124, 158, 204, 205, 213, 217, 218, 224, 233, 237, 254, 255, 256, 259, 265, 273, 283, 299, 302, 303

Wired News 299, 314, 351

Wismer, Michael 11, 19, 21, 22, 27, 31, 32, 34, 35, 49

X

X-Division 1, 2, 318, 321, 322, 326, 341, 342, 343

Z

Zambrea, Marcellaa 89, 90, 91, 207, 216, 226, 233, 270, 271,272

ZIP Disks 318, 321, 322, 332, 341, 343